The Foundations of Belief;

THE

FOUNDATIONS OF BELIEF

BEING

NOTES INTRODUCTORY TO THE STUDY OF THEOLOGY

BY THE

RIGHT HON. ARTHUR JAMES BALFOUR

AUTHOR OF "A DEFENCE OF PHILOSOPHIC DOUBT," ETC.

EIGHTH EDITION, REVISED

WITH A NEW INTRODUCTION AND SUMMARY

LONGMANS, GREEN, AND CO.

91 AND 93 FIFTH AVENUE, NEW YORK

LONDON AND BOMBAY

1902

CONTENTS

PART III

SOME CAUSES OF BELIEF

PART IV

SUGGESTIONS TOWARDS A PROVISIONAL PHILOSOPHY

INTRODUCTION

THE EIGHTH EDITION

EXCEPT for three or four explanatory notes and a few verbal corrections, the body of the following essay remains what it was in the preceding editions. But I have added a summary of the argument, and transferred to an appendix two chapters which are somewhat parenthetical in character. I propose now to say a few words by way of introduction, in the hope of preventing some of the misconceptions to which experience has shown this presentation of my views to be peculiarly liable.

I am far from thinking that these misconceptions are mainly due to the carelessness of the reader. Surveying the work after an interval of years, with a rested eye, I perceive in it certain peculiarities or, if it be preferred, errors of construction, which may well leave the reader more impressed—favourably or unfavourably—by particular arguments and episodes than by the ordered sequence of the whole. A well-known theologian (who, by the way, has himself completely failed to catch my general drift) observed

in a review, which he has since republished, that the
book is redeemed by its digressions;[1] and though I
cannot be expected gratefully to accept so dubious .
a compliment, I admit that the interest of certain
branches of the subject has occasionally betrayed
me into giving them a relative prominence which
the bare necessities of the general argument hardly
seem to justify. Examples in point are the æsthetic
discussion in the second chapter of Part I., and the
chapter on Authority in Part III.

I have made no attempt to correct this fault, if
fault it be. Had I done so the book would, no doubt,
have been a good deal altered, but I doubt whether
it would on the whole have been altered for the
better. It might have gained in proportion and
balance; but it would, perhaps, have lost whatever
freshness and spontaneity it may ever have possessed.
I have, therefore, contented myself with providing,
in the argumentative summary mentioned above, a
corrective to the too detailed treatment of certain
portions of the work, hoping that by thus unspar-
ingly thinning out the trees I shall enable the most
careless wayfarer to understand without difficulty
the general lie of the wood. I desire, however,
emphatically to express a (perhaps not unbiassed)
opinion that the book is something more than the expansion of its summary, and that no extract or essence

---

[1] *Catholicism, Roman and Anglican*, by Principal Fairbairn,
p. 384.

can really reproduce the qualities of the original preparation—whatever those qualities may be worth.

To turn now from the form of the essay to its substance. The objection which seems most readily to suggest itself to my critics, is that the whole argument is a long endeavour to find in doubt the foundation of belief, to justify an excess of credulity by an excess of scepticism. If all creeds, whether scientific or theological (it is thus I am supposed to argue), are equally irrational, all may be equally accepted. If there is no reason for believing anything, and yet something must in fact be believed, let that something be what we like rather than what we dislike. If constructive reason is demonstrably barren, why should we be ashamed to find contentment in prejudice?

I am not concerned to defend a theory which, whatever be its merits, is by no means the one which the following essay is intended to advocate. But it may be worth while to dwell for a moment on the causes to which this misconception of the argument is probably due. The first of these, though by much the least important, is, I imagine, to be found in the avowedly tentative character of the scheme of thought I have endeavoured to expound. This scheme certainly claims, rightly or wrongly, to be philosophical, but it does not claim to constitute a philosophy; nor do I for a moment desire to enter ·into the humblest competition with the great architects of metaphysical systems. The world owes much to these remarkable men, but it does not owe them as yet a generally accepted theory of the knowable; nor can I perceive any satisfactory indication that we are on the high-road to such a measure of agreement, either about the method of philosophy or its results, as has prevailed for two centuries in the case of science. Kant was of opinion that 'metaphysic, notwithstanding its high pretension, had' (up to the publication of the 'Critique of Pure Reason') 'been wandering round and round the same point without gaining a step.' If Kant's criterion of progress, namely, universal and permanent approval, is to be as rigorously applied to the period subsequent to 1781 as he applied it to the preceding twenty centuries, I fear that in *this* respect the publication of his masterpiece can hardly be said to open a new philosophic epoch. But without fully accepting this pessimistic view, it is surely permitted to those who do not feel themselves able either to frame a fresh system of philosophy or to acknowledge the jurisdiction of any old one, candidly to confess the fact, without thereby laying themselves open to the charge of being dangerous sceptics masquerading for some sinister purpose as defenders of the faith! No doubt this unambitious procedure has its difficulties. It carries with it, as an almost inevitable corollary, the admission, not only that the provisional theory advocated is incomplete, but that to a certain

extent its various parts are not entirely coherent.
For if our ideal philosophy is, as I think it ought to
be, a system of thought co-extensive with the knowable and the real, whose various elements are shown
not only to be consistent, but to be interdependent,
then it seems highly probable that anything short of
this would not only be incomplete, but to a certain
extent obscure and contradictory. It does not seem
likely, nay, it seems almost impossible, that our
knowledge of what is only a fragment could be exact
knowledge even of that fragment. Divorced from
the context which it explains, and by which it is itself explained, it must surely present incongruities
and mysteries incapable of complete solution. To
know in part must not merely be to know something
less than the whole, but to know that something
loosely and imperfectly.

Now this modest estimate of the present reach of
speculation may, no doubt, be contrasted with two
others, both of which seem at first sight more in
harmony with the dignity of reason. That dignity
is, of course, not impaired by a mere admission of
ignorance. It is on all hands allowed that by far the
largest portion of the knowable is yet unknown, and,
so far as mankind on this planet are concerned, is
likely to remain so. But our ignorance and our correlative knowledge may be pictured in more than
one way. We might, for example, conceive ourselves
as in possession of a general outline of the knowable,

though ignorant of its details—as understanding in a broad but thoroughly consistent fashion the mutual relation of its principal provinces, though minutely acquainted with but a small corner of one of them. We should in that case be like geographers who had determined by an accurate triangulation the position of a few high mountain peaks dominating some vast continent, while avowedly unable to explore its interior, to penetrate its forests, or navigate its streams. Their knowledge would thus be small; yet in a certain sense it would cover the ground, it would be thoroughly coherent, and neither the progress of thought nor accumulating discoveries, however they might fill up its outlines, could seriously modify them.

Something not much less than this has from time to time been claimed for the great metaphysical and theological systems by their disciples, perhaps even by their founders. And though I cannot persuade myself that we have as yet reached anything like this breadth and sureness of vision, it is not with those who think otherwise that my main controversy has to be fought out. The vital issue lies rather with those (in this book termed Naturalists) who map out the world of knowledge in a very different fashion. Unlike the metaphysicians, they glory in the limitations of their system. The narrower range of their vision is, they think, amply redeemed by its superior certitude. They admit, or rather proclaim, that the area of reality open to their investigation is small compared with that over which Metaphysics or Theology profess to range. But though small, it is admittedly accessible; such surveys as have already been made of it are allowed on all hands to be trustworthy; and it yields up its treasures of knowledge to methods of exploration which, valid though they be, can never, from the nature of the case, be employed in searching out the secrets of the surrounding solitudes.

It is, I imagine, by those whose philosophy conforms to this type, who are naturalistic rather than metaphysical, that the charge against the following essay of misusing sceptical methods is principally urged. And this is what might have been expected. Scepticism in the field of Theology or Metaphysic is too common to excite remark. Believers in Naturalism are sceptical about all theology and all metaphysics. Theologians and Metaphysicians are sceptical about all theology and all metaphysics but their own. The one subject which sceptical criticism usually spares is the one subject against which, in this essay, it is directed, namely, the current beliefs about the world of phenomena. No wonder therefore that those to whom beliefs of this character represent the sum of all actual and all possible knowledge find ground of suspicion against this method of conducting controversy. No wonder they suggest that freedom of thought when thus employed is in some danger of degenerating into licence; that at the best it is useless, and may easily become harmful.

Objections like these compel us to enquire into the legitimate uses of sceptical or destructive criticism. That it has its uses is denied by none. To hasten the final disintegration of dying superstition would be one, I suppose, universally approved of. But there will be less agreement about its value when ap-plied, as it is applied in the following pages, to beliefs which are neither dead nor likely to die. Everybody is gratified by the refutation of theories from which they differ; but they are apt to receive with im-patience any criticism of statements on the truth of which (it may be) both they and the critic are agreed. Such questionings of the unquestionable are judged not only to be superfluous, but to be of dubious ex-pediency—disquieting yet unproductive, a profitless display of more or less ingenious argumentation.

Now, it may readily be acknowledged that philo-sophic scepticism which neither carries with it, nor is intended to carry with it, any practical doubt, finds its chief uses within the region of pure specu-lation. *There* it may be a valuable measure of the success which speculative effort has already attained, a needful corrective of its exaggerated pretensions. It is at once a spur to philosophic curiosity and a touchstone of philosophic work. But even outside the sphere of pure speculation this sceptical criticism has its uses—humbler, no doubt, yet not without

their value.   Though it provides no material out of
which a creed can be formed, it may yet give a much-
needed warning that the apparent stability of some
very solid-looking beliefs cannot be shown to extend
to their foundations.   It may thus most wholesomely
disturb a certain kind of intellectual dogmatism,
which is often a real hindrance to free speculation,
and so prepare the ground for constructive labours,
to which directly it contributes nothing.

This is the use to which I have endeavoured to
put it; and surely not without ample justification.
How many persons are there who acquiesce in the
limitations of the Naturalistic creed, not because it
appeals to them as adequate—responsive and satisfying to their whole nature—but because loyalty to
reason seems to require their acceptance of it, and to
require their acceptance of nothing else? 'Positive
knowledge' they are taught to believe is really
knowledge, and is the only knowledge.   All else is
but phantasie, unverified and unverifiable—speculative ore, unminted by experience, which each man
may arbitrarily assess at his own valuation, which
no man can force into general circulation.   Naturalism, on the other hand, provides them with a system
of beliefs which, with all its limitations, is in their
judgment rational, self-consistent, sure.   It may not
give them all they ask; but what it promises it gives;
and what it gives may be accepted in all security.

Now critical scepticism is the leading remedy

indicated for this mood of dogmatic serenity. If it does nothing else, it should destroy the illusion that Naturalism is a creed in which mankind may find intellectual repose. It suggests the question whether, after all, there is, from the point of view of disinterested reason, this profound distinction between the beliefs which Naturalism accepts and those which it rejects, and, if not, whether it can be legitimate to suppose that the so-called ' conflict between religion and science' touches more than the fringe of the deeper problems with which we are really confronted in our endeavour to comprehend the world in which we live.

I have no doubt myself how this question should be answered. In spite of the importunate clamour which this ' conflict' has so often occasioned since the revival of learning, drowning at times even the domestic quarrelling of the Churches, the issues decided have, after all, been but secondary and unessential. It is true, no doubt, that high ecclesiastical authorities have seen fit from time to time to denounce the teaching of astronomy, or geology, or morphology, or anthropology, or historical criticism. It is also true that in the long run science is seen to be justified of all her children. But do not on this account let us fall into the vulgar error of supposing that these skirmishings decide, or help to decide, the great cause which is in debate between naturalism and religion. It is not so. The difficulties and obscurities which beset the attempt to fuse into a coherent whole the living beliefs of men are not to be found on one side only of the line dividing religion from science. Naturalism is not the goal towards which we are being driven by the intellectual endeavour of the ages; nor is anything gained either for philosophy or science by attempting to minimise its deficiencies.

Some may think that in the following pages I have preached from this text with too persistent an iteration. At any rate, I seem to have given certain of my critics the impression that the principal, if not the sole, object of this work was to show that our beliefs concerning the material world and those concerning the spiritual world are equally poverty-stricken in the matter of philosophic proof, equally embarrassed by philosophic difficulties. This, however, is not so; and if any think that by over-emphasis I have given just occasion for the suspicion, let them remember how deeply rooted is the prejudice that had to be combated, how persistently it troubles the conscience of the religious, how blatantly it triumphs in the popular literature of infidelity.

But, of course, the dissipation of a prejudice, however fundamental, can at best be but an indirect contribution to the work of philosophic construction. Concede the full claims of the argument just referred to, it yet amounts to no more than this—that while it *is* irrational to adopt the procedure of

Naturalism, and elevate scientific methods and conclusions into the test and measure of universal truth, it is *not* necessarily irrational for those who accept the general methods and conclusions of science, to accept also ethical and theological beliefs which cannot be reached by these methods, and which, it may be, harmonise but imperfectly with these conclusions. This is indeed no unimportant result: yet if the argument stopped here it might not be untrue, though it would assuredly be misleading, to say that the following essay only contributed to belief in one department of thought, by suggesting doubt in another. But the argument does not stop here. The most important part has still to be noted—that in which an endeavour is made to show that science, ethics, and (in its degree) æsthetics, are severally and collectively more intelligible, better fitted to form parts of a rational and coherent whole, when they are framed in a theological setting, than when they are framed in one which is purely naturalistic.

The method of proof depends essentially upon the principle that for a creed to be truly consistent, there must exist a correspondence between the account it gives of the origin of its beliefs and the estimate it entertains of their value; in other words, there must be a harmony between the accepted value of results and the accepted theory of causes. This compressed, and somewhat forbidding, formula will receive ample

illustration in succeeding chapters, but even here it
may perhaps be expanded and elucidated with advantage.

What, then, is meant by the phrase 'an accepted
value' in (say) the case of scientific beliefs; and
how can this be out of 'harmony with their origin'?
The chief 'accepted value,' the only one which we
need here consider, is *truth*. And what the formula
asserts is that no creed is really harmonious which
sets this high value on truth, or on true beliefs, and
at the same time holds a theory as to the ultimate
origin of beliefs which suggests their falsity. If,
underlying the rational apparatus by which scientific
beliefs are formally justified, there is a wholly non-
rational machinery by which they are in fact produced, if we are of opinion that in the last resort
our stock of convictions is determined by the blind
interaction of natural forces and, so far as we know,
by these alone, then there is a discord between
one portion of our scheme of thought and another,
between our estimate of values and our theory of
origins, which may properly be described as inconsistency.

Again, if in the sphere of æsthetics we try to
combine the 'accepted value' of some great work of
art or some moving aspect of Nature, with a theory
which traces our feeling for the beautiful to a blind
accident or an irresponsible freak of fashion, a like
collision between our estimate of worth and our

theory of origins must inevitably occur. The emotions stirred in us by loveliness or grandeur wither in the climate produced by such a doctrine, and the message they seem to bring us—not, as we would fain hope, of less import because it is inarticulate—becomes meaningless or trivial.

A precisely parallel argument may be applied with even greater force in the sphere of ethics. The ordinarily 'accepted value' of the moral law, of moral sentiments, of responsibility, of repentance, self-sacrifice, and high resolve, clashes hopelessly with any doctrine of origins which should trace the pedigree of ethics through the long-drawn developments produced by natural selection, till it be finally lost in some material, and therefore non-moral, beginning. In this case, as in the other two, we can only reach a consistency (relative, indeed, and imperfect at the best) if we assume behind, or immanent in, the chain of causes cognisable by science, a universal Spirit shaping them to a foreseen end.

The line of argument thus indicated is the exact opposite of one with which we are all very familiar. We are often told—and it may be properly told—that this or that statement is true, this or that practice laudable, because it comes to us with a Divine sanction, or because it is in accordance with Nature. In the argument on which I am insisting the movement of thought is reversed. Starting from the conception that knowledge is indeed real, that the moral law does indeed possess authority, it travels towards the conviction that the source from which they spring can itself be neither irrational nor unmoral. In the one case we infer validity from origin: in the other, origin from validity.

It is of course evident that in strictness the 'validity' from which 'origin' is thus inferred, is not so much the absolute validity of even the most widely accepted conclusion, as the valid tendency of the general processes out of which these conclusions have arisen. To base our views of the universe on the finality and adequacy of particular scientific and ethical propositions or groups of propositions, might well be considered hazardous. Not only is the secular movement of thought constantly requiring of us to restate our beliefs, but as I have shown in a later portion of this volume, even in those cases where no restatement is necessary, this is not because the beliefs to be expressed remain unchanged, but because our mode of expressing them is elastic. No such admission, however, really touches the essence of the argument. It is enough for my purpose to establish that we cannot plausibly assume a truthward tendency in the belief-forming processes, a growing approximation to verity in their results, unless we are prepared to go further, and to rest that hypothesis itself on a theistic and spiritual foundation.

On the argument thus barely and imperfectly

outlined two further observations may perhaps be
made. The first is that, like every other appeal
to consistency, it is essentially an *argumentum ad
hominem*. It can only affect the man who 'accepts'
both the 'estimate of value' and the 'theory of
origin.' On him who is unmoved by beauty, or who
regards morality and moral sentiments as no more
than a device for the preservation of society or the
continuation of the race, neither the æsthetic nor the
ethic branch of the argument can have any hold or
purchase. For him, again, if any such there be,
whose agnosticism requires him to cut down his
creed to the bare acceptance of a perceiving Self and
a perceived series of subjective states, there can be
no conflict between the theory of origins and the
accepted value of the consequent beliefs, since by
hypothesis he neither has, nor could have, any theory
of origins at all. He lives in a world of shadows
related to each other only as events succeeding each
other in time; a world in which there is no room for
contradiction as there is no room for anything that
deserves to be called knowledge. The man who
makes profession of such doctrines may justly be
suspected of lying, but he is not open, in this con-
nexion at least, to any charge of philosophic inconsistency.

It may in the second place be worth noting that
the preceding argument is both suggested by the
modern theory of universal development, and is

(as I think) its necessary philosophic complement. Before this general point of view was reached, the interest taken in the causes which produced beliefs as distinguished from the reasons which also justify them, was confined to particular cases, and suggested as a rule by a controversial or historical motive. This or that doctrine was inspired (*i.e.* immediately caused) by God, and therefore it was true; by the Devil, and therefore it was false: was due to the teaching of a power-loving priesthood; was unconsciously suggested by self-interested motives; was born of parental influence or the subtle power of social surroundings—such and such like comments have always been sufficiently common. But until the theory of evolution began to govern our reconstruction of the past, observations like these were but detached and episodical notes. They represented no generalised or universal view as to the genesis of human opinions. To regard all beliefs whatever, be they true or false, our own or other people's, as having a natural history as well as a logical or philosophical status; to see them not merely as conclusions, but as effects, conditioned, like all other effects, by a succession of causes stretching back into an illimitable past; to recognise the fact that, so far as induction and observation can inform us, only a fraction of these causes, and those not the most fundamental, can be described as rational—all this is new. New also (at least in degree) is it to realise that the beginnings of morality are lost among the self-preserving and race-prolonging instincts which we share with the animal creation; that religion in its higher forms is a development of infantine, and often brutal, superstitions; that in the pedigree of the noblest and most subtle of our emotions are to be discovered primitive strains of coarsest quality.

But though these truths are now admitted as truths of anthropology, I do not think their full philosophical consequences have yet been properly worked out. Their true bearing on the theory of scientific belief seems scarcely to have been recognised. In the domain of religious speculations there are many who suppose that to explain the natural genesis of some belief or observance, to trace its growth from a lower to a higher form in different races and widely separated countries, is in some way to throw it into discredit. In the sphere of Ethics a like suspicion has perhaps prompted the various attempts to construct 'intuitive' systems of morals which shall owe nothing to historical development and psychological causation. I cannot believe that this is philosophically to be defended. Nothing, and least of all what most we value, has come to us ready made from Heaven. Yet if we are still to value it, the modern conception of its natural growth requires us more than ever to believe that from Heaven in the last resort it comes.

There is one more point on which I desire to throw

light before bringing this Introduction to a close, one other class of objector whom, if possible, I should wish to conciliate.   To these critics it may seem that, whatever be the value of the argumentative scheme herein set forth, it does not even pretend to give them that for which they have been looking. Compared with the philosophy of which they dream, it appears mere tinkering. It not only suffers, on its own confession, from rents and gaps, imperfect cohesion, unsolved antinomies, but it is infected by the vice inherent in all apologetics—the vice of foregone conclusions. It travels towards a predestined end. Not content simply to follow reason where reason freely leads, it endeavours to cajole it into uttering oracles about the universe which shall do no violence to what are conceived to be the moral and emotional needs of man: a course which may be rational, but the rationality of which should (they think) be proved, but ought by no means to be assumed.

Now a criticism like this raises a most important question, which, in its full generality, does not perhaps receive all the attention it deserves. Since belief necessarily precedes the theory of belief, what is the proper relation which theory in the making should bear to beliefs already made? It may at first seem that any serious attempt to devise a philosophy should be preceded not merely by a suspension of judgment as to the truth of all pre-philosophic assumptions, but by their complete elimination as factors in the enquiry. From the nature of the case, they can as yet be no more than guesses, and in the eyes of philosophy a mere guess is as if it were not. The examination into what we ought to believe should therefore be wholly unaffected by what we do in fact believe. The seeker after truth should set forth on his speculative voyage neither commit، ted to a predetermined course nor bound for any port of predilection, and it،should seem to him a far smaller evil to lie stagnant and becalmed in univer، sal doubt than to move towards the most attractive goal on any impulse but that of strictly disinterested reason.

The policy is an attractive one; but its immediate consequence would be a total and absolute sundering of theory and practice. In so far as he was theorist, the philosopher acting on these principles would, or should, regard himself as discredited if he believed anything which was not either self-evident or ra-tionally involved in that which was self-evident. In so far as he was a citizen of the world, he could not live ten minutes without acting on some principle which still waits in vain for rational proof; and he would do so, be it observed, although (on his own principles) there is *no probability whatever* that when he has reached the philosophic theory of which he is in quest, it will be in any kind of agreement with his pre-philosophic practice. If such a probability exists, it should evidently have guided him in his investigations, and there would be at once an end of the 'clean slate and disinterested reason.'

For myself indeed I doubt whether this method is possible, or, if possible, likely to be fruitful. And I am fortified in this conviction by the reflection that those to whose constructive suggestions the world owes most have favoured a different procedure. They have not thus speculated in the void. In their search for a world-theory wherein they might find repose, they have been guided by some pre-conceived ideal, borrowed in its main outlines from the thought of their age, to which by excisions, modifications, or additions, they have sought to give definiteness and a rational consistency. I do not, of course, suggest that they were advocates speaking from a brief, or that their conclusions were explicitly formulated before their arguments were devised. My meaning rather is that we must think of them as working over, and shaping afresh, a body of doctrine (empirical, ethical, metaphysical, or meta-physico-theological, as the case may be), which in the main they *found*, but did not *make;* that, judged by their practice, they have not regarded 'disinterested reason' as the proper instrument of philosophic construction; nor have they in fact disdained to struggle towards foreseen and wished for conclusions.

Is this not plainly true, for example, of such men as Locke, Leibnitz, Berkeley, Kant, Hegel? Is it not confessed in the very name of the 'common-sense' school? Should it not be admitted even of thinkers whose conclusions deviate so much from the normal as Spinoza or Schopenhauer? I say nothing of the many schools of moralists who teach an identic morality, though on the most divergent grounds, nor of those who, in their endeavours to frame a logic of experience assume (quite rightly, in my opinion) that the empirical methods which we actually employ are those which it is their business if possible to justify. It is sufficiently evident that their example, if not their profession, amply supports my contention.

This is not the place, however, to labour the historic point; and it is the less necessary because I think the reader will probably agree with me that, in its complete and consistent purity, this method of 'disinterested reason' never has been, and probably never will be, employed. What has been, and constantly is, employed, is a partial and bastard adaptation of it—an adaptation under which 'disinterested reason,' or what passes for such, is only exercised for purposes of destructive criticism, in arbitrarily selected portions of the total area of belief. On this subject, however, the reader endowed with sufficient patience will hear much in the sequel. For the present it is only necessary to state, by way of contrast, what I conceive to be the mode in which philosophy can most profitably order its course in the presence of those living beliefs which precede it in order of time, though not in order of logic.

In my view, then, it should do avowedly, and with open eyes, what in fact it has constantly done, though silently and with hesitation. It should provisionally assume, not of course that the general body of our beliefs are in conformity with reality, but that they represent a stage in the movement towards such conformity; that in particular the great presuppositions (such as, for example, the uniformity of Nature or the existence of a persistent reality capable of being experienced by us but independent of our experience) which form as it were the essential skeleton of our working creed, should be regarded as matters which it is our business, if possible, rationally to establish, but not necessarily our business to ignore until such time as our efforts shall have succeeded.

No doubt this method assumes a kind of harmony between the knowing Self and the reality to be known, which seems only plausible if both are part of a common design; while again, if such a design is to be accepted at all, it can hardly be confined to the Self as knowing subject, but must embrace other and not less notable aspects of our complex personality.[1]

[1] It might at first seem as if this postulated harmony might be due not to design, but to the material universe having, in the process of development, somehow evolved a mind, or rather a multitude of minds, in this kind of correspondence with itself. The inadequacy of such a theory is shown in a later chapter of this volume. But it

I may observe that this, and no more than this, is the doctrine of 'needs' to which, as expounded in the following pages,[1] serious objection has been taken by a certain number of my critics.

We have thus again reached the point of view to which, by a slightly different route, we had already travelled. Whether, taking as our point of departure beliefs as they are, we look for the setting which shall bind them into the most coherent whole; or whether, in searching out what they ought to be, we ask in what direction we had best start our explorations, we seem equally moved towards the hypothesis of a Spiritual origin common to the knower and the known.

Now it will be observed that in both cases the creed aimed at is an inclusive one. There is, I mean, an admitted desire that no great department of knowledge (real or supposed) in which there are living and effective beliefs, shall be excluded from the final co-ordination. But inasmuch as this final co-ordination has not been reached, has indeed, as we fear, been scarcely approached, we are not only compelled in our gropings after a philosophy to accept guidance from beliefs which as yet possess no

may be here observed that it is not very satisfactory to assume, even provisionally, the truth of a full-fledged and very complex scientific theory at the starting point of an investigation into the proof of the fundamental principles on which that theory, and other empirical doctrines, ultimately depend.

[1] See below pp 243–260.

rational warranty, but to tolerate some which it seems impossible at present to harmonise.

This seems a hard saying, and it inevitably suggests the question whether happier results might not be obtained by abandoning the attempt at comprehension, and boldly expunging a number of the conflicting opinions sufficient to secure immediate consistency.

I am not aware, however, that any operation of this kind has so far been attended with the smallest success, nor does it seem very easy to justify it in the name of reason, unless on examination it turns out that the opinions retained have a better claim to reasonable acceptance than their rivals, a contingency more remote than is often supposed. Even from the purely empirical point of view, a consideration of the natural history of knowledge, or what is accepted as knowledge, gives fair warning that this procedure (were it indeed practicable) would not be without its dangers. For knowledge does not grow merely by the addition of new discoveries: nor is it purified merely by the subtraction of detected errors. Truth and falsehood are often too intimately combined to be dissociated by any simple method of filtration. It is by a subtler process that new verities, while increasing the sum of our beliefs, act even more effectively as a kind of ferment, impressing on those that already exist a novel and previously unsuspected character; just as a fresh touch of colour added to a

picture, though it immediately affects but one **corner**
of the canvas, may yet change the whole from un-
likeness to likeness, from confusion to significance.

Now if this be a faithful representation of what
actually occurs, it seems plain that to amputate important departments of belief in order to free what
remains from any trace of incoherence, might, even
if it succeeded, be to hinder, not to promote, the
cause of truth.   Nothing, indeed, which is incoherent
can be true.   But though it cannot be true, it may
not only contain much truth, but may contain more
than any system in which both the true and the false
are abandoned in the premature and, at this stage of
development, hopeless endeavour after a creed which,
within however narrow limits, shall be perfectly clear
and self-consistent.   Most half-truths are half-errors;
but who is there who would refrain from grasping
the half-truth although he could not obtain it at a
less cost than that of taking the half-error with it?

There are those who would accept the historical
application of this doctrine, who would admit that
logical laxity had often in fact been of service to
intellectual progress, but would altogether deny the
propriety of admitting that such a theory could have
any practical bearing on their own case.   They would
draw a distinction between a detected and an unde-
tected incoherence.   The unconscious acquiescence
in the latter may happen to aid the cause of knowledge: the conscious acquiescence in the former must

be a sin against reason. I do not think the distinction will hold. Our business is to reach as much truth as we can; and neither observation nor reflection[1] give any countenance to the notion that this end will best be attained by turning the merely critical understanding into the undisputed arbiter in all matters of belief. Its importance for the clarification of knowledge cannot indeed be exaggerated. As a commentator it should be above control. As cross-examiner its rights should be unlimited. But it cannot arrogate to itself the duties of a final court of appeal. Should it, for example, show, as I think it does, that neither the common-sense views of ordinary men, nor the modification of these on which science proceeds, nor the elaborated systems of metaphysics, are more than temporary resting-places, seen to be insecure almost as soon as they are occupied, yet we must still hold them to be stages on a journey towards something better than a futile scepticism which, were it possible in practice, would be ruinous alike to every form of conviction, whether scientific, ethical, or religious. When that journey is accomplished, but only then, can we hope that all difficulties will be smoothed away, all anomalies be reconciled, and the certainty and rational interdependence of all its parts made manifest in the transparent Whole of Knowledge.

I have now endeavoured to present in isolation,

[1] See this Introduction, *ante*, p. xi.

those scientific and philosophical questions which have a more profound and permanent bearing on Theology even than the results of critical and historical scholarship.

Whether any single individual is fully competent either to acquire or successfully to manipulate so formidable an apparatus of learning, I do not know. But in any case I am very far indeed from being even among that not inconsiderable number who are qualified to put the reader in the way of profitably cultivating some portion of this vast and always increasing field of research. The following pages, therefore, scarcely claim to deal with the substance of Theology at all. They are in the narrowest sense of the word an 'introduction' to it. They deal for the most part with preliminaries; and it is only towards the end of the volume, where the Introduction begins insensibly to merge into that which it is designed to introduce, that purely theological doctrines are mentioned, except by way of illustration.

Although what follows might thus be fitly described as 'Considerations preliminary to a study of Theology,' I do not think the subjects dealt with are less important on that account. For, in truth, the decisive battles of Theology are fought beyond its frontiers. It is not over purely religious controversies that the cause of Religion is lost or won. The judgments we shall form upon its special problems are commonly settled for us by our general mode of looking at the Universe; and this again, in so far as it is determined by arguments at all, is determined by arguments of so wide a scope that they can seldom be claimed as more nearly concerned with Theology than with the philosophy of Science or of Ethics.

My object, then, is to recommend a particular way of looking at the World-problems, which, whether we like it or not, we are compelled to face. I wish, if I can, to lead the reader up to a point of view whence the small fragments of the Infinite Whole, of which we are able to obtain a glimpse, may appear to us in their true relative proportions. This is, therefore, no work of 'Apologetics' in the ordinary sense of that word. Theological doctrines are not taken up in turn and defended from current objections; nor is there any endeavour here made specifically to solve the 'doubts' or allay the 'difficulties' which in this, as in every other, age perplex the minds of a certain number of religious persons. Yet, as I think that perhaps the greater number of these doubts and difficulties would never even present themselves in that character were it not for a certain superficiality and one-sidedness in our habitual manner of considering the wider problems of belief, I cannot help entertaining the hope that by what is here said the work of the Apologist proper may indirectly be furthered.

It is a natural, if not an absolutely necessary consequence of this plan, that the subjects alluded to in the following pages are, as a rule, more secular than the title of the book might perhaps at first suggest, and also that the treatment of some of them has been brief even to meagreness. If the reader is tempted to complain of the extreme conciseness with which some topics of the greatest importance are touched on, and the apparent irrelevance with which others have been introduced, I hope he will reserve his judgment until he has read to the end, should his patience hold out so long. If he then thinks that the 'particular way of looking at the World-problems' which this book is intended to recommend is not rendered clearer by any portion of what has been written, I shall be open to his criticism; but not otherwise. What I have tried to do is not to write a monograph, or a series of monographs, upon Theology, but to delineate, and, if possible, to recommend, a certain attitude of mind; and I hope that in carrying out this less ambitious scheme I have put in few touches that were superfluous and left out none that were necessary.

If it be asked, 'For whom is this book intended?' I answer, that it is intended for the general body of readers interested in such subjects rather than for the specialist in Philosophy. I do not, of course, mean that I have either desired or been able to avoid questions which in essence are strictly philosophical. Such an attempt would have been wholly absurd. But no knowledge either of the history or the technicalities of Philosophy is assumed in the reader, nor do I believe that there is any train of thought here suggested which, if he thinks it worth his while, he will have the least difficulty in following. He may, and very likely will, find objection both to the substance of my arguments and their form. But I shall be disappointed if, in addition to their other deficiencies, he finds them unintelligible or even obscure.[1]

There is one more point to be explained before these prefatory remarks are brought to a conclusion. In order that the views here advocated may be seen in the highest relief, it is convenient to exhibit them against the background of some other and contrasted system of thought. What system shall that be? In Germany the philosophies of Kant and his successors may be (I know not whether they are) matters of such common knowledge that they fittingly supply a standard of reference, by the aid of which the relative positions of other and more or less differing systems may be conveniently determined. As to whether this state of things, if it anywhere exists, is desirable or not, I offer no opinion. But I am very sure that it does not at present exist in any English-speaking community, and probably never will, until the ideas of these speculative giants are throughout rethought by Englishmen, and reproduced in a shape which ordinary Englishmen will consent to assimilate. Until this occurs Transcendental Idealism must continue to be what it is

[1] These observations must not be taken as applying to Part II., Chapter II., which the general reader is recommended to omit.

now—the intellectual possession of a small minority of philosophical specialists. Philosophy cannot, under existing conditions, become, like Science, absolutely international. There is in matters speculative, as in matters poetical, a certain amount of natural protection for the home-producer, which commentators and translators seem unable altogether to overcome.

Though, therefore, I have devoted a chapter to the consideration of Transcendental Idealism as represented in some recent English writings, it is not with overt or tacit reference to that system that I have arranged the material of the following Essay. I have, on the contrary, selected a system with which I am in much less sympathy, but which under many names numbers a formidable following, and is in reality the only system which ultimately profits by any defeats which Theology may sustain, or which may be counted on to flood the spaces from which the tide of Religion has receded. Agnosticism, Positivism, Empiricism, have all been used more or less correctly to describe this scheme of thought; though in the following pages, for reasons with which it is not necessary to trouble the reader, the term which I shall commonly employ is Naturalism.[1]

[1] [This sentence has greatly excited the wrath of Mr. Frederic Harrison. But whether his indignation is directed against my description of the meaning in which the word ' Positivism ' is frequently used, or against that meaning itself, is not quite so clear. If my description is accurate, I see no reason why he should be angry with me ; and that it is accurate seems beyond doubt. I commend to Mr.

But whatever the name selected, the thing itself is sufficiently easy to describe. For its leading doctrines are that we may know 'phenomena'[1] and the laws

Harrison's attention the following passage from John Mill's volume on 'Auguste Comte and Positivism:'* 'The character by which he (Comte) defines Positive Philosophy is the following: We have no knowledge of anything but Phenomena; and our knowledge of Phenomena is relative, not absolute. . . . The laws of Phenomena are all we know respecting them. Their essential nature and their ultimate causes, either efficient or final, are unknown and inscrutable to us.'

Mill's account of the 'character by which Comte defines Positive Philosophy' (which, as the reader will see, is almost identical with my account of Naturalism) may, in Mr. Harrison's elegant language,† be a 'coagulated clot of confusions and mis-statements,' but passages of a like import (which could easily be multiplied) fully account for the use of the term 'Positivism' to which I have referred in the text. 'Positivism,' says Mr. Harrison, 'is the religion of humanity resting on the philosophy of human nature.'‡ Very possibly; but if so, Positivism as described by Mr. Harrison is a strangely different thing from 'Positive Philosophy' as described by John Mill; and it is hardly to be wondered at that these words are sometimes employed in a manner displeasing to the religious sect of which Mr. Harrison is so distinguished a member. This, however, is no fault of mine.

Let me add that Mr. Harrison's ill humour may in part be due to his supposing that I regard Positivists as being *ipso facto* materialists. I need not say to the attentive reader of the following essay that I do nothing of the sort.]

[1] I feel that explanation, and perhaps apology, is due for this use of the word 'phenomena' In its proper sense the term implies, I suppose, that which *appears*, as distinguished from something, presumably more real, which does *not appear*. I neither use it as carrying this metaphysical implication, nor do I restrict it to things which appear, or even to things which *could* appear to beings endowed with senses like ours. The ether, for instance, though it is impossible that we should ever know it except by its effects, I should call a phenom-

* P. 6, ed. 1865.   † *Positivist Review*, No. 29, p 79.
‡ *Positivist Review* for May 1895, p. 79.

by which they are connected, but nothing more. 'More' there may or may not be; but if it exists we can never apprehend it : and whatever the World may be 'in its reality' (supposing such an expression to be otherwise than meaningless), the World for us, the World with which alone we are concerned, or of which alone we can have any cognisance, is that World which is revealed to us through perception, internal and external, and which is the subject-matter of the Natural Sciences. Here, and here only, are we on firm ground. Here, and here only, can we discover anything which deserves to be described as Knowledge. Here, and here only, may we profitably exercise our reason or gather the fruits of Wisdom.

Such, in rough outline, is Naturalism. My first task will be the preparatory one of examining certain of its consequences in various departments of human thought and emotion; and to this in the next four chapters I proceed to devote myself.

enon. The coagulation of nebular meteors into suns and planets I should call a phenomenon, though nobody may have existed to whom it could appear. Roughly speaking, things and events, the general subject-matter of Natural Science, are what I endeavour to indicate by a term for which, as thus used, there is, unfortunately, no substitute, however little the meaning which I give to it can be etymologically justified.

While I am on the subject of definitions, it may be as well to say that, generally speaking, I distinguish between Philosophy and Metaphysics. To Philosophy I give an *epistemological* significance. I regard it as the systematic exposition of our grounds of knowledge. Thus, the philosophy of Religion or the philosophy of Science would mean the theoretic justification of our theological or scientific beliefs. By Metaphysics, on the other hand, I usually mean the knowledge that we have, or suppose ourselves to have, respecting realities which are not phenomenal, *e.g.* God, and the Soul.

PART I

SOME CONSEQUENCES OF BELIEF

CHAPTER I

NATURALISM AND ETHICS

I

THE two subjects on which the professors of every creed, theological and anti-theological, seem least anxious to differ, are the general substance of the Moral Law, and the character of the sentiments with which it should be regarded. That it is worthy of all reverence; that it demands our ungrudging submission; and that we owe it not merely obedience, but love — these are common-places which the preachers of all schools vie with each other in proclaiming. And they are certainly right. Morality is more than a bare code of laws, than a *catalogue raisonné* of things to be done or left undone. Were it otherwise, we must change something more important than the mere customary language of exhortation. The old ideals of the world would have to be uprooted, and no new ones could spring up and flourish in their stead; the very soil on which they grew would be sterilised, and the phrases in which all that has hitherto been regarded as best and noblest in human life has been expressed, nay, the words 'best' and 'noblest' themselves, would become as foolish and unmeaning as the incantation of a forgotten superstition.

This unanimity, familiar though it be, is surely very remarkable. And it is the more remarkable because the unanimity prevails only as to conclusions, and is accompanied by the widest divergence of opinion with regard to the premises on which these conclusions are supposed to be founded. Nothing but habit could blind us to the strangeness of the fact that the man who believes that morality is based on *a priori* principles, and the man who believes it to be based on the commands of God, the transcendentalist, the theologian, the mystic, and the evolutionist, should be pretty well at one both as to what morality teaches, and as to the sentiments with which its teaching should be regarded.

It is not my business in this place to examine the Philosophy of Morals, or to find an answer to the charge which this suspicious harmony of opinion among various schools of moralists appears to suggest, namely, that in their speculations they have taken current morality for granted, and have squared their proofs to their conclusions, and not their conclusions to their proofs. I desire now rather to direct the reader's attention to certain questions relating to the origin of ethical systems, not to their justification; to the natural history of morals, not to its philosophy; to the place which the moral law occupies in the general chain of causes and effects, not to the nature of its claim on the unquestioning obedience of mankind. I am aware, of course, that many persons have been, and are, of opinion that these two sets of questions are not merely related, but identical; that the validity of a command depends only on the source from which it springs; and that in the investigation into the character and authority of this source consists the principal business of the moral philosopher. I am not concerned here to controvert this theory, though, as thus stated, I do not agree with it. It will be sufficient if I lay down two propositions of a much less dubious character:—(1) That, practically, human beings being what they are, no moral code can be effective which does not inspire, in those who are asked to obey it, emotions of reverence; and (2) that, practically, the capacity of any code to excite this or any other elevated emotion cannot be wholly independent of the origin from which those who accept that code suppose it to emanate.[1]

Now what, according to the naturalistic creed, is the origin of the generally accepted, or, indeed, of any other possible, moral law? What position does it occupy in the great web of interdependent phenomena by which the knowable 'Whole' is on this hypothesis constituted? The answer is plain: as

[1] These are statements, it will be noted, not relating to ethics proper. They have nothing to do either with the contents of the moral law or with its validity; and if we are to class them as belonging to any special department of knowledge at all, it is to psychology or anthropology that they should in strictness be assigned.

life is but a petty episode in the history of the
universe; as feeling is an attribute of only a fraction of things that live, so moral sentiments and the
apprehension of moral rules are found in but an
insignificant minority of things that feel.   They are
not, so to speak, among the necessities of Nature; no
great spaces are marked out for their accommodation;
were they to vanish to-morrow, the great machine
would move on with no noticeable variation; the
sum of realities would not suffer sensible diminution;
the organic world itself would scarcely mark the
change.   A few highly developed mammals, and
chiefest among these *man*, would lose instincts and
beliefs which have proved of considerable value in
the struggle for existence, if not between individuals,
at least between tribes and species.   But put it at
the highest, we can say no more than that there
would be a great diminution of human happiness,
that civilisation would become difficult or impossible,
and that the 'higher' races might even succumb and
disappear.

These are considerations which to the 'higher'
races themselves may seem not unimportant, however trifling to the universe at large.   But let it be
noted that every one of these propositions can be
asserted with equal or greater assurance of all the
bodily appètites, and of many of the vulgarest forms
of desire and ambition.   On most of the processes, indeed, by which consciousness and life are maintained
in the individual and perpetuated in the race we are

never consulted; of their intimate character we are
for the most part totally ignorant, and no one is in
any case asked to consider them with any other
emotion than that of enlightened curiosity. But in
the few and simple instances in which our co-operation is required, it is obtained through the stimulus
supplied by appetite and disgust, pleasure and pain,
instinct, reason, and morality; and it is hard to see,
on the naturalistic hypothesis, whence any one of
these various natural agents is to derive a dignity or
a consideration not shared by all the others, why
morality should be put above appetite, or reason
above pleasure.

It may, perhaps, be replied that the sentiments
with which we choose to regard any set of actions
or motives do not require special justification, that
there is no disputing about this any more than about
other questions of 'taste,' and that, as a matter of
fact, the persons who take a strictly naturalistic view
of man and of the universe are often the loudest
and not the least sincere in the homage they pay to
the 'majesty of the moral law.' This is, no doubt,
perfectly true; but it does not meet the real difficulty. I am not contending that sentiments of the
kind referred to may not be, and are not, frequently
entertained by persons of all shades of philosophical
or theological opinion. My point is, that in the case
of those holding the naturalistic creed the sentiments
and the creed are antagonistic; and that the more
clearly the creed is grasped, the more thoroughly

the intellect is saturated with its essential teaching, the more certain are the sentiments thus violently and unnaturally associated with it to languish or to die.

For not only does there seem to be no ground, from the point of view of biology, for drawing a distinction in favour of any of the processes, physiological or psychological, by which the individual or the race is benefited; not only are we bound to consider the coarsest appetites, the most calculating selfishness, and the most devoted heroism, as all sprung from analogous causes and all evolved for similar objects, but we can hardly doubt that the august sentiments which cling to the ideas of duty and sacrifice are nothing better than a device of Nature to trick us into the performance of altruistic actions.[1] The working ant expends its life in labouring, with more than maternal devotion, for a progeny not its own, and, so far as the race of ants is concerned, doubtless it does well. Instinct, the inherited impulse to follow a certain course with no developed consciousness of its final goal, is here the instrument selected by Nature to attain her ends. But in the case of man, more flexible if less certain methods have to be employed. Does conscience, in bidding us to do or to refrain, speak with an authority from which there seems no appeal? Does

[1] It is scarcely necessary to state that by this phrase I do not wish to suggest that Biology necessarily is teleological. Naturalism of course cannot be.

our blood tingle at the narrative of some great deed? Do courage and self-surrender extort our passionate sympathy, and invite, however vainly, our halting imitation? Does that which is noble attract even the least noble, and that which is base repel even the basest? Nay, have the words 'noble' and 'base' a meaning for us at all? If so, it is from no essential and immutable quality in the deeds themselves. It is because, in the struggle for existence, the altruistic virtues are an advantage to the family, the tribe, or the nation, but *not* always an advantage to the individual; it is because man comes into the world richly endowed with the inheritance of self-regarding instincts and appetites required by his animal progenitors, but poor indeed in any inbred inclination to the unselfishness necessary to the well-being of the society in which he lives; it is because in no other way can the original impulses be displaced by those of late growth to the degree required by public utility, that Nature, indifferent to our happiness, indifferent to our morals, but sedulous of our survival, commends disinterested virtue to our practice by decking it out in all the splendour which the specifically ethical sentiments alone are capable of supplying. Could we imagine the chronological order of the evolutionary process reversed: if courage and abnegation had been the qualities first needed, earliest developed, and therefore most deeply rooted in the ancestral organism; while selfishness, cowardice, greediness, and lust

2

represented impulses required only at a later stage
of physical and intellectual development, doubtless
we should find the 'elevated' emotions which now
crystallise round the first set of attributes transferred
without alteration or amendment to the second; the
preacher would expend his eloquence in warning
us against excessive indulgence in deeds of self-
immolation, to which, like the 'worker' ant, we
should be driven by inherited instinct, and in ex-
horting us to the performance of actions and the
cultivation of habits from which we now, unfortunately, find it only too difficult to abstain.

Kant, as we all know, compared the Moral Law
to the starry heavens, and found them both sublime.
It would, on the naturalistic hypothesis, be more
appropriate to compare it to the protective blotches
on the beetle's back, and to find them both ingenious.
But how on this view is the 'beauty of holiness' to
retain its lustre in the minds of those who know so
much of its pedigree? In despite of theories, mankind—even instructed mankind—may, indeed, long
preserve uninjured sentiments which they have
learned in their most impressionable years from
those they love best; but if, while they are being
taught the supremacy of conscience and the austere
majesty of duty, they are also to be taught that
these sentiments and beliefs are merely samples of
the complicated contrivances, many of them mean
and many of them disgusting, wrought into the
physical or into the social organism by the shaping

forces of selection and elimination, assuredly much of the efficacy of these moral lessons will be destroyed, and the contradiction between ethical sentiment and naturalistic theory will remain intrusive and perplexing, a constant stumbling-block to those who endeavour to combine in one harmonious creed the bare explanations of Biology and the lofty claims of Ethics.[1]

II

Unfortunately for my reader, it is not possible wholly to omit from this section some references to the questionings which cluster round the time-worn debate on Determinism and Free Will; but my remarks will be brief, and as little tedious as may be.

[1] It may perhaps be thought that in this section I have too confidently assumed that morality, or, more strictly, the moral sentiments (including among these the feeling of authority which attaches to ethical imperatives), are due to the working of natural selection. I have no desire to dogmatise on a subject on which it is the business of the biologist and anthropologist to pronounce. But it seems difficult to believe that natural selection should not have had the most important share in producing and making permanent things so obviously useful. If the reader prefers to take the opposite view, and to regard moral sentiments as ' accidental,' he may do so, without on that account being obliged to differ from my general argument. He will then, of course, class moral sentiments with the æsthetic emotions dealt with in the next chapter.

Of course I make no attempt to trace the causes of the variations on which selective action has worked, nor to distinguish between the moral sentiments, an inclination to or an aptitude for which has been bred into the *physical* organism of man or some races of men, and those which have been wrought only into the *social* organism of the family, the tribe, or the State.

I have nothing here to do with the truth or un-truth of either of the contending theories. It is sufficient to remind the reader that on the naturalis-tic view, at least, free will is an absurdity, and that those who hold that view are bound to believe that every decision at which mankind have arrived, and every consequent action which they have performed, was implicitly determined by the quantity and dis-tribution of the various forms of matter and energy which preceded the birth of the solar system. The fact, no doubt, remains[1] that every individual, while balancing between two courses, is under the inevi-table impression that he is at liberty to pursue either, and that it depends upon 'himself' and himself alone, 'himself' as distinguished from his character, his desires, his surroundings, and his antecedents, which of the offered alternatives he will elect to pursue. I do not know that any explanation has been proposed of what, on the naturalistic hypothe-sis, we must regard as a singular illusion. I vent-ure with some diffidence to suggest, as a theory pro-visionally adequate, perhaps, for scientific purposes, that the phenomenon is due to the same cause as so many other beneficent oddities in the organic world, namely, to natural selection. To an animal with no self-consciousness a sense of freedom would evidently be unnecessary, if not, indeed, absolutely unmeaning. But as soon as self-consciousness is developed, as

[1] At least, so it seems to me. There are, however, eminent psychologists who differ.

soon as man begins to reflect, however crudely and imperfectly, upon himself and the world in which he lives, then deliberation, volition, and the sense of responsibility become wheels in the ordinary machinery by which species-preserving actions are produced; and as these psychological states would be weakened or neutralised if they were accompanied by the immediate consciousness that they were as rigidly determined by their antecedents as any other effects by any other causes, benevolent Nature steps in, and by a process of selective slaughter makes the consciousness in such circumstances practically impossible. The spectacle of all mankind suffering under the delusion that in their decision they are free, when, as a matter of fact, they are nothing of the kind, must certainly appear extremely ludicrous to any superior observer, were it possible to conceive, on the naturalistic hypothesis, that such observers should exist; and the comedy could not be otherwise than greatly relieved and heightened by the performances of the small sect of philosophers who, knowing perfectly as an abstract truth that freedom is an absurdity, yet in moments of balance and deliberation invariably conceive themselves to possess it, just as if they were savages or idealists.

The roots of a superstition so ineradicable must lie deep in the groundwork of our inherited organism, and must, if not now, at least in the first beginning of self-consciousness, have been essential to the welfare of the race which entertained it. Yet it may, perhaps, be thought that this requires us to attribute to the dawn of intelligence ideas which are notoriously of late development; and that as the primitive man knew nothing of 'invariable sequences' or 'universal causation,' he could in nowise be embarrassed in the struggle for existence by recognising that he and his proceedings were as absolutely determined by their antecedents as sticks and stones. It is, of course, true that in any formal or philosophical shape such ideas would be as remote from the intelligence of the savage as the differential calculus. But it can, nevertheless, hardly be denied that, in some shape or other, there must be implicitly present to his consciousness the sense of freedom, since his fetichism largely consists in attributing to inanimate objects the spontaneity which he finds in himself; and it seems equally certain that the sense, I will not say of *constraint*, but of *inevitableness*, would be as embarrassing to a savage in the act of choice as it would to his more cultivated descendant, and would be not less productive of that moral impoverishment which, as I proceed briefly to point out, Determinism is calculated to produce.[1]

[1] It seems to be regarded as quite simple and natural that this attribution of human spontaneity to inanimate objects should be the first stage in the interpretation of the external world, and that it should be only after the uniformity of material Nature had been conclusively established by long and laborious experience that the same principles were applied to the inner experience of man himself. But, in truth, unless man in the very earliest stages of his development had believed himself to be free, precisely the opposite order of discovery might have been anticipated. Even now our means of external

And here I am anxious to avoid any appearance of the exaggeration which, as I think, has sometimes characterised discussions upon this subject. I admit that there is nothing in the theory of determinism which need modify the substance of the moral law. That which duty prescribes, or the 'Practical Reason' recommends, is equally prescribed and recommended whether our actual decisions are or are not irrevocably bound by a causal chain which reaches back in unbroken retrogression through a limitless past. It may also be admitted that no argument

investigation are so imperfect that it is rather a stretch of language to say that the theory of uniformity is in accordance with experience, much less that it is established by it. On the contrary, the more refined are our experiments, the more elaborate are our precautions, the more difficult it is to obtain results absolutely identical with each other, qualitatively as well as quantitatively. So far, therefore, as mere observation goes, Nature seems to be always aiming at a uniformity which she never quite succeeds in attaining, and though it is no doubt true that the differences are due to errors in the observations and not to errors in Nature, this manifestly cannot be proved by the observations themselves, but only by a theory established independently of the observations, and by which these may be corrected and interpreted But a man's own motives for acting in a particular way at a particular time are simple compared with the complexities of the material world, and to himself at least might be known (one would suppose) with reasonable certainty. Here, then (were it not for the inveterate illusion, old as self-consciousness itself, that at the moment of choice no uniformity of antecedents need insure a uniformity of consequences) would have been the natural starting-point and suggestion of a theory of causation which, as experience ripened and knowledge grew, might have gradually extended itself to the universe at large. Man would, in fact, have had nothing more to do than to apply to the chaotic complex of the macrocosm the principles of rigid and unchanging law by which he had discovered the microcosm to be governed against good resolutions or virtuous endeavours can fairly be founded upon necessitarian doctrines. No doubt he who makes either good resolutions or virtuous endeavours does so (on the determinist theory) because he could not do otherwise; but none the less may these play an important part among the antecedents by which moral actions are ultimately produced. An even stronger admission may, I think, be properly made. There is a fatalistic temper of mind found in some of the greatest men of action, religious and irreligious, in which the sense that all that happens is fore-ordained does in no way weaken the energy of volition, but only adds a finer temper to the courage. It nevertheless remains the fact that the persistent realisation of the doctrine that voluntary decisions are as completely determined by external and (if you go far enough back) by material conditions as involuntary ones, does really conflict with the sense of personal responsibility, and that with the sense of personal responsibility is bound up the moral will. Nor is this all. It may be a small matter that determinism should render it thoroughly irrational to feel righteous indignation at the misconduct of other people. It cannot be wholly without importance that it should render it equally irrational to feel righteous indignation at our own. Self-condemnation, repentance, remorse, and the whole train of cognate emotions, are really so useful for the promotion of virtue that it is a pity to find them at a stroke thus deprived of all reasonable foundation, and reduced, if they are to survive at all, to the position of amiable but unintelligent weaknesses. It is clear, moreover, that these emotions, if they are to fall, will not fall alone. What is to become of moral admiration? The virtuous man will, indeed, continue to deserve and to receive admiration of a certain kind—the admiration, namely, which we justly accord to a well-made machine; but this is a very different sentiment from that at present evoked by the heroic or the saintly; and it is, therefore, much to be feared that, at least in the region of the higher feelings, the world will be no great gainer by the effective spread of sound naturalistic doctrine.

No doubt this conflict between a creed which claims intellectual assent and emotions which have their root and justification in beliefs which are deliberately rejected, is greatly mitigated by the precious faculty which the human race enjoys of quietly ignoring the logical consequences of its own accepted theories. If the abstract reason by which such theories are contrived always ended in producing a practice corresponding to them, natural selection would long ago have killed off all those who possessed abstract reason. If a complete accord between practice and speculation were required of us, philosophers would long ago have been eliminated. Nevertheless, the persistent conflict between that which is thought to be true, and that which is felt to be noble and of good report, not only produces a sense of moral unrest in the individual, but makes it impossible for us to avoid the conclusion that the creed which leads to such results is, somehow, unsuited for 'such beings as we are in such a world as ours.'

III

There is thus an incongruity between the sentiments subservient to morality, and the naturalistic account of their origin.   It remains to inquire whether any better harmony prevails between the demands of the ethical imagination and what Naturalism tells us concerning the final goal of all human endeavour.

This is plainly not a question of small or subsidiary importance, though it is one which I shall make no attempt to treat with anything like completeness.   Two only of these ethical demands is it necessary, indeed, that I should here refer to: that which requires the ends prescribed by morality to be consistent; and that which requires them to be adequate.   Can we say that either one or the other is of a kind which the naturalistic theory is able to satisfy?

The first of these questions — that relating to consistency—will no doubt be dealt with in different ways by various schools of moralists; but by whatever path they travel, all should arrive at a negative conclusion.   Those who hold as I do, that 'reasonable self-love' has a legitimate position among ethical ends; that as a matter of fact it is a virtue wholly incompatible with what is commonly called selfishness; and that society suffers not from having too much of it, but from having too little, will probably take the view that, until the world undergoes a very remarkable transformation, a complete harmony between 'egoism' and 'altruism,' between the pursuit of the highest happiness for one's self and the highest happiness for other people, can never be provided by a creed which refuses to admit that the deeds done and the character formed in this life can flow over into another, and there permit a reconciliation and an adjustment between the conflicting principles which are not always possible here. To those, again, who hold (as I think, erroneously), both that the 'greatest happiness of the greatest number' is the right end of action, and also that, as a matter of fact, every agent invariably pursues his own, a heaven and a hell, which should make it certain that principle and interest were always in agreement, would seem almost a necessity. Not otherwise, neither by education, public opinion, nor positive law, can there be any assured harmony produced between that which man must do by the constitution of his will, and that which he ought to do according to the promptings of his conscience. On the other hand, it must be acknowledged that those moralists who are of opinion that 'altruistic' ends alone are

worthy of being described as moral, and that man is
not incapable of pursuing them without any self-
regarding motives, require no future life to eke out
their practical system.   But even they would probably not be unwilling to admit, with the rest of the
world, that there is something jarring to the moral
sense in a comparison between the distribution of
happiness and the distribution of virtue, and that no
better mitigation of the difficulty has yet 'been
suggested than that which is provided by a system
of 'rewards and punishments,' impossible in any universe constructed on strictly naturalistic principles.

With this bare indication of some of the points
which naturally suggest themselves in connection
with the first question suggested above, I pass on to
the more interesting problem raised by the second:
that which is concerned with the *emotional* adequacy
of the ends prescribed by Naturalistic Ethics.   And
in order to consider this to the best advantage I
will assume that we are dealing with an ethical system which puts these ends at their highest; which
charges them, as it were, to the full with all that,
on the naturalistic theory, they are capable of con-
taining.   Taking, then, as my text no narrow or
egoistic scheme, I will suppose that in the perfection and felicity of the sentient creation we may
find the all-inclusive object prescribed by morality
for human endeavour.   Does this, then, or does it
not, supply us with all that is needed to satisfy our
ethical imagination?   Does it, or does it not, pro-

vide us with an ideal end, not merely big enough to exhaust our energies, but great enough to satisfy our aspirations?

At first sight the question may seem absurd. The object is admittedly worthy; it is admittedly beyond our reach. The unwearied efforts of countless generations, the slow accumulation of inherited experience, may, to those who find themselves able to read optimism into evolution, promise some faint approximation to the millennium at some far distant epoch. How, then, can we, whose own contribution to the great result must be at the best insignificant, at the worst nothing or worse than nothing, presume to think that the prescribed object is less than adequate to our highest emotional requirements? The reason is plain: our ideals are framed, not according to the measure of our performances, but according to the measure of our thoughts; and our thoughts about the world in which we live tend, under the influence of increasing knowledge, constantly to dwarf our estimate of the importance of man, if man be indeed, as Naturalism would have us believe, no more than a phenomenon among phenomena, a natural object among other natural objects.

For what is man looked at from this point of view? Time was when his tribe and its fortunes were enough to exhaust the energies and to bound the imagination of the primitive sage.[1] The gods'

---

[1] The line of thought here is identical with that which I pursued in an already published essay on the *Religion of Humanity.* I

peculiar care, the central object of an attendant universe, that for which the sun shone and the dew fell, to which the stars in their courses ministered, it drew its origin in the past from divine ancestors, and might by divine favour be destined to an indefinite existence of success and triumph in the future. These ideas represent no early or rudimentary stage in the human thought, yet have we left them far behind. The family, the tribe, the nation, are no longer enough to absorb our interests. Man— past, present, and future—lays claim to our devotion. What, then, can we say of him? Man, so far as natural science by itself is able to teach us, is no longer the final cause of the universe, the Heaven-descended heir of all the ages. His very existence is an accident, his story a brief and transitory episode in the life of one of the meanest of the planets. Of the combination of causes which first converted a dead organic compound into the living progenitors of humanity, science, indeed, as yet knows nothing. It is enough that from such beginnings famine, disease, and mutual slaughter, fit nurses of the future lords of creation, have gradually evolved, after infinite travail, a race with conscience enough to feel that it is vile, and intelligence enough to know that it is insignificant. We survey the past, and see that its history is of blood and tears, of helpless blundering, of wild revolt, of stupid ac-

have not hesitated to borrow the phraseology of that essay wherever it seemed convenient.

quiescence, of empty aspirations. We sound the future, and learn that after a period, long compared with the individual life, but short indeed compared with the divisions of time open to our investigation, the energies of our system will decay, the glory of the sun will be dimmed, and the earth, tideless and inert, will no longer tolerate the race which has for a moment disturbed its solitude. Man will go down into the pit, and all his thoughts will perish. The uneasy consciousness, which in this obscure corner has for a brief space broken the contented silence of the universe, will be at rest. Matter will know itself no longer. 'Imperishable monuments' and 'immortal deeds,' death itself, and love stronger than death, will be as though they had never been. Nor will anything that *is* be better or be worse for all that the labour, genius, devotion, and suffering of man have striven through countless generations to effect.

It is no reply to say that the substance of the Moral Law need suffer no change through any modification of our views of man's place in the universe. This may be true, but it is irrelevant. We desire, and desire most passionately when we are most ourselves, to give our service to that which is Universal, and to that which is Abiding. Of what moment is it, then (from this point of view), to be assured of the fixity of the moral law when it and the sentient world, where alone it has any significance, are alike destined to vanish utterly away within periods trifling beside those with which the geologist and the astronomer lightly deal in the course of their habitual speculations? No doubt to us ordinary men in our ordinary moments considerations like these may seem far off and of little meaning. In the hurry and bustle of every-day life death itself—the death of the individual—seems shadowy and unreal; how much more shadowy, how much less real, that remoter but not less certain death which must some day overtake the race! Yet, after all, it is in moments of reflection that the worth of creeds may best be tested; it is through moments of reflection that they come into living and effectual contact with our active life. It cannot, therefore, be a matter to us of small moment that, as we learn to survey the material world with a wider vision, as we more clearly measure the true proportions which man and his performances bear to the ordered Whole, our practical ideal gets relatively dwarfed and beggared, till we may well feel inclined to ask whether so transitory and so unimportant an accident in the general scheme of things as the fortunes of the human race can any longer satisfy aspirations and emotions nourished upon beliefs in the Everlasting and the Divine.

CHAPTER II

NATURALISM AND ÆSTHETIC

I

In the last chapter I considered the effects which Naturalism must tend to produce upon the sentiments associated with Morality. I now proceed to consider the same question in connection with the sentiments known as æsthetic; and as I assumed that the former class were, like other evolutionary utilities, in the main produced by the normal operation of selection, so I now assume that the latter, being (at least in any developed stage) quite useless for the preservation of the individual or species, must be regarded, upon the naturalistic hypothesis, as mere by-products of the great machinery by which organic life is varied and sustained. It will not, I hope, be supposed that I propose to offer this distinction as a material contribution towards the definition either of ethic or of æsthetic sentiments. This is a question in which I am in no way interested; and I am quite prepared to admit that some emotions which in ordinary language would be described as 'moral,' are useless enough to be included in the class of natural accidents; and also that this class may,

3

indeed does, include many emotions which no one following common usage would characterise as æsthetic. The fact remains, however, that the capacity for every form of feeling must in the main either be, or not be, the direct result of selection and elimination; and whereas in the first section of the last chapter I considered the former class, taking moral emotion as their type, so now I propose to offer some observations on the second class, taking as their type the emotions excited by the Beautiful. Whatever value these Notes may have will not necessarily be affected by any error that I may have made in the apportionment between the two divisions, and the reader may make what redistribution he thinks fit, without thereby necessarily invalidating the substance of the conclusions which I offer for his acceptance.

I do not, however, anticipate that there will be any serious objection raised from the scientific side to the description of developed æsthetic emotion as 'accidental,' in the sense in which that word is here employed. The obstacle I have to deal with in conducting the argument of this chapter is of a different kind. My object is to indicate the consequences which flow from a purely naturalistic treatment of the theory of the Beautiful; and I am at once met with the difficulty that, so far as I am aware, no such treatment has ever been attempted on a large scale, and that the fragmentary contributions which have been made to the subject do not meet

with general acceptance on the part of scientific investigators themselves. To say that certain capacities for highly complex feeling are not the direct
result of natural selection, and were not evolved to
aid the race in the struggle for existence, may be a
true, but is a purely negative account of the matter,
and gives but little help in dealing with the two
questions to which an answer is especially required :
namely, What are the causes, historical, psychological, and physiological, which enable us to derive æsthetic gratification from some objects, and forbid us
to derive it from others ? and, Is there any fixed and
permanent element in Beauty, any unchanging reality which we perceive in or through beautiful objects,
and to which normal æsthetic feelings correspond ?

Now, it is clear that on the naturalistic hypothesis
the second question cannot be properly dealt with
till some sort of answer has been given to the first ;
and the answers given to the first seem so unsatisfactory that they can hardly be regarded as even
provisionally adequate.

In order to realise the difficulties and, as I think,
the shortcomings of existing theories on the subject, let us take the case of Music—by far the most
convenient of the Fine Arts for our purpose, partly because, unlike Architecture, it serves no very
obvious purpose,[1] and we are thus absolved from

---

[1] I may be permitted to ignore Mr. Spencer's suggestion that
the function of music is to promote sympathy by improving our
modulation in speech.

giving any opinion on the relation between beauty and utility; partly because, unlike Painting and Poetry, it has no external reference, and we are thus absolved from giving any opinion on the relation between beauty and truth. Of the inestimable blessings which these peculiarities carry with them, anyone may judge who has ever got bogged in the barren controversies concerning the Beautiful and the Useful, the Real and the Ideal, which fill so large a space in certain classes of æsthetic literature. Great indeed will he feel the advantages to be of dealing with an Art whose most characteristic utterances have so little directly to do, either with utility or truth.

What, then, is the cause of our delight in Music? It is sometimes hastily said to have originated in the ancestors of man through the action of sexual selection. This is of course impossible. Sexual selection can only work on materials already in existence. Like other forms of selection, it can improve, but it cannot create; and the capacity for enjoying music (or noise) on the part of the female, and the capacity for making it on the part of the male, must both have existed in a rudimentary state before matrimonial preferences can have improved either one gift or the other. I do not in any case quite understand how sexual selection is supposed even to improve the capacity for *enjoyment*. If the taste exist, it can no doubt develop the means required for its gratification; but how can it improve the taste itself? The females of certain species of spiders, I believe, like to see good dancing. Sexual selection, therefore, no doubt may gradually improve the dancing of the male. The females of many animals are, it seems, fond of particular kinds of noise. Sexual selection may therefore gradually furnish the male with the apparatus by which appropriate noises may be produced. In both cases, however, a pre-existing taste is the cause of the variation, not the variation of the taste; nor, except in the case of the advanced arts, which do not flourish at a period when those who successfully practise them have any advantage in the matrimonial struggle, does taste appear to be one of the necessary qualifications of the successful artist. Of course, if violin - playing were an important aid to courtship, sexual selection would tend to develop that musical feeling and discrimination, without which good violin-playing is impossible. But a grasshopper requires no artistic sensibility before it can successfully rub its wing-cases together; so that Nature is only concerned to provide the anatomical machinery by which such rubbing may result in a sibilation gratifying to the existing æsthetic sensibilities of the female, but cannot in any way be concerned in developing the artistic side of those sensibilities themselves.

Sexual selection, therefore, however well it may be fitted to give an explanation of a large number of animal noises and of the growth of the organs by

which they are produced, throws but little light on
the origin and development of musical feeling, either
in animals or men. And the other explanations I
have seen do not seem to me much better. Take,
for instance, Mr. Spencer's modification of Rousseau's
theory. According to Mr. Spencer, strong emotions
are naturally accompanied by muscular exertion, and,
among other muscular exertions, by contractions
and extensions of 'the muscles of the chest, abdomen,
and vocal cords.' The resultant noises recall by
association the emotions which gave them birth, and
from this primordial coincidence sprang, as we are
asked to believe, first cadenced speech, and then
music. Now I do not desire to quarrel with the
'primordial coincidence.' My point is, that even if
it ever took place, it affords no explanation of any
modern feeling for music. Grant that a particular
emotion produced a 'contraction of the abdomen,'
that the 'contraction of the abdomen' produced a
sound or series of sounds, and that, through this
association with the originating emotion, the sound
ultimately came to have independent æsthetic value,
how are we advanced towards any explanation of
the fact that quite different sound-effects now please
us, and that the nearer we get to the original noises,
the more hideous they appear? How does the 'primordial coincidence' account for our ancestors liking the tom-tom? And how does the fact that our
ancestors liked the tom-tom account for our liking
the Ninth Symphony?

The truth is that Mr. Spencer's theory, like all others which endeavour to trace back the pleasure-giving qualities of art to some simple and original association, slurs over the real difficulties of the problem. If it is the primitive association which produces the pleasure-giving quality, the further this is left behind by the developing art, the less pleasure should be produced. Of course, if the art is continually fed from other associations and different experiences, if fresh emotional elements are constantly added to it capable of being worn and weathered into the fitting soil for an æsthetic harvest, in that case, no doubt, we may suppose that with each new development its pleasure - giving qualities may be enriched and multiplied. But then, it is to these new elements and to these new experiences, not to the 'primordial coincidence,' that we should mainly look for the causal explanation of our æsthetic feeling. In the case of music, where are these new elements and experiences to be found? None can tell us; few theorists even try. Indeed, the procedure of those who account for music by searching for the primitive association which first in the history of man or of his ancestors conferred æsthetic value upon noise, is as if one should explain the Amazon in its flood by pointing to the rivulet in the far Andes which, as the tributary most distant from its mouth, has the honour of being called its source. This may be allowed to stand as a geographical description, but it is very

inadequate as a physical explanation. Dry up the
rivulet, and the huge river would still flow on,
without abatement or diminution. Only its titular
origin has been touched; and if we would know the
Amazon in its beginnings, and trace back the history
of the vast result through all the complex ramifica-
tions of its contributory causes, each great confluent
must be explored, each of the countless streams
enumerated whose gathered waters sweep into the
sea four thousand miles across the plain.

The imperfection of this mode of procedure will
become clear if we compare it with that adopted
by the same school of theorists when they endeavour
to explain the beauty of landscape. I do not mean
to express any assent to their account of the causes
of our feelings for scenery; on the contrary, these
accounts seem to me untenable. But though untenable, they are not on the face of them inadequate.
Natural objects—the sky and hills, woods and waters
—are spread out before us as they were spread out
before our remotest ancestors, and there is no obvious absurdity (if the hereditary transmission of
acquired qualities be granted) in conceiving them,
through the secular experience of mankind, to become charged with associations which reappear for
us in the vague and massive form of æsthetic pleasure. But according to all association theories of
music, that which is charged with the raw material of
æsthetic pleasure is not the music we wish to have
explained, but some primeval howl, or at best the

unmusical variations of ordinary speech, and no solution whatever is offered of the paradox that the sounds which give musical delight have no associations, and that the sounds which have associations give no musical delight.

It is, perhaps, partly in consequence of these or analogous difficulties, but mainly in consequence of his views on heredity, which preclude him from accepting any theory which involves the transmission of acquired qualities, that Weismann gives an account of the musical sense which is practically equivalent to the denial that any explanation of the pleasure we derive from music is possible at all. For him, the faculties which enable us to appreciate and enjoy music were evolved for entirely different purposes, and it is a mere accident that, when they come into relation with certain combinations of sound, we obtain through their means æsthetic gratification. Mankind, no doubt, are continually inventing new musical devices, as they are continually inventing new dishes. But as the second process implies an advance in the art of cookery, but no transmitted modification in the human palate, so the former implies musical progress, but no change in the innate capacities of successive generations of listeners.[1]

[1] I have made no allusion to Helmholtz's classic investigations, for these deal chiefly with the physical character of the sounds, or combinations of sound, which give us pleasure, but do not pretend fully to answer the question *why* they give pleasure.

II

This is, perhaps, a sufficiently striking example of
the unsatisfactory condition of scientific æsthetics,
and may serve to show how difficult it is to find in
the opinions of different authorities a common body
of doctrine on which to rest the argument of this
chapter.   I should imagine, however, both from
the speculations to which I have just briefly adverted, and from any others with which I am acquainted, that no person who is at all in sympathy
with the naturalistic view of things would maintain
that there anywhere exists an intrinsic and essential
quality of beauty, independent of the feelings and
the taste of the observer.   The very nature, indeed,
of the senses principally engaged indicates that on
the naturalistic hypothesis they cannot, in most cases,
refer to any external and permanent object of beauty.
For Naturalism (as commonly held) is deeply committed to the distinction between the *primary* and
the *secondary* qualities of matter ; the former (extension, solidity, and so forth) being supposed to exist as
they are perceived, while the latter (such as sound and
colour) are due to the action of the primary qualities
upon the sentient organism, and apart from the sentient organism have no independent being.   Every
scene in Nature, therefore, and every work of art,
whose beauty consists either directly or indirectly,
either presentatively or representatively, in colour or

in sound, has, and can have, no more permanent existence than is possessed by that relation between the
senses and our material environment which gave
them birth, and in the absence of which they perish.
If we could perceive the succession of events which
constitute a sunset exactly as they occur, as they
are (physically, not metaphysically speaking) *in
themselves*, they would, so far as we can guess, have
no æsthetic merit, or even meaning. If we could
perform the same operation on a symphony, it
would end in a like result. The first would be no
more than a special agitation of the ether; the
second would be no more than a special agitation
of the air. However much they might excite the
curiosity of the physicist or the mathematician, for
the artist they could no longer possess either interest or significance.

It might, however, be said that the Beautiful,
although it cannot be called permanent as compared
with the general framework of the external world,
is, nevertheless, sufficiently permanent for all human
purposes, inasmuch as it depends upon fixed relations between our senses and their material surroundings. Without at present stopping to dispute
this, let us consider whether we have any right to
suppose that even this degree of 'objectivity' can
be claimed for the quality of beauty. In order to
settle the question we can, on the naturalistic
hypothesis, appeal, it would seem, to only one
authority, namely, the experience of mankind.

Does this, then, provide us with any evidence that beauty is more than the name for a miscellaneous flux of endlessly varying causes, possessing no property in common, except that at some place, at some time, and in some person, they have shown themselves able to evoke the kind of feeling which we choose to describe as æsthetic?

Put thus there seems room for but one answer. The variations of opinion on the subject of beauty are notorious. Discordant pronouncements are made by different races, different ages, different individuals, the same individual at different times. Nor does it seem possible to devise any scheme by which an authoritative verdict can be extracted from this chaos of contradiction. An appeal, indeed, is sometimes made from the opinion of the vulgar to the decision of persons of ' trained sensibility '; and there is no doubt that, as a matter of fact, through the action of those who profess to belong to this class, an orthodox tradition has grown up which may seem at first sight almost to provide some faint approximation to the ' objective ' standard of which we are in search. Yet it will be evident on consideration that it is not simply on their ' trained sensibility ' that experts rely in forming their opinion. The ordinary critical estimate of a work of art is the result of a highly complicated set of antecedents, and by no means consists in a simple and naked valuation of the ' æsthetic thrill ' which the aforesaid work produces in the critic, now and here. If it were so, clearly it could not be of any importance to the art critic when and by whom any particular work of art was produced. Problems of age and questions of authorship would be left entirely to the historian, and the student of the beautiful would, as such, ask himself no question but this: How and why are my æsthetic sensibilities affected by this statue, poem, picture, as it is in itself? or (to put the same thing in a form less open to metaphysical disputation), What would my feelings towards it be if I were totally ignorant of its date, its author, and the circumstances of its production?

As we all know, these collateral considerations are never in practice ignored by the critic. He is preoccupied, and rightly preoccupied, by a multitude of questions beyond the mere valuation of the outstanding amount of æsthetic enjoyment which, in the year 1892, any artistic or literary work, taken *simpliciter*, is, as a matter of fact, capable of producing. He is much concerned with its technical peculiarities. He is anxious to do justice to its author, to assign him his true rank among the productive geniuses of his age and country, to make due allowance for his 'environment,' for the traditions in which he was nurtured, for the causes which make his creative genius embody itself in one form rather than in another. Never for one instant does the critic forget, or allow his reader to forget, that the real magnitude of the foreshortened object under observation must be estimated by the rules of historical perspective. Never does he omit, in dealing with the artistic legacies of bygone times, to take account of any long - accepted opinion which may exist concerning them. He endeavours to make himself the exponent of the 'correct view.' His judgment is, consciously or unconsciously, but not, I think, wrongly, a sort of compromise between that which he would form if he drew solely from his own inner experience, and that which has been formed for him by the accumulated wisdom of his predecessors on the bench. He expounds case-made law. He is partly the creature and partly the creator of a critical tradition; and we can easily conjecture how devious his course would be, were his orbit not largely controlled by the attraction of received views, if we watch the disastrous fate which so often overtakes him when he pronounces judgment on new works, or on works of which there is no estimate embodied in any literary creed which he thinks it necessary to respect. Voltaire's opinion of Shakespeare does not make one think less of Voltaire, but it throws an interesting light on the genesis of average critical decisions and the normal growth of taste.

From these considerations, which might easily be supplemented, it seems plain that the opinions of critical experts represent, not an objective standard, if such a thing there be, but an historical compromise. The agreement among them, so far as such a thing is to be found, is not due solely to the fact

that with their own eyes they all see the same
things, and therefore say the same things; it is not
wholly the result of a common experience: it arises
in no small measure from their sympathetic endeavours to see as others have seen, to feel as others
have felt, to judge as others have judged. This
may be, and I suppose is, the fairest way of compar-
ing the merits of deceased artists. But, at the same
time, it makes it impossible for us to attach much
weight to the assumed consensus of the ages, or to
suppose that this, so far as it exists, implies the
reality of a standard independent of the varying
whims and fancies of individual critics. In truth,
however, the consensus of the ages, even about the
greatest works of creative genius, is not only in part
due to the process of critical manufacture indicated
above, but its whole scope and magnitude are absurdly exaggerated in the phrases which pass current on the subject. This is not a question, be it
observed, of æsthetic right and wrong, of good taste
or bad taste; it is a question of statistics. We are
not here concerned with what the mass of mankind,
even of educated mankind, ought to feel, but with
what as a matter of fact they do feel, about the
works of literature and art which they have inherited from the past. And I believe that every impartial observer will admit that, of the æsthetic
emotion actually experienced by any generation, the
merest fraction is due to the 'immortal' productions
of the generations which have long preceded it.

Their immortality is largely an immortality of libraries and museums; they supply material to critics and historians, rather than enjoyment to mankind; and if it were to be maintained that one music-hall song gives more æsthetic pleasure in a night than the most exquisite compositions of Palestrina in a decade, I know not how the proposition could be refuted.

The ancient Norsemen supposed that besides the soul of the dead, which went to the region of departed spirits, there survived a ghost, haunting, though not for ever, the scenes of his earthly labours. At first vivid and almost lifelike, it slowly waned and faded, until at length it vanished, leaving behind it no trace or memory of its spectral presence amidst the throng of living men. So, it seems to me, is the immortality we glibly predicate of departed artists. If they survive at all, it is but a shadowy life they live, moving on through the gradations of slow decay to distant but inevitable death. They can no longer, as heretofore, speak directly to the hearts of their fellow-men, evoking their tears or laughter, and all the pleasures, be they sad or merry, of which imagination holds the secret. Driven from the market-place, they become first the companions of the student, then the victims of the specialist. He who would still hold familiar intercourse with them must train himself to penetrate the veil which, in ever-thickening folds, conceals them from the ordinary gaze; he must catch the tone of a vanished society, he must move in a circle of alien associations, he must think in a language not his own. Need we, then, wonder that under such conditions the outfit of a critic is as much intellectual as emotional, or that if from off the complex sentiments with which they regard the 'immortal legacies of the past' we strip all that is due to interests connected with history, with biography, with critical analyses, with scholarship, and with technique, but a small modicum will, as a rule, remain which can with justice be attributed to pure æsthetic sensibility.

III

I have, however, no intention of implying by the preceding observations that the æsthetic feelings of 'the vulgar' are less sophisticated than those of the learned. A very cursory examination of 'public taste' and its revolutions may suffice to convince anyone of the contrary. And, in the first place, let us ask why every 'public' has a taste? And why, at least in Western communities, that taste is so apt to alter? Why, in other words, do communities or sections of communities so often feel the same thing at the same time, and so often feel different things at different times? Why is there so much uniformity, and why is there so much change?

These questions are of great interest, although they have not, perhaps, met with all the attention

4

they deserve. In these Notes it would not be fitting
to attempt to deal with them at length, and I shall
only offer observations on two points which seem
relevant to the design of the present chapter.

The question of Uniformity is best approached
at the humbler end of the æsthetic scale, in connection, not with art in its narrower and loftier sense,
but with *dress*. Everybody is acquainted, either
by observation or by personal experience, with the
coercive force of fashion; but not everybody is
aware what an instructive and interesting phenomenon it presents. Consider the case of bonnets.
During the same season all persons belonging, or
aspiring to belong, to the same ' public,' if they wear
bonnets at all, wear bonnets modelled on the same
type. Why do they do this? If we were asking a
similar question, not about bonnets, but about steam-
engines, the answer would be plain. People tend
at the same date to use the same kind of engine for
the same kind of purpose because it is the best avail-
able. They change their practice when a better one
is invented. But as so used the words ' better' and
' best' have no application to modern dress. Neither
efficiency nor economy, it will at once be admitted,
supplies the grounds of choice or the motives for
variation.

If, again, we were asking the question about some
great phase of art, we should probably be told that
the general acceptance of it by a whole generation
was due to some important combination of historic

causes, acting alike on artist and on public. Such causes no doubt exist and have existed; but the case of fashion proves that uniformity is not produced by them alone, since it will hardly be pretended that there is any widely diffused cause in the social environment, except the coercive operation of fashion itself, which should make the bonnets which were thought becoming in 1881 unbecoming in the year 1892.

Again, we might be told that art contains essential principles of self-development, which require one productive phase to succeed another by a kind of inner necessity, and determine not merely that there shall be variation, but what that variation shall be. This also may be, and is, in a certain sense, true. But it can hardly be supposed that we can explain the fashions which prevail in any year by assuming, not merely that the fashions of the previous years were foredoomed to change, but also that, in the nature of the case, only one change was possible, that, namely, which actually took place. Such a doctrine would be equivalent to saying that if all the bonnet-wearers were for a space deprived of any knowledge of each other's proceedings (all other things remaining the same), they would, on the resumption of their ordinary intercourse, find that they had all inclined towards much the same modification of the type of bonnet prevalent before their separation—a conclusion which seems to me, I confess, to be somewhat improbable.

It may perhaps be hazarded, as a further explanation, that this uniformity of practice is indeed a fact,
and is really produced by a complex group of causes
which we denominate 'fashion,' but that it is a
uniformity of *practice* alone, not of *taste* or *feeling*,
and has no real relation to any æsthetic problem
whatever. This is a question the answer to which
can be supplied, I apprehend, by observation alone ;
and the answer which observation enables us to give
seems to me quite unambiguous. If, as is possible, my readers have but small experience in such
matters themselves, let them examine the experiences of their acquaintance. They will find, if I
mistake not, that by whatever means conformity to
a particular pattern may have been brought about,
those who conform are not, as a rule, conscious of
coercion by an external and arbitrary authority.
They do not act under penalty ; they yield no unwilling obedience. On the contrary, their admiration for a 'well-dressed person,' *quâ* well-dressed, is
at least as genuine an æsthetic approval as any they
are in the habit of expressing for other forms of
beauty ; just as their objection to an outworn fashion is based on a perfectly genuine æsthetic dislike.
They are repelled by the unaccustomed sight, as a
reader of discrimination is repelled by turgidity or
false pathos. It appears to them ugly, even gro-
tesque, and they turn from it with an aversion as
disinterested, as unperturbed by personal or 'society' considerations, as if they were critics contem-

plating the production of some pretender in the region of Great Art.

In truth this tendency in matters æsthetic is only a particular case of a general tendency to agreement which plays an even more important part in other departments of human activity. Its operation, beneficent doubtless on the whole, may be traced through all social and political life. We owe to it in part that deep-lying likeness in tastes, in opinions, and in habits, without which cohesion among the individual units of a community would be impossible, and which constitutes the unmoved platform on which we fight out our political battles. It is no contemptible factor among the forces by which nations are created and religions disseminated and maintained. It is the very breath of life to sects and coteries. Sometimes, no doubt, its results are ludicrous. Sometimes they are unfortunate. Sometimes merely insignificant. Under which of these heads we should class our ever-changing uniformity in dress I will not take upon me to determine. It is sufficient for my present purpose to point out that the æsthetic likings which fashion originates, however trivial, are perfectly genuine; and that to an origin similar in kind, however different in dignity and permanence, should be traced much of the characteristic quality which gives its special flavour to the higher artistic sentiments of each successive generation.

IV

It is, of course, true that this ' tendency to agreement,'[1] this principle of drill, cannot itself determine
the objects in respect of which the agreement is to
take place.   It can do much to make every member
of a particular ' public' like the same bonnet, or the
same epic, at the same time; but it cannot determine what that bonnet or that epic is to be.   A
fashion, as the phrase goes, has to be ' set,' and the
persons who set it manifestly do not follow it.   What,
then, do they follow?   We note the influences that
move the flock.   What moves the bell-wether?

Here again much might conveniently be learnt
from an examination of fashion and its changes, for
these provide us with a field of research where we
are disturbed by no preconceived theories or inconvenient admirations, and where we may dissect our
subject with the cold impartiality which befits
scientific investigation.   The reader, however, may
think that enough has been done already by this
method; and I shall accordingly pursue a more
general treatment of the subject, premising that in
the brief observations which follow no complete

[1] **Of** course the ' tendency to agreement' is not presented to the
reader as a simple, undecomposable social force.   It is, doubtless,
highly complex, one of its most important elements being, I suppose, the instinct of uncritical imitation, which is the very basis of all
effective education.   The line of thought hinted at in this paragraph
is pursued much further in the Third Part of this Essay.

analysis of the complexity of concrete Nature is attempted, or is, indeed, necessary for my purpose.

It will be convenient, in the first place, to distinguish between the mode in which the public who enjoy, and the artists who produce, respectively promote æsthetic change. That the public are often weary and expectant—weary of what is provided for them, and expectant of some good thing to come—will hardly be denied. Yet I do not think they can be usually credited with the conscious demand for a fresh artistic development. For though they often want some new thing, they do not often want a *new kind* of thing; and accordingly it commonly, though not invariably, happens that, when the new thing appears, it is welcomed at first by the few, and only gradually — by the force of fashion and otherwise —conquers the genuine admiration of the many.

The artist, on the other hand, is moved in no small measure by a desire that his work should be his own, no pale reflection of another's methods, but an expression of himself in his own language. He will vary for the better if he can, yet, rather than be conscious of repetition, he will vary for the worse; for vary he must, either in substance or in form, unless he is to be in his own eyes, not a creator, but an imitator; not an artist, but a copyist.[1]

It will be observed that I am not obliged to

[1] No doubt it is an echo of this feeling that makes purchasers commonly prefer a bad original to the best copy of the best original— a preference which in argument it would be exceedingly difficult to justify.

draw the dividing-line between originality and pla-
giarism; to distinguish between the man who is one
of a school, and the man who has done no more
than merely catch the trick of a master. It is
enough that the artist himself draws the distinction,
and will never consciously allow himself to sink from
the first category into the second.

We have here, then, a general cause of change,
but not a cause of change in any particular direction,
or of any particular amount. These I believe to be
determined in part by the relation between the
artists and the public for whom they produce, and in
part by the condition of the art itself at the time the
change occurs. As regards the first, it is commonly
said that the artist is the creation of his age, and the
discovery of this fact is sometimes thought to be a
momentous contribution made by science to the
theory of æsthetic evolution. The statement, however, is unfortunately worded. The action of the
age is, no doubt, important, but it would be more
accurate, I imagine, to describe it as destructive
than as creative; it does not so much produce as
select. It is true, of course, that the influence of
'the environment' in moulding, developing, and
stimulating genius within the limits of its original
capacity is very great, and may seem, especially in
the humbler walks of artistic production, to be all-
powerful. But innate and original genius is not the
creation of any age. It is a biological accident, the
incalculable product of two sets of ancestral ten-

dencies; and what the age does to these biological accidents is not to create them, but to choose from them, to encourage those which are in harmony with its spirit, to crush out and to sterilise the rest. Its action is analogous to that which a plot of ground exercises on the seeds which fall upon it. Some thrive, some languish, some die; and the resulting vegetation is sharply characterised, not because few kinds of seed have there sown themselves, but because few kinds have been allowed to grow up. Without pushing the parallel too far, it may yet serve to illustrate the truth that, as a stained window derives its character and significance from the absorption of a large portion of the rays which endeavour to pass through it, so an age is what it is, not only by reason of what it fosters, but as much, perhaps, by reason of what it destroys. We may conceive, then, that from the total but wholly unknown number of men of productive capacity born in any generation, those whose gifts are in harmony with the tastes of their contemporaries will produce their best; those whose gifts are wholly out of harmony will be extinguished, or, which is very nearly the same thing, will produce only for the benefit of the critics in succeeding generations; while those who occupy an intermediate position will, indeed, produce, but their powers will, consciously or unconsciously, be warped and thwarted, and their creations fall short of what, under happier circumstances, they might have been able to achieve.

Here, then, we have a tendency to change arising out of the artist's insistence on originality, and
a limitation on change imposed by the character
of the age in which he lives. The kind of change
will be largely determined by the condition of
the art which he is practising. If it be in an
early phase, full as yet of undeveloped possibilities, then in all probability he will content himself with improving on his predecessors, without
widely deviating from the lines they have laid
down. For this is the direction of least resistance:
here is no public taste to be formed, here are no
great experiments to be tried, here the pioneer's
rough work of discovery has already been accomplished. But if this particular fashion of art has
culminated, and be in its decline; if, that is to say,
the artist feels more and more difficulty in expressing himself through it, without saying worse what
his predecessors have said already, then one of
three things happens—either originality is perforce
sought for in exaggeration; or a new style is-
invented; or artistic creation is abandoned and the
field is given up to mere copyists. Which of these
events shall happen depends, no doubt, partly on
the accident of genius, but it depends, I think, still
more on the prevailing taste. If, as has frequently
happened, that taste be dominated by the memory
of past ideals; if the little public whom the big
public follow are content with nothing that does
not conform to certain ancient models, a period of

artistic sterility is inevitable. But if circumstances
be more propitious, then art continues to move;
the direction and character of its movement being
due partly to the special turn of genius possessed
by the artist who succeeds in producing a public
taste in harmony with his powers, and partly to the
reaction of the taste thus created, or in process of
creation, upon the general artistic talent of the
community.

Even, however, in those periods when the
movement of art is most striking, it is dangerous
to assume that movement implies progress, *if by
progress be meant increase in the power to excite
æsthetic emotion.* It would be rash to assume this
even as regards Music, where the movement has
been more remarkable, more continuous, and more
apparently progressive over a long period of time
than in any other art whatever. In music, the
artist's desire for originality of expression has been
aided generation after generation by the discovery
of new methods, new forms, new instruments. From
the bare simplicity of the ecclesiastical chant or the
village dance to the ordered complexity of the modern
score, the art has passed through successive stages
of development, in each of which genius has discovered devices of harmony, devices of instrumenta-
tion, and devices of rhythm which would have been
musical paradoxes to preceding generations, and
became musical commonplaces to the generations
that followed after. Yet, what has been the net

gain? Read through the long *catena* of critical judgments, from Wagner back (if you please) to Plato, which every age has passed on its own performances, and you will find that to each of them its music has been as adequate as ours is to us. It moved them not less deeply, nor did it move them differently; and compositions which for us have lost their magic, and which we regard as at best but agreeable curiosities, contained for them the secret of all the unpictured beauties which music shows to her worshippers.

Surely there is here a great paradox. The history of Literature and Art is tolerably well known to us for many hundreds of years. During that period Poetry and Sculpture and Painting have been subject to the usual mutations of fashion; there have been seasons of sterility and seasons of plenty; schools have arisen and decayed; new nations and languages have been pressed into the service of Art; old nations have fallen out of line. But it is not commonly supposed that at the end of it all we are much better off than the Greeks of the age of Pericles in respect of the technical dexterity of the artist, or of the resources which he has at his command. During the same period, and measured by the same external standard, the development of Music has been so great that it is not, I think, easy to exaggerate it. Yet, through all this vast revolution, the position and importance of the art as compared with other arts seem, so far as I can discover, to have .

suffered no sensible change. It was as great four hundred years before Christ as it is at the present moment. It was as great in the sixteenth, seventeenth, and eighteenth centuries as it is in the nineteenth. How, then, can we resist the conclusion that this amazing musical development, produced by the expenditure of so much genius, has added little to the felicity of mankind; unless, indeed, it so happens that in his particular art a steady level of æsthetic sensation can only be maintained by increasing doses of æsthetic stimulant.

V

These somewhat desultory observations do not, it must be acknowledged, carry us very far towards that of which we are in search, namely, a theory of æsthetics in harmony with naturalism. Yet, on recapitulation, negative conclusions of some importance will, I think, be seen to follow from them. It is clear, for instance, that those who, like Goethe, long to dwell among ' permanent relations,' wherever else they may find them, will at least not find them in or behind the feeling of beauty. Such permanent relations do, indeed, exist, binding in their unchanging framework the various forms of energy and matter which make up the physical universe; but it is not the perception of these which, either in Nature or in art, stirs within us æsthetic emotion—else should we find our surest guides to beauty in

an astronomical chart or a table of chemical equiva-
lents, and nothing would seem to us of less æsthetic significance than a symphony or a love-song.
That which is beautiful is not the object as we
know it to be—the vibrating molecule and the un-
dulating ether—but the object as we know it not
to be—glorious with qualities of colour or of sound.
Nor can its beauty be supposed to last any longer
than the transient reaction between it and our special senses, which are assuredly not permanent or
important elements in the constitution of the world
in which we live.

But even within these narrow limits—narrow, I
mean, compared with the wide sweep of our scientific
vision—there seemed to be no ground for supposing
that there is in Nature any standard of beauty to
which all human tastes tend to conform, any beautiful objects which all normally constituted individuals
are moved to admire, any æsthetic judgments which
can claim to be universal. The divergence between
different tastes is, indeed, not only notorious, but is
what we should have expected. As our æsthetic
feelings are not due to natural selection, natural selection will have no tendency to keep them uniform and stable. In this respect they differ, as I
have said, from ethical sentiments and beliefs. De-
viations from sound morality are injurious either
to the individual or to the community—those who
indulge in them are at a disadvantage in the struggle
for existence; hence, on the naturalistic hypothesis,

the approximation to identity in the accepted codes of different nations. But there is, fortunately, no natural punishment annexed to bad taste; and accordingly the variation between tastes has passed into a proverb.

Even in those cases where some slender thread of similarity seemed to bind together the tastes of different times or different persons, further consideration showed that this was largely due to causes which can by no possibility be connected with any supposed permanent element in beauty. The agreement, for example, between critics, in so far as it exists, is to no small extent an agreement in statement and in analysis, rather than an agreement in feeling; they have the same opinion as to the cooking of the dinner, but they by no means all eat it with the same relish. In few cases, indeed, do their estimates of excellence correspond with the living facts of æsthetic emotion as shown either in themselves or in anybody else. Their whole procedure, necessary though it may be for the comparative estimate of the worth of individual artists, unduly conceals the vast and arbitrary[1] changes by which the taste of one generation is divided from that of another. And when we turn from critical tradition to the æsthetic likes and dislikes of men and women; when we leave the admirations which are professed for the emotions which are felt, we find

---

[1] 'Arbitrary,' *i.e.* not due to any causes which point to the existence of objective beauty.

in vast multitudes of cases that these are not connected with the object which happens to excite them by any permanent æsthetic bond at all. Their true determining cause is to be sought in fashion, in that 'tendency to agreement' which plays so large and beneficent a part in social economy. Nor, in considering the causes which produce the rise and fall of schools, and all the smaller mutations in the character of æsthetic production, did we perceive more room for the belief that there is somewhere to be found a permanent element in the beautiful. There is no evidence that these changes constitute stages in any process of gradual approximation to an unchanging standard; they are not born of any strivings after some ideal archetype; they do not, like the movements of science, bring us ever nearer to central and immutable truth. On the contrary, though schools are born, mature, and perish, though ancient forms decay, and new ones are continually devised, this restless movement is, so far as science can pronounce, without meaning or purpose, the casual product of the quest after novelty, determined in its course by incalculable forces, by accidents of genius, by accidents of public humour, involving change but not progress, and predestined, perhaps, to end universally, as at many times and in many places it has ended already, in a mood of barren acquiescence in the repetition of ancient models, the very *Nirvana* of artistic imagination, without desire and without pain.

And yet the persistent and almost pathetic endeavours of æsthetic theory to show that the beautiful is a necessary and unchanging element in the general scheme of things, if they prove nothing else, may at least convince us that mankind will not easily reconcile themselves to the view which the naturalistic theory of the world would seemingly compel them to accept. We feel no difficulty, perhaps, in admitting the full consequences of that theory at the lower end of the æsthetic scale, in the region, for instance, of bonnets and wall-papers. We may tolerate it even when it deals with important elements in the highest art, such as the sense of technical excellence, or sympathy with the craftsman's skill. But when we look back on those too rare moments when feelings stirred in us by some beautiful object not only seem wholly to absorb us, but to raise us to the vision of things far above the ken of bodily sense or discursive reason, we cannot acquiesce in any attempt at explanation which confines itself to the bare enumeration of psychological and physiological causes and effects. We cannot willingly assent to a theory which makes a good composer only differ from a good cook in that he deals in more complicated relations, moves in a wider circle of associations, and arouses our feelings through a different sense. However little, therefore, we may be prepared to accept any particular scheme of metaphysical æsthetics—and most of these appear to me to be very absurd—we must

5

believe that somewhere and for some Being there shines an unchanging splendour of beauty, of which in Nature and in Art we see, each of us from our own standpoint, only passing gleams and stray reflections, whose different aspects we cannot now co-ordinate, whose import we cannot fully comprehend, but which at least is something other than the chance play of subjective sensibility or the far-off echo of ancestral lusts. No such mystical creed can, however, be squeezed out of observation and experiment; Science cannot give it us; nor can it be forced into any sort of consistency with the Naturalistic Theory of the Universe.

CHAPTER III

NATURALISM AND REASON

I

AMONG those who accept without substantial modification the naturalistic theory of the universe are some who find a compensation for the general non-rationality of Nature in the fact that, after all, reason, human reason, is Nature's final product. If the world is not made by Reason, Reason is at all events made by the world; and the unthinking interaction of causes and effects has at least resulted in a consciousness wherein that interaction may be reflected and understood. This is not Teleology. Indeed it is a doctrine which leaves no room for any belief' in design. But in the minds of some who have but imperfectly grasped their own doctrines, it appears capable of partially meeting the sentimental needs to which teleology gives a fuller satis. faction, inasmuch as reason thus finds an assured place in the scheme cš things, and is enabled, after the fashion of the Chinese, in some sort to ennoble its ignoble progenitors.

This theory of the non-rational origin of reason, which is a necessary corollary of the naturalistic

scheme, has philosophical consequences of great interest, to some of which I have alluded elsewhere,[1]
and which must occupy our attention in a later
chapter of these Notes. In the meanwhile, there
are other aspects of the subject which deserve a
moment's consideration.

From the point of view of organic evolution
there is no distinction, I imagine, to be drawn between the development of reason and that of any
other faculty, physiological or psychical, by which
the interests of the individual or the race are pro-
moted. From the humblest form of nervous irritability at one end of the scale, to the reasoning
capacity of the most advanced races at the other,
everything, without exception—sensation, instinct,
desire, volition—has been produced, directly or indirectly, by natural causes acting for the most part
on strictly utilitarian principles. Convenience, not
knowledge, therefore, has been the main end to
which this process has tended. ' It was not for purposes of research that our senses were evolved,' nor
was it in order to penetrate the secrets of the universe that we are endowed with reason.

Under these circumstances it is not surprising
that the faculties thus laboriously created are but
imperfectly fitted to satisfy that speculative curiosity which is one of the most curious by-products of
the evolutionary process. The inadequacy of our
intellect, indeed, to resolve the questions which it

---

[1] *Philosophic Doubt*, Pt. iii., ch. xiii.

is capable of asking is acknowledged (at least in
words) both by students of science and by students
of theology.   But they do not seem so much impressed with the inadequacy of our senses.   Yet, if
the current doctrine of evolution be true, we have
no choice but to admit that with the great mass of
natural fact we are probably brought into no sensible relation at all.   I am not referring here merely
to the limitations imposed upon such senses as we
possess, but to the total absence of an indefinite
number of senses which conceivably we might possess, but do not.   There are sounds which the ear
cannot hear, there are sights which the eye cannot
see.   But besides all these there must be countless ·
aspects of external Nature of which we have no
knowledge; of which, owing to the absence of appropriate organs, we can form no conception; which
imagination cannot picture nor language express.
Had Voltaire been acquainted with the theory of
evolution, he would not have put forward his Mi-
cromegas so much as an illustration of a paradox
which cannot be disproved, as of a truth which cannot be doubted.   For to suppose that a course of
development carried out, not with the object of ex-
tending knowledge or satisfying curiosity, but solely
with that of promoting life, on an area so insignificant as the surface of the earth, between limits
of temperature and pressure so narrow, and under
general conditions so exceptional, should have ended in supplying us with senses even approximately

adequate to the apprehension of Nature in all her complexities, is to believe in a coincidence more astounding than the most audacious novelist has ever employed to cut the knot of some entangled tale.

For it must be recollected that the same natural forces which tend to the evolution of organs which are useful tend also to the suppression of organs that are useless. Not only does Nature take no interest in our general education, not only is she quite indifferent to the growth of enlightenment, unless the enlightenment improve our chances in the struggle for existence, but she positively objects to the very existence of faculties by which these ends might, perhaps, be attained. She regards them as mere hindrances in the only race which she desires to see run; and not content with refusing directly to create any faculty except for a practical purpose, she immediately proceeds to destroy faculties already created when their practical purpose has ceased; for thus does the eye of the cave-born fish degenerate and the instinct of the domesticated animal decay. Those, then, who are inclined to the opinion that between our organism and its environments there is a correspondence which, from the point of view of general knowledge, is even approximately adequate, must hold, in the *first* place, that samples or suggestions of every sort of natural manifestation are to be found in our narrow and limited world; in the *second* place, that these samples are of a character which would permit of nervous tissue

being so modified by selection as to respond specifically to their action; in the *third* place, that such
specific modifications were not only possible, but
would have proved useful at the period of evolution
during which our senses in their present shape were
developed; and in the *fourth* place, that these modifications would have proved useful enough to make
it worth while to use up, for the purpose of producing them, material which might have been, and has
been, otherwise employed.

All these propositions seem to me improbable,
the first two of them incredible.[1] It is impossible,

[1] It may perhaps be said that it is not necessary that we should be
specifically affected by each particular kind of energy in order either
to discover its existence or to investigate its character. It is enough
that among its effects should be some which are cognisable by our
actual senses, that it should modify in some way the world we know,
that it should intervene perceptibly in that part of the general system
to which our organism happens to be immediately connected. This
is no doubt true, and our knowledge of electricity and magnetism
(among other things) is there to prove it. But let it be noted how
slender and how accidental was the clue which led us to the first
beginnings, from which all our knowledge of these great phenomena
is derived. *Directly* they can hardly be said to be in relation with
our organs of perception at all (notwithstanding the fact that light is
now regarded as an electro-magnetic phenomenon) and their *indirect*
relation with them is so slight that probably no amount of mere observation could, in the absence of experiment, have given us a notion of
their magnitude or importance. They were not sought for to fill a
gap whose existence had been demonstrated by calculation. Their
discovery was no inevitable step in the onward march of scientific
knowledge. They were stumbled upon by accident; and few would
be bold enough to assert that if, for example, the human race had
not happened to possess iron, magnetism would ever have presented
itself as a subject requiring investigation at all.

therefore, to resist the conviction that there must be an indefinite number of aspects of Nature respecting which science never can give us any information, even in our dreams. We must conceive ourselves as feeling our way about this dim corner of the illimitable world, like children in a darkened room, encompassed by we know not what; a little better endowed with the machinery of sensation than the protozoon, yet poorly provided indeed as compared with a being, if such a one could be conceived, whose senses were adequate to the infinite variety of material Nature. It is true, no doubt, that we are possessed of reason, and that protozoa are not. But even reason, on the naturalistic theory, occupies no elevated or permanent position in the hierarchy of phenomena. It is not the final result of a great process, the roof and crown of things. On the contrary, it is, as I have said, no more than one of many experiments for increasing our chance of survival, and, among these, by no means the most important or the most enduring.

II

People sometimes talk, indeed, as if it was the difficult and complex work connected with the maintenance of life that was performed by intellect. But there can be no greater delusion. The management of the humblest organ would be infinitely beyond our mental capacity, were it possible for us to be

entrusted with it; and as a matter of fact, it is only
in the simplest jobs that discursive reason is permitted to have a hand at all; our tendency to take
a different view being merely the self-importance of
a child who, because it is allowed to stamp the let-
ters, imagines that it conducts the correspondence.
The best way of looking at mind on the naturalistic
hypothesis is, perhaps, to regard it as an instrument
for securing a flexibility of adaptation which instinct
alone is not able to attain. Instinct is incomparably the better machine in every respect save one.
It works more smoothly, with less friction, with far
greater precision and accuracy.   But it is not adapt-
able.   Many generations and much slaughter are required to breed it into a race.   Once acquired, it can
be modified or expelled only by the same harsh and
tedious methods.   Mind, on the other hand, from
the point of view of organic evolution, may be considered as an inherited faculty for self-adjustment;
and though, as I have already had occasion to note,
the limits within which such adjustment is permitted are exceedingly narrow, within those limits it is
doubtless exceedingly valuable.

But even here one of the principal functions of
mind is to create habits by which, when they are
fully formed, it is itself supplanted. If the conscious
adaptation of means to ends was always necessary
in order to perform even those few functions for the
first performance of which conscious adaptation was
originally required, life would be frittered away in

doing badly, but with deliberation, some small fraction of that which we now do well without any
deliberation at all. The formation of habits is, therefore, as has often been pointed out, a necessary preliminary to the 'higher' uses of mind; for it, and it
alone, sets attention and intelligence free to do work
from which they would otherwise be debarred by
their absorption in the petty needs of daily existence.

But while it is thus plain that the formation of
habits is an essential pre-requisite of mental development, it would also seem that it constitutes the
first step in a process which, if thoroughly successful, would end in the destruction, if not of consciousness itself, at least of the higher manifestation of
consciousness, such as will, attention, and discursive reason.[1] All these, as we may suppose, will be
gradually superseded in an increasing number of
departments of human activity by the growth of instincts or inherited habits, by which even such adjustments between the organism and its surroundings as
now seem most dependent on self-conscious mind
may be successfully effected.

These are prophecies, however, which concern
themselves with a very remote future, and for my
part I do not ask the reader to regard their fulfilment as an inexorable necessity. It is enough if

[1] Empirical psychologists are not agreed as to whether the apparent unconsciousness which accompanies completed habits is real
or not. It is unnecessary for the purpose of my argument that this
point should be determined.

they mark with sufficient emphasis the place which Mind, in its higher manifestations, occupies in the scheme of things, as this is presented to us by the naturalistic hypothesis. Mr. Spencer, who pierces the future with a surer gaze than I can make the least pretence to, looks confidently forward to a time when the relation of man to his surroundings will be so happily contrived that the reign of absolute right-eousness will prevail; conscience, grown unneces-sary, will be dispensed with; the path of least resistance will be the path of virtue; and not the 'broad,' but the 'narrow way,' will 'lead to destruc-tion.' These excellent consequences seem to me to flow very smoothly and satisfactorily from his particular doctrine of evolution, combined with his particular doctrine of morals. But I confess that my own personal gratification at the prospect is some-what dimmed by the reflection that the same kind of causes which make conscience superfluous will relieve us from the necessity of intellectual effort, and that by the time we are all perfectly good we shall also be all perfectly idiotic.

I know not how it may strike the reader; but I at least am left sensibly poorer by this deposition of Reason from its ancient position as the Ground of all existence, to that of an expedient among other expedients for the maintenance of organic life ; an ex-pedient, moreover, which is temporary in its charac-ter and insignificant in its effects. An irrational Universe which accidentally turns out a few reasoning animals at one corner of it, as a rich man may experiment at one end of his park with some curious 'sport' accidentally produced among his flocks and herds, is a Universe which we might well despise if we did not ourselves share its degradation. But must we not inevitably share it? Pascal somewhere observes that Man, however feeble, is yet in his very feebleness superior to the blind forces of Nature; for he knows himself, and they do not. I confess that on the naturalistic hypothesis I see no such superiority. If, indeed, there were a Rational Author of Nature, and if in any degree, even the most insignificant, we shared His attributes, we might well conceive ourselves as of finer essence and more intrinsic worth than the material world which we inhabit, immeasurable though it may be. But if we be the creation of that world; if it made us what we are, and will again unmáke us; how then? The sense of humour, not the least precious among the gifts with which the clash of atoms has endowed us, should surely prevent us assuming any airs of superiority over members of the same family of 'phenomena,' more permanent and more powerful than ourselves.

CHAPTER IV

SUMMARY AND CONCLUSION OF PART I

I HAVE now completed my survey of certain opinions which naturalism seems to require us to hold respecting important matters connected with Righteousness, Beauty, and Reason. The survey has necessarily been concise; but, concise though it has been, it has, perhaps, sufficiently indicated the inner antagonism which exists between the Naturalistic system and the feelings which the best among mankind, including many who may be counted as adherents of that system, have hitherto considered as the most valuable possessions of our race. If naturalism be true, or, rather, if it be the whole truth, then is morality but a bare catalogue of utilitarian precepts; beauty but the chance occasion of a passing pleasure; reason but the dim passage from one set of unthinking habits to another. All that gives dignity to life, all that gives value to effort, shrinks and fades under the pitiless glare of a creed like this; and even curiosity, the hardiest among the nobler passions of the soul, must languish under the conviction that neither for this generation nor for any that shall come after it, neither in this life nor in another, will the tie be wholly loosened by which reason, not less than appetite, is held in hereditary bondage to the service of our material needs.

I am anxious, however, not to overstate my case. It is of course possible, to take for a moment æsthetics as our text, that whatever be our views concerning naturalism, we shall still like good poetry and good music, and that we shall not, perhaps, find if we sum up our pleasures at the year's end, that the total satisfaction derived from the contemplation of Art and Nature is very largely diminished by the fact that our philosophy allows us to draw no important distinction between the beauties of a sauce and the beauties of a symphony. Both may continue to afford the man with a good palate and a good ear a considerable amount of satisfaction; and if all we desire is to find in literature and in art something that will help us either 'to enjoy life or to endure it,' I do not contend that, by any theory of the beautiful, of this we shall wholly be deprived.

Nevertheless there is, even so, a loss not lightly to be underrated, a loss that falls alike on him that produces and on him that enjoys. Poets and artists have been wont to consider themselves, and to be considered by others, as prophets and seers, the revealers under sensuous forms of hidden mysteries, the symbolic preachers of eternal truths. All this is, of course, on the naturalistic theory, very absurd. They minister, no doubt, with success to some phase, usually a very transitory phase, of public taste; but they have no mysteries to reveal, and what they tell us, though it may be very agreeable, is seldom true, and never important. This is a conclusion which, howsoever it may accord with sound philosophy, is not likely to prove very stimulating to the artist, nor does it react with less unfortunate effect upon those to whom the artist appeals. Even if their feeling of delight in the beautiful is not marred for them in immediate experience, it must suffer in memory and reflection. For such a feeling carries with it, at its best, an inevitable reference, not less inevitable because it is obscure, to a Reality which is eternal and unchanging; and we cannot accept without suffering the conviction that in making such a reference we were merely the dupes of our emotions, the victims of a temporary hallucination induced, as it were, by some spiritual drug.

But if on the naturalistic hypothesis the sentiments associated with beauty seem like a poor jest played on us by Nature for no apparent purpose, those that gather round morality are, so to speak, a deliberate fraud perpetrated for a well-defined end. The consciousness of freedom, the sense of responsibility, the authority of conscience, the beauty of holiness, the admiration for self-devotion, the sympathy with suffering—these and all the train of beliefs and feelings from which spring noble deeds and generous ambitions are seen to be mere devices for securing to societies, if not to individuals, some competitive advantage in the struggle for existence.

They are not worse, but neither are they better than the thousand-and-one appetites and instincts, many of them, as I have said, cruel, and many of them disgusting, created by similar causes in order to carry out through all organic Nature the like unprofitable ends; and if we think them better, as in our unreflecting moments we are apt to do, this, on the Naturalistic hypothesis, is only because some delusion of the kind is necessary in order to induce us to perform actions which in themselves can contribute nothing to our personal gratification.

The inner discord which finds expression in conclusions like these largely arises, as the reader sees, from a want of balance or proportion between the range of our intellectual vision and the circumstances of our actual existence. Our capacity for standing outside ourselves and taking stock of the position which we occupy in the universe of things has been enormously and, it would seem, unfortunately, increased by recent scientific discovery. We have learned too much. We are educated above that station in life in which it has pleased Nature to place us. We can no longer accept it without criticism and without examination. We insist on interrogating that material system which, according to naturalism, is the true author of our being as to whence we come and whither we go, what are the causes which have made us what we are, and what are the purposes which our existence subserves. And it must be confessed that the answers given to this question by our oracle are extremely unsatisfactory. We have learned to measure space, and we perceive that our dwelling-place is but a mere point, wandering with its companions, apparently at random, through the wilderness of stars. We have learned to measure time, and we perceive that the life not merely of the individual or of the nation, but of the whole race, is brief, and apparently quite unimportant. We have learned to unravel causes, and we perceive that emotions and aspirations whose very being seems to hang on the existence of realities of which naturalism takes no account, are in their origin contemptible and in their suggestion mendacious.

To me it appears certain that this clashing between beliefs and feelings must ultimately prove fatal to one or the other. Make what allowance you please for the stupidity of mankind, take the fullest account of their really remarkable power of letting their speculative opinions follow one line of development and their practical ideals another, yet the time must come when reciprocal action will perforce bring opinions and ideals into some kind of agreement and congruity. If, then, naturalism is to hold the field, the feelings and opinions inconsistent with naturalism must be foredoomed to suffer change; and how, when that change shall come about, it can do otherwise than eat all nobility out of our conception of conduct and all worth out of our conception of life, I am wholly unable to understand.

6

I am aware that many persons are in the habit of subjecting these views to an experimental refutation by pointing to a great many excellent people who hold, in more or less purity, the naturalistic creed, but who, nevertheless, offer prominent examples of that habit of mind with which, as I have been endeavouring to show, the naturalistic creed is essentially inconsistent. Naturalism—so runs the argument—co-exists in the case of Messrs. A., B., C., &c., with the most admirable exhibition of unselfish virtue. If this be so in the case of a hundred individuals, why not in the case of ten thousand? If in the case of ten thousand, why not in the case of humanity at large? Now, to the facts on which this reasoning proceeds I raise no objection. I desire neither to ignore the existence nor to minimise the merits of these shining examples of virtue unsupported by religion. But though the facts be true, the reasoning based on them will not bear close examination. Biologists tell us of parasites which live, and can only live, within the bodies of animals more highly organised than they. For them their luckless host has to find food, to digest it, and to convert it into nourishment which they can consume without exertion and assimilate without difficulty. Their structure is of the simplest kind. Their host sees for them, so they need no eyes; he hears for them, so they need no ears; he works for them and contrives for them, so they need but feeble muscles and an undeveloped nervous system.   But are we to conclude from this that for the animal kingdom eyes and ears, powerful limbs and complex nerves, are superfluities?   They are superfluities for the parasite only because they have first been necessities for the host, and when the host perishes the parasite, in their absence, is not unlikely to perish also.

So it is with those persons who claim to show by their example that naturalism is practically consistent with the maintenance of ethical ideals with which naturalism has no natural affinity.   Their spiritual life is parasitic: it is sheltered by convictions which belong, not to them, but to the society of which they form a part; it is nourished by processes in which they take no share.   And when those convictions decay, and those processes come to an end, the alien life which they have maintained can scarce be expected to outlast them.

I am not aware that anyone has as yet endeavoured to construct the catechism of the future, purged of every element drawn from any other source than the naturalistic creed.   It is greatly to be desired that this task should be undertaken in an impartial spirit; and as a small contribution to such an object, I offer the following pairs of contrasted propositions, the first member, of each pair representing current teaching, the second representing the teaching which ought to be substituted for it if the naturalistic theory be accepted.

A. The universe is the creation of Reason, and

all things work together towards a reasonable end.

B. *So far as we are concerned, reason is to be found neither in the beginning of things nor in their end; and though everything is predetermined, nothing is fore-ordained.*

A. Creative reason is interfused with infinite love.

B. *As reason is absent, so also is love. The universal flux is ordered by blind causation alone.*

A. There is a moral law, immutable, eternal; in its governance all spirits find their true freedom and their most perfect realisation. Though it be adequate to infinite goodness and infinite intelligence, it may be understood, even by man, sufficiently for his guidance.

B. *Among the causes by which the course of organic and social development has been blindly determined are pains, pleasures, instincts, appetites, disgusts, religions, moralities, superstitions; the sentiment of what is noble and intrinsically worthy; the sentiment of what is ignoble and intrinsically worthless. From a purely scientific point of view these all stand on an equality; all are action-producing causes developed, not to improve, but simply to perpetuate, the species.*

A. In the possession of reason and in the enjoyment of beauty, we in some remote way share the nature of that infinite Personality in Whom we live and move and have our being.

B. *Reason is but the psychological expression of certain physiological processes in the cerebral hemispheres; it is no more than an expedient among many expedients by which the individual and the race are preserved; just as Beauty is no more than the name for such varying and accidental attributes of the material or moral worlds as may happen for the moment to stir our æsthetic feelings.*

A. Every human soul is of infinite value, eternal, free; no human being, therefore, is so placed as not to have within his reach, in himself and others, objects adequate to infinite endeavour.

B. *The individual perishes; the race itself does not endure. Few can flatter themselves that their conduct has any appreciable effect upon its remoter destinies; and of those few, none can say with reasonable assurance that the effect which they are destined to produce is the one which they desire. Even if we were free, therefore, our ignorance would make us helpless; and it may be almost a consolation to reflect that our conduct was determined for us by unthinking forces in a remote past, and that if we are impotent to foresee its consequences, we were not less impotent to arrange its causes.*

The doctrines embodied in the second member of each of these alternatives may be true, or may at least represent the nearest approach to truth of which we are at present capable. Into this question I do not yet inquire. But if they are to constitute the dogmatic scaffolding by which our educational system is to be supported; if it is to be in harmony with principles like these that the child is to be taught at its mother's knee, and the young man is to build up the ideals of his life, then, unless I greatly mistake, it will be found that the inner discord which exists, and which must gradually declare itself, between the emotions proper to naturalism and those which have actually grown up under the shadow of traditional convictions, will at no distant date most unpleasantly translate itself into practice.

PART II

SOME REASONS FOR BELIEF

CHAPTER I

THE PHILOSOPHIC BASIS OF NATURALISM

I

So far we have been occupied in weighing certain indirect and collateral consequences which seem likely to flow from a particular theory of the world in which we live. The theory itself was taken for granted. No attempt was made to examine its foundations or to test their strength; no comparison between its different parts was instituted for the purpose of determining how far they really constituted a coherent and intelligible whole. We accepted it as we found it, turning with averted eyes even from the speculative problems which lay closest to the track of our immediate investigation.

This course is not the most logical; and it might perhaps appear a more fitting procedure to reserve our consideration of the consequences of a system until some conclusion had been arrived at concerning its truth. Such, however, is not the ordinary habit of mankind in dealing with problems in which questions of abstract theory and daily practice are closely intertwined; and even philosophers show a kindly reluctance too closely to examine the claims of creeds whose consequences are in strict accord with contemporary sentiment. I have a better reason, however, to offer for the order here selected than can be derived from precedent or example, a reason based on the fact that, had I begun these Notes with the discussion on which I am about to embark, their whole character would probably have been misunderstood. They would have been regarded as contributions to philosophical discussion of a kind which would only interest the specialist; and the general reader, to whom I desire particularly to appeal, would have abandoned their perusal in disgust. For I cannot deny, either that I am about to ask him to accompany me in a search after first principles; or (which is, perhaps, worse) that the search is destined to be ineffectual. He will not only have to occupy himself with arguments of a remote and abstract kind, and for a moment to disturb the placid depths of ordinary thought with unaccustomed soundings, but the arguments will be to all appearance barren, and the soundings will not find bottom. The full justification for a procedure seemingly so futile can only be found in the chapters which follow, and in the general drift of the discussion taken as a whole; but in the meanwhile the reader will be able to appreciate my immediate object if he will bear in mind the precise point at which we have arrived.

Let him remember, then, that the result of the inquiry instituted into the practical tendencies of the naturalistic theory is to show them to be well-nigh intolerable. The theory, no doubt, may for all that be true, since it must candidly be admitted that there is no naturalistic reason for anticipating any pre-established harmony between truth and expediency in the higher regions of speculation. But at least we are called upon to make a very searching inquiry before we admit that it is true. We are not here concerned with any mere curiosity of dialectics, with the quest for a kind of knowledge which, however interesting to the few, yet bears no fruit for ordinary human use. On the contrary, the issues that have to be decided are practical, if anything is practical. They touch at every point the most permanent interests of man, individual and social; and any procedure is preferable to a complacent acquiescence in the loss of all the fairest provinces in our spiritual inheritance.

This is a fact which has long been perceived by the defenders of all the creeds, philosophical or theological, with which the pretensions of naturalism are in conflict. You will not open a modern work of apologetics, for instance, without finding in it some endeavour to show that the naturalistic theory is insufficient, and that it requires to be supplemented by precisely the very system in whose interests that particular work was written. This, no doubt, is as it should be; and on this plan a great deal of valuable criticism and interesting speculation has been produced. It is not, however, exactly the plan which can be here pursued, partly because these Notes contain, not a system of theology, but only an introduction to theology; and partly because I have always found it easier to satisfy myself of the insufficiency

of naturalism than of the absolute sufficiency of any
of the schemes by which it has been sought to modify
or to complete it.

In this chapter, however, I shall follow an easier
line of march, the nature of which the reader will
readily understand if he considers the two elements
composing the naturalistic creed: the one *positive*,
consisting, broadly speaking, of the teaching contained in the general body of the natural sciences;
the other *negative*, expressed in the doctrine that
beyond these limits, wherever they may happen to
lie, nothing is, and nothing can be, known. Now,
the usual practice with those who dissent from this
general view is, as I have said, to choose the second, or negative, half of it for attack. They tell us,
for example, that the knowledge of phenomena
given by science carries with it by necessary implication the knowledge of that which is above phenomena; or, again, that the moral nature of man
points to the reality of ends and principles which
cannot be exhausted by any investigation into a
merely natural world of causally related objects.
Without the least underrating such lines of investigation, I purpose here to consider, not the negative,
but the positive half of the naturalistic system. I
shall leave for the moment unchallenged the statement that beyond the natural sciences knowledge is
impossible; but I shall venture, instead, to ask a few
questions as to the character of the knowledge
which is thought to be obtained within those limits.

I shall not endeavour to prove that a scheme of merely positive beliefs, admirable, no doubt, as far as it goes, is yet intellectually insufficient unless it be supplemented by a metaphysical or theological appendix. But I shall examine the foundations of the scheme itself; and though such criticisms on it as I shall be able to offer can never be a substitute for the real work of philosophic construction, they would seem to be its fitting preliminary, and a preliminary which the succeeding chapters may show to be not without a profit of its own.

One great metaphysician has described the system of another as 'shot out of a pistol,' meaning thereby that it was presented for acceptance without introductory proof. The criticism is true not only of the particular theory of the Absolute about which it was first used, but about every system, or almost every system, of belief which has ever passed current among mankind. Some subtle analogy with accepted doctrines, some general harmony with existing sentiments and modes of thought, has not uncommonly been deemed sufficient to justify the most audacious conjectures; and the history of speculation is littered with theories whose authors seem never to have suffered under any overmastering need to prove the opinions which they advanced. No such overmastering need has, at least, been felt in the case of 'positive knowledge,' and the very circumstance that, alike in its methods and in its results, all men are practically agreed to accept it without demur, has blinded them to the fact that it, too, has been 'shot out of a pistol,' and that, like some more questionable beliefs, it is still waiting for a rational justification.

[1] [For our too easy acquiescence in this state of things I do not think science is itself to blame. It is no part of its duty to deal with first principles. Its business is to provide us with a theory of Nature; and it should not be required, in addition, to provide us with a theory of itself. This is a task which properly devolves upon the masters of speculation; though it is one which, for various reasons, they have not as yet satisfactorily accomplished. I doubt, indeed, whether any metaphysical philosopher before Kant can be said to have made contributions to this subject which at the present day need be taken into serious account; and, as I shall endeavour to indicate in the next chapter, Kant's doctrines, even as modified by his successors, do not, so it seems to me, provide a sound basis for an 'epistemology of Nature.'

But if in this connection we owe little to the metaphysical philosophers, we owe still less to those in whom we had a better right to trust, namely, the empirical ones. If the former have to some extent neglected the theory of science for theories of the Absolute, the latter have always shown an inclination

---

[1] The remarks on the history of philosophy which occupy the remainder of this section are not essential to the argument, and may be omitted by readers uninterested in that subject. The strictly necessary discussion is resumed on p. 100.

to sacrifice the theory of knowledge itself to theories
as to the genesis or growth of knowledge.   They
have contented themselves with investigating the
primitive elements from which have been developed
in the race and in the individual the completed
consciousness of ourselves and of the world in which
we live.   They have, therefore, dealt with the origins
of what we believe rather than with its justification.
They have substituted psychology for philosophy ;
they have presented us, in short, with studies in a
particular branch or department of science, rather
than with an examination into the grounds of science
in general.   And when perforce they are brought
face to face with some of the problems connected
with the philosophy of science which most loudly
clamour for solution, there is something half-pathetic
and half-humorous in their methods of cutting a knot
which they are quite unable to untie.   Can anything,
for example, be more naive than the undisturbed
serenity with which Locke, towards the end of his
great work, assures his readers that he 'suspects that
natural philosophy is not capable of being made a
science'; or, as I should prefer to state it, that natural science is not capable of being made a philosophy ?   Or can anything be more characteristic than
the moral which he draws from this rather surprising
admission, namely, that as we are so little fitted to
frame theories about this present world, we had better devote our energies to preparing for the next ?
This remarkable display of philosophic resignation

in the father of modern empiricism has been imi-
tated, with differences, by a long line of distinguished successors. Hume, for example, though
naturally enough he declined to draw Locke's edifying conclusion, did more than anyone else to establish Locke's despairing premise; and his inferences
from it are at least equally singular. Having reduced our belief in the fundamental principles of scientific interpretation to expectations born of habit;
having reduced the world which is to be interpreted
to an unrelated series of impressions and ideas; having by this double process made experience impossible and turned science into foolishness, he quietly
informs us, as the issue of the whole matter, that
outside experience and science knowledge is impossible, and that all except 'mathematical demonstration' and 'experimental reasoning' on 'matters of
fact' is sophistry and illusion!

I think too well of Hume's speculative genius
and too ill of his speculative sincerity to doubt that
in making this statement he spoke, not as a philosopher, but as a man of the world, making formal
obeisance to the powers that be. But what he said
half ironically, his followers have said with an unshaken seriousness. Nothing in the history of speculation is more astonishing, nothing—if I am to speak
my whole mind—is more absurd than the way in
which Hume's philosophic progeny—a most distinguished race—have, in spite of all their differences,
yet been able to agree, *both* that experience is essen-

tially as Hume described it, *and* that from such an experience can be rationally extracted anything even in the remotest degree resembling the existing system of the natural sciences.   Like Locke, these gentlemen, or some of them, have, indeed, been assailed by momentary misgivings.   It seems occasionally to have occurred to them that if their theory of knowledge were adequate, 'experimental reasoning,' as Hume called it, was in a very parlous state; and that, on the merits, nothing less deserved to be held with a positive conviction than what some of them are wont to describe as 'positive' knowledge. But they have soon thrust away such unwelcome thoughts.   The self-satisfied dogmatism which is so convenient, and, indeed, so necessary a habit in the daily routine of life, has resumed its sway.   They have forgotten that they were philosophers, and with true practical instincts have reserved their 'obstinate questionings' exclusively for the benefit of opinions from which they were already predisposed to differ.

Whether these historic reasons fully account for the comparative neglect of a philosophy of science I will not venture to pronounce.   But that the neglect has been real I cannot doubt.   Admirable generalisations of the actual methods of scientific research, usually under some such name as ' Inductive Logic,' we have no doubt had in abundance. But a full and systematic attempt, first to enumerate, and then to justify, the presuppositions on which all

7

science finally rests, has, it seems to me, still to be made, and must form no insignificant or secondary portion of the task which philosophy has yet to perform.   To some, perhaps to most, it may, indeed, appear as if such a task were one of perverse futility; not more useful and much less dignified than metaphysical investigations into the nature of the Absolute.   However profitless in the opinion of the objector these may be, at least it seems better to strain after the transcendent than to demonstrate the obvious.   And science, it may well be thought, is quite sure enough of its ground to be justified in politely bowing out those who thus officiously tender it a perfectly superfluous assistance.

This is a contention on the merits of which it will only be possible to pronounce after the critical examination into the presuppositions of science which I desiderate has been thoroughly carried out. It may then appear that nothing stands more in need of demonstration than the obvious; that at the very root of our scientific system of belief lie problems of which no satisfactory solution has hitherto been devised; and that, so far from its being possible to ignore the difficulties which these involve, no general theory of knowledge has the least chance of being successful which does not explicitly include within the circuit of its criticism, not only the beliefs which seem to us to be dubious, but those also which we hold with the most perfect practical assurance.

So much, at least, I have endeavoured to establish in another work to which reference has been already made.[1]   And to this I must venture to refer those readers who either wish to see this position elaborately developed, or who are of opinion that I have in the preceding remarks treated the philosophy of the empirical school with too scant a measure of respect. The very technical discussion, however, which it contains could not, I think, be made interesting, or perhaps intelligible, to the majority of those for whom this book is intended, and, even were it otherwise, they could not appropriately be introduced into the body of these Notes. Yet, though this is impossible, it ought not, I think, to be quite impossible to convey some general notion of the sort of difficulty with which any empirical theory of science would seem to be beset, and this without requiring on the part of the reader any special knowledge of philosophic terminology, or, indeed, any knowledge at all except that of some few very general scientific doctrines. If I could succeed, however imperfectly, in such a task, it might be of some slight service even to the reader conversant with empirical theories in all their various forms. For though he will, of course, recognise in what follows the familiar faces of many old controversies, the circumstance that they are here approached, not from the accustomed side of the psychology of perception, but from that of physics and physiology,

. L. of C.

[1] Cf. Prefatory Note.

may perhaps give them a freshness they would not otherwise possess.]

II

In order to fix our ideas let us recall, in however rough and incomplete a form, the broad outlines of scientific doctrine as it at present exists, and as it has been developed from that unorganised knowledge of a world of objects—animals, mountains, men, planets, trees, water, fire, and so forth—which in some degree or other all mankind possess. These objects science conceives as ordered and mutually related in one unlimited space and one unlimited time; all in their true reality independent of the presence or absence of any observer, all governed in their behaviour by rigid and unvarying laws. These are its material; these it is its business to describe. Their appearance, their inner constitution, their environment, the process of their development, the modes in which they act and are acted upon—such and such-like subjects of inquiry constitute the problems which science has set itself to investigate.

The result of its investigations is now embodied in a general, if provisional, view of the (phenomenal) universe which may be accepted at least as a working hypothesis. According to this view, the world consists essentially of innumerable small particles of definite mass, endowed with a variety of mechanical, chemical, and other qualities, and forming by their mutual association the various bodies which we can handle and see, and many others which we can neither handle nor see. These ponderable particles have their being in a diffused and all-penetrating medium, or ether, which possesses, or behaves as if it possessed, certain mechanical properties of a very remarkable character; while the whole of this material[1] system, ponderable particles and ether alike, is animated (if the phrase may be permitted me) by a quantity of energy which, though it varies in the manner and place of its manifestation, yet never varies in its total amount. It only remains to add, as a fact of considerable importance to ourselves, though of little apparent importance to the universe at large, that a few of the material particles above alluded to are arranged into living organisms, and that among these organisms are a small minority which have the remarkable power of extracting from the changes which take place in certain of their tissues psychical phenomena of various kinds; some of which are the reflection, or partial reproduction

[1] This ambiguity in the use of the word ' matter ' is apt to be a nuisance in these discussions. The term is sometimes, and quite properly, used only of ponderable matter, and in opposition to ether. But when we talk of the ' material universe,' it is absurd to exclude from our meaning the ether, which is the most important part of that universe. The context will, I hope, always show in which sense the word is used. I should perhaps add that I have deliberately refrained from complicating the text by any allusion to recent hypotheses as to the nature of the ether and its relation to ponderable matter or to recent discoveries respecting the divisibility of the atom.

in perception and in thought, of fragments and aspects of that material world to which they owe their being.

Secure in this general view of things, the great co-operative work of scientific investigation moves swiftly on. The psychologist deals with the laws governing mental phenomena and with the relations of mind and body; the physiologist endeavours to surprise the secrets of the living organ; the biologist traces the development of the individual and the mutations of the species; the chemist searches out the laws which govern the combination and reactions of atoms and molecules; the astronomer investigates the movements and the life-histories of suns and planets; while the physicist explores the inmost mysteries of matter and energy, not unprepared to discover behind the invisible particles and the insensible movements with which he familiarly deals, explanations of the material universe yet more remote from the unsophisticated perceptions of ordinary mankind.

˙ The philosophic reader is of course aware that many of the terms which I have used, and been obliged to use, in this outline of the scientific view of the universe may be, and have been, subjected to philosophic analysis, and often with very curious results. Space, time, matter, energy, cause, quality, idea, perception—all these, to mention no others, are expressions without the aid of which no account could be given of the circle of the sciences; though

every one of them suggests a multitude of speculative problems, of which speculation has not as yet
succeeded in giving us the final and decisive solution. These problems, for the most part, however,
I put on one side.[1] I take these terms as I find
them; in the sense, that is, which everybody attributes to them until he begins to puzzle himself with
too curious inquiries into their precise meaning. No
such embarrassing investigations do I here wish to
impose upon my reader. It shall for the present be
agreed between us that the body of doctrine sum-
marised above is, so far as it goes, clear and intelligible; and all I shall now require of him is to look at
it from a new point of view, to approach it, as it were,
from a different side, to study it with a new intention.
Instead, then, of asking what are the beliefs which
science inculcates, let us ask why, in the last resort,
we hold them to be true. Instead of inquiring how
a thing happens, or what it is, let us inquire how we
know that it does thus happen, and why we believe
that so in truth it is. Instead of enumerating causes,
let us set ourselves to investigate reasons.

III

Now it is at once evident that the very same
general body of doctrines, the very same set of propositions about the 'natural' world, arranged according to the principles suggested by these questions, would fall into a wholly different order from

[1 See, however, *infra*, the chapter on 'Ultimate Scientific
Ideas.']

that which would be observed if its distribution were governed merely by considerations based upon the convenience of scientific exposition. Indeed, we may say that there are at least four quite different orders, theoretically distinguishable, though usually mixed up in practice, in which scientific truth may be expounded. There is, first, the order of discovery. This is governed by no rational principle, but depends on historic causes, on the accidents of individual genius and the romantic chances of experiment and observation. There is, secondly, the rhetorical order, useful enough in its proper place, in which, for example, we proceed from the simple to the difficult, or from the striking to the important, according to the needs of the hearer. There is, thirdly, the scientific order, in which, could we only bring it to perfection, we should proceed from the abstract to the concrete, and from the general law to the particular instance, until the whole world of phenomena was gradually presented to our gaze as a closely woven tissue of causes and effects, infinite in its complexity, incessant in its changes, yet at each moment proclaiming to those who can hear and understand the certain prophecy of its future and the authentic record of its past. Lastly, there is what, according to the terminology here employed, must be called the philosophic order, in which the various scientific propositions or dogmas are, or rather should be, arranged as a series of premises and conclusions, starting from those which are axiomatic, *i.e.* for which proof can be neither given nor required, and moving on through a continuous series of binding inferences, until the whole of knowledge is caught up and ordered in the meshes of this all-inclusive dialectical network.

In its perfected shape it is evident that the philosophic series, though it reaches out to the farthest confines of the known, must for each man trace its origin to something which *he* can regard as axiomatic and self-evident truth. There is no theoretical escape for any of us from the ultimate 'I.' What 'I' believe as conclusive must be drawn, by some process which 'I' accept as cogent, from something which 'I' am obliged to regard as intrinsically self-sufficient, beyond the reach of criticism or the need for proof. The philosophic order and the scientific order of statement, therefore, cannot fail to be wholly different. While the scientific order may start with the dogmatic enunciation of some great generalisation valid through the whole unmeasured range of the material universe, the philosophic order is perforce compelled to find its point of departure in the humble personality of the inquirer. *His* grounds of belief, not the things believed in, are the subject-matter of investigation. *His* reason, or, if you like to have it so, his share of the Universal Reason, but in any case something which is *his*, must sit in judgment, and must try the cause. The rights of this tribunal are inalienable, its authority incapable of delegation; nor is there any superior court by which the verdict it pronounces can be reversed.

If now the question were asked, 'On what sort of premises rests ultimately the scientific theory of the world?' science and empirical philosophy, though they might not agree on the meaning of terms, would agree in answering, 'On premises supplied by experience.' It is experience which has given us our first real knowledge of Nature and her laws. It is experience, in the shape of observation and experiment, which has given us the raw material out of which hypothesis and inference have slowly elaborated that richer conception of the material world which constitutes perhaps the chief, and certainly the most characteristic, glory of the modern mind.

What, then, is this experience? or, rather, let us ask (so as to avoid the appearance of trenching on Kantian ground) what are these experiences? Putting psychology on one side, these experiences, the experiences on which are alike founded the practice of the savage and the theories of the man of science, are for the most part observations of material things or objects, and of their behaviour in the presence of or in relation to each other. These, on the empirical theory of knowledge, supply the direct information, the immediate data from which all our wider knowledge ultimately draws its sanction. Behind these it is impossible to go; impossible, but also unnecessary.

For as the 'evidence of the senses' does not derive its authority from any higher source, so it is useless to dispute its full and indefeasible title to command our assent. According to this view, which is thoroughly in accordance with common-sense, science rests in the main upon the immediate judgments we form about natural objects in the act of seeing, hearing, and handling them. This is the solid, if somewhat narrow, platform which provides us with a foothold whence we may reach upward into regions where the 'senses' convey to us no direct knowledge, where we have to do with laws remote from our personal observation, and with objects which can neither be seen, heard, nor handled.

IV

But although such a theory seems simple and straightforward enough, in perfect harmony with the habitual sentiments and the universal practice of mankind, it would evidently be rash to rest satisfied with it as a philosophy of science until we had at least heard what science itself has to say upon the subject. What, then, is the account which science gives of these 'immediate judgments of the senses'? Has it anything to tell us about their nature, or the mode of their operation? Without doubt it has; and its teaching provides a curious, and at first sight an even startling, commentary on the common-sense version of that philosophy of experience

whose general character has just been indicated
above.

For whereas common-sense tells us that our experience of objects provides us with a knowledge of
their nature which, so far as it goes, is immediate
and direct, science informs us that each particular
experience is itself but the final link in a long chain
of causes and effects, whose beginning is lost amid
the complexities of the material world, and whose
ending is a change of some sort in the 'mind' of
the percipient. It informs us, further, that among
these innumerable causes, the thing 'immediately
experienced' is but one; and is, moreover, one
separated from the 'immediate experience' which it
modestly assists in producing by a very large number of intermediate causes which are never experienced at all.

Take, for example, an ordinary case of vision.
What are the causes which ultimately produce the
apparently immediate experience of (for example) a
green tree standing in the next field? There are,
first (to go no further back), the vibrations among
the particles of the source of light, say the sun.
Consequent on these are the ethereal undulations
between the sun and the objects seen, namely, the
green tree. Then follows the absorption of most of
these undulations by the object; the reflection of the
'green' residue; the incidence of a small fraction of
these on the lens of the eye; their arrangement on
the retina; the stimulation of the optic nerve; and,

finally, the molecular change in a certain tract of the cerebral hemispheres by which, in some way or other wholly unknown, through predispositions in part acquired by the individual, but chiefly inherited through countless generations of ancestors, is produced the complex mental fact which we describe by saying that 'we have an immediate experience of a tree about fifty yards off.'

Now the experience, the causes and conditions of which I have thus rudely outlined, is typical of all the experiences, without exception, on which is based our knowledge of the material universe. Some of these experiences, no doubt, are incorrect. The 'evidence of the senses,' as the phrase goes, proves now and then to be fallacious. But it is proved to be fallacious by other evidence of precisely the same kind; and if we take the trouble to trace back far enough our reasons for believing any scientific truth whatever, they always end in some 'immediate experience' or experiences of the type described above.

But the comparison thus inevitably suggested between 'immediate experiences' considered as the ultimate basis of all scientific belief, and immediate experience considered as an insignificant and, so to speak, casual product of natural laws, suggests some curious reflections. I do not allude to the difficulty of understanding how a mental effect can be produced by a physical cause—how matter can act on mind. The problem I wish to dwell on is of quite a different kind. It is concerned, not with the nature of the laws by which the world is governed, but with their proof. It arises, not out of the difficulty of feeling our way slowly along the causal chain from physical antecedents to mental consequents, but from the difficulty of harmonising this movement with the opposite one, whereby we jump by some instantaneous effort of inferential activity from these mental consequents to an immediate conviction as to the reality and character of some of their remoter physical antecedents. I am 'experiencing' (to revert to our illustration) the tree in the next field. While looking at it I begin to reflect upon the double process I have just described. I remember the long-drawn series of causes, physical and physiological, by which my perception of the object has been produced. I realise that each one of these causes might have been replaced by some other cause without altering the character of the consequent perception; and that if it had been so replaced, my judgment about the object, though it would have been as confident and as immediate as at present, would have been wrong. Anything, for instance, which would distribute similar green rays on the retina of my eyes in the same pattern as that produced by the tree, or anything which would produce a like irritation of the optic nerve or a like modification of the cerebral tissues, would give me an experience in itself quite indistinguishable from my experience of the tree, though with the unfortunate peculiarity of being wholly incorrect. The same message would be delivered, in the same terms and on the same authority, but it would be false. And though we are quite familiar with the fact that illusions are possible and that mistakes will occur in the simplest observation, yet we can hardly avoid being struck by the incongruity of a scheme of belief whose premises are wholly derived from witnesses admittedly untrustworthy, yet which is unable to supply any criterion, other than the evidence of these witnesses themselves, by which the character of their evidence can in any given case be determined.

The fact that even the most immediate experiences carry with them no inherent guarantee of their veracity is, however, by far the smallest of the difficulties which emerge from a comparison of the causal movement from object to perception, with the cognitive leap through perception to object. For a very slight consideration of the teaching of science as to the nature of the first is sufficient to prove, not merely the possible, but the habitual inaccuracy of the second. In other words, we need only consider carefully our perceptions regarded as psychological results, in order to see that, regarded as sources of information, they are not merely occasionally inaccurate, but habitually mendacious. We are dealing, recollect, with a theory of science according to which the ultimate stress of scientific proof is thrown wholly upon our immediate experience of objects. But nine-tenths of our immediate experiences of objects are visual; and all visual experiences, without exception, are, according to science, erroneous. As everybody knows, colour is not a property of the thing seen: it is a sensation produced in us by that thing. The thing itself consists of uncoloured particles, which become visible solely in consequence of their power of either producing or reflecting ethereal undulations. The degrees of brightness and the qualities of colour perceived in the thing, and in virtue of which alone any visual perception of the thing is possible, are, therefore, according to optics, no part of its reality, but are mere feelings produced in the mind of the percipient by the complex movements of material molecules, possessing mass and extension, but to which it is not only incorrect but unmeaning to attribute either brightness or colour.

From the side of science these are truisms. From the side of a theory or philosophy of science, however, they are paradoxes. It was sufficiently embarrassing to discover that the messages conveyed to us by sensible experiences which the observer treats as so direct and so certain are, when considered in transit, at one moment nothing but vibrations of imperceptible particles, at another nothing but periodic changes in an unimaginable ether, at a third nothing but unknown, and perhaps unknowable, modifications of nervous tissue; and that none of these various messengers carry with them any warrant that the judgment in which they

finally issue will prove to be true. But what are we
to say about these same experiences when we discover, not only that they may be wholly false, but
that they are never wholly true? What sort of a
system is that which makes haste to discredit its
own premises? In what entanglements of contradiction do we not find ourselves involved by the
attempt to rest science upon observations which
science itself asserts to be erroneous? By what
possible title do we proclaim the same immediate
experience to be right when it testifies to the independent reality of something solid and extended,
and to be wrong when it testifies to the independent reality of something illuminated and coloured?

V

There is, of course, an answer to all this, simple
enough if only it be true. The whole theory, it
may be said, on which we have been proceeding is
untenable, the undigested product of crude common-sense. The bugbear which frightens us is of
our own creation. We have no immediate experience of independent things such as has been
gratuitously supposed. What science tells us of the
colour element in our visual perceptions, namely,
that it is merely a feeling or sensation, is true of
every element in every perception. We are directly cognisant of nothing but mental states: all
else is a matter of inference; a hypothetical ma-

chinery devised for no other purpose than to account for the existence of the only realities of which we have first-hand knowledge—namely, the mental states themselves.

Now this theory does at first sight undoubtedly appear to harmonise with the general teaching of science on the subject of mental physiology. This teaching, as ordinarily expounded, assumes throughout a material world of objects and a psychical world of feelings and ideas. The latter is in all cases the product of the former. In some cases it may be a copy or partial reflection of the former. In no case is it identified with the former. When, therefore, I am in the act of experiencing a tree in the next field, what on this theory I am really doing is inferring from the fact of my having certain feelings the existence of a cause having qualities adequate to produce them. It is true that the process of inference is so rapid and habitual that we are unconscious of performing it. It is also true that the inference is quite differently performed by the natural man in his natural moments and the scientific man in his scientific moments. For, whereas the natural man infers the existence of a material object which in all respects resembles his idea of it, the scientific man knows very well that the material object only resembles his ideas of it in certain particulars—extension, solidity, and so forth—and that in respect of such attributes as colour and illumination there is no resemblance at all. Nevertheless, in all cases, whether there be resemblance between them or not, the material fact is a conclusion from the mental fact, with which last alone we can be said to be, so to speak, in any immediate empirical relation.

As this theory regarding the sources of our knowledge of the material world fits in with the habitual language of mental physiology, so also it fits in with the first instincts of speculative analysis. It is, I suppose, one of the earliest discoveries of the metaphysically minded youth that he can, if he so wills it, change his point of view, and thereby sud-denly convert what in ordinary moments seem the solid realities of this material universe, into an un-ending pageant of feelings and ideas, moving in long procession across his mental stage, and having from the nature of the case no independent being before they appear, nor retaining any after they vanish.

But however plausible be this correction of com-mon-sense, it has its difficulties. In the first place, it involves a complete divorce between the practice of science and its theory. It is all very well to say that the scientific account of mental physiology in general, and of sense-perception in particular, re-quires us to hold that what is immediately expe-rienced are mental facts, and that our knowledge of physical facts is but mediate and inferential. Such a conclusion is quite out of harmony with its own premises, since the propositions on which, as a matter of historical verity, science is ultimately founded are not propositions about states of mind, but about material things. The observations on which are built, for example, our knowledge of anatomy or our knowledge of chemistry were not, in the opinion of those who originally made them or have since confirmed them, observations of their own feelings, but of objects thought of as wholly independent of the observer. They may have been mistaken. Such observations may be impossible. But, possible or impossible, they were believed to have occurred, and on that belief depends the whole empirical evidence of science as scientific discoverers themselves conceive it.

The reader will, I hope, understand that I am not here arguing that the theory of experience now under consideration, the theory, that is, which confines the field of immediate experience to our own states of mind, is inconsistent with science, or even that it supplies an inadequate empirical basis for science. On these points I may have a word to say presently. My present contention simply is, that it is not experience *thus understood* which has supplied men of science with their knowledge of the physical universe. They have never suspected that, while they supposed themselves to be perceiving independent material objects, they were in reality perceiving quite another set of things, namely, feelings and sensations of a particular kind, grouped in particular ways, and succeeding each other in a particular order. Nor, if this idea had ever occurred to them, would they have admitted that these two classes of things could by any merely verbal manipulation be made the same. So that if this particular account of the nature of experience be accurate, the system of thought represented by science presents the singular spectacle of a creed which is believed in practice for one set of reasons, though in theory it can only be justified by another; and which, through some beneficent accident, turns out to be true, though its origin and each subsequent stage in its gradual development are the product of error and illusion.

This is perplexing enough. Yet an even stronger statement would seem to be justified. We must not only say that the experiences on which science is founded have been invariably misinterpreted by those who underwent them, but that, if they had not been so misinterpreted, science as we know it would never have existed. We have not merely stumbled on the truth in spite of error and illusion, which is odd, but because of error and illusion, which is odder. For if the scientific observers of Nature had realised from the beginning that all they were observing was their own feelings and ideas, as empirical idealism and mental physiology alike require us to hold, they surely would never have taken the trouble to invent a Nature (*i.e.* an independently existing system of material things) for no other purpose than to provide a machinery by which the occurrence of feelings and ideas might be adequately accounted for. To go through so much to get so little, to bewilder themselves in the ever-increasing intricacies of this hypothetical wheel-work, to pile world on world and add infinity to infinity, and all for no more important object than to find an explanation for a few fleeting impressions, say of colour or resistance, would, indeed, have seemed to them a most super-fluous labour. Nor is it possible to doubt that this task has been undertaken and partially accomplished only because humanity has been, as for the most part it still is, under the belief not merely that there ex-ists a universe possessing the independence which science and common-sense alike postulate, but that it is a universe immediately, if imperfectly, revealed to us in the deliverances of sense-perception.

VI

We can scarcely deny, then, though the paradox be hard of digestion, that, historically speaking, if the theory we are discussing be true, science owes its being to an erroneous view as to what kind of information it is that our experiences directly convey to us. But a much more important question than the merely historical one remains behind, namely, whether, from the kind of information which our ex-periences do thus directly convey to us, anything at all resembling the scientific theory of Nature can be reasonably extracted. Can our revised conception of the material world really be inferred from our revised conception of the import and limits of experience? Can we by any possible treatment of sensations and feelings legitimately squeeze out of them trustworthy knowledge of the permanent and independent material universe of which, according to science, sensations and feelings are but transient and evanescent effects?

I cannot imagine the process by which such a result may be attained, nor has it been satisfactorily explained to us by any apologist of the empirical theory of knowledge. We may, no doubt, argue that sensations and feelings, like everything else, must have a cause; that the hypothesis of a material world suggests such a cause in a form which is agreeable to our natural beliefs; and that it is a hypothesis we are justified in adopting when we find that it enables us to anticipate the order and character of that stream of perceptions which it is called into existence to explain. But this is a line of argument which really will not bear examination. Every one of the three propositions of which it consists is, if we are to go back to fundamental principles, either disputable or erroneous. The principle of causation cannot be extracted out of a succession of individual experiences, as is implied by the first. The world described by science is not congruous with our natural beliefs, as is alleged by the second. Nor can we legitimately reason back from effect to cause in the manner required by the third.

A very brief comment will, I think, be sufficient to make this clear, and I proceed to offer it on each of the three propositions, taking them, for convenience, in the reverse order, and beginning, therefore, with the third. This in effect declares that as the material world described by science would, if it existed, produce sensations and impressions in the very manner in which our experiences assure us that they actually occur, we may assume that such a world exists. But may we? Even supposing that there was this complete correspondence between theory and fact, which is far, unfortunately, from being at present the case, are we justified in making so bold a logical leap from the known to the unknown? I doubt it. Recollect that by hypothesis we are strictly imprisoned, so far as direct experiences are concerned, within the circle of sensations or impressions. It is in this self-centred universe alone, therefore, that we can collect the premises of further knowledge. How can it possibly supply us with any principles of selection by which to decide between the various kinds of cause that may, for anything we know to the contrary, have had a hand in its production? None of these kinds of cause are open to observation. All must, from the nature of the case, be purely conjectural. Because, therefore, we happen to have thought of one which, with a little goodwill, can be forced into a rude correspondence with the observed facts, shall we, oblivious of the million possible explanations which a superior intelligence

might be able to devise, proceed to decorate our
particular fancy with the title of the 'Real World'?
If we do so, it is not, as the candid reader will be
prepared to admit, because such a conclusion is
justified by such premises, but because we are predisposed to a conclusion of this kind by those
instinctive beliefs which, in unreflective moments,
the philosopher shares with the savage. In such
moments all men conceive themselves (by hypothesis erroneously) as having direct experiences of
an independent material universe. When, therefore,
science, or philosophers on behalf of science, proceed to infer such a universe from impressions of
extension, resistance, and so forth, they find themselves, so far, in an unnatural and quite illegitimate
alliance with common-sense. By procedures which
are different, and essentially inconsistent, the two
parties have found it possible to reach results which
at first sight look very much the same. Immediate
intuitions wrongly interpreted come to the aid of
mediate inferences illegitimately constructed; we
find ourselves quite prepared to accept the conclusions of bad reasoning, because they have a partial
though, as I shall now proceed to show, an illusory
resemblance to the deliverances of uncriticised experience.

This, it will be observed, is the subject dealt
with in the second of the three propositions on
which I am engaged in commenting. It alleges that
the world described by science is congruous with

our natural beliefs; a thesis not very important in itself, which I only dwell on now because it affords a convenient text from which to preach the great oddity of the creed which science requires us to adopt respecting the world in which we live. This creed is evidently in its origin an amendment or modification of our natural or instinctive view of things, a compromise to which we are no doubt compelled by considerations of conclusive force, but a compromise, nevertheless, which, if we did not know it to be true, we should certainly find it difficult not to abandon as absurd.

For, consider what kind of a world it is in which we are asked to believe—a world which, so far as most people are concerned, can only be at all adequately conceived in terms of the visual sense, but which in its true reality possesses neither of the qualities characteristically associated with the visual sense, namely, illumination and colour. A world which is half like our ideas of it and half unlike them. Like our ideas of it, that is to say, so far as the so-called primary qualities of matter, such as extension and solidity, are concerned; unlike our ideas of it so far as the so-called secondary qualities, such as warmth and colour, are concerned. A hybrid world, a world of inconsistencies and strange anomalies. A world one-half of which may commend itself to the empirical philosopher, and the other half of which may commend itself to the plain man, but which as a whole can commend itself to

neither.   A world which is rejected by the first because it arbitrarily selects what he regards as modes
of sensation, and hypostatises them into permanent
realities; while it is scarcely intelligible to the
second, because it takes what he regards as permanent realities, and evaporates them into modes of
sensation.   A world, in short, which seems to
harmonise neither with the conclusions of critical
empiricism nor with the 'unmistakable evidence of
the senses'; which outrages the whole psychology
of the one, and is in direct contradiction with the
deliverances of the other.

So far as the leading philosophic empiricists are
concerned—and it is only with them that we need
deal—the result of these difficulties has been extraordinary.   They have found it impossible to swal-
low this strange universe, consisting partly of
microcosms furnished with impressions and ideas
which, as such, are of course transient and essentially mental, partly of a macrocosm furnished with
material objects whose qualities exactly resemble
impressions and ideas, with the embarrassing exception that they are neither transient nor mental.
They have, therefore, been compelled by one device
or another to sweep the macrocosm *as conceived by
science* altogether out of existence.   In the name of
experience itself they have destroyed that which
professes to be experience systematised.   And we
are presented with the singular spectacle of thinkers
whose claim to our consideration largely consists in

their uncompromising empiricism playing unconscious havoc with the most solid results which empirical methods have hitherto attained.

I say 'unconscious' havoc, because, no doubt, the
truth of this indictment would not be admitted by
the majority of those against whom it is directed.
Yet there can, I think, be no real question as to its
truth.   In the case of Hume it will hardly be
denied; and Hume, perhaps, would himself have
been the last to deny it.   But in the case of John
Mill, of Mr. Herbert Spencer,[1] and of Professor
Huxley, it is an allegation which would certainly be
repudiated, though the evidence for it seems to me
to lie upon the surface of their speculations.   The
allegation, be it observed, is this—that while each
of these thinkers has recognised the necessity for
some independent reality in relation to the ever-
moving stream of sensations which constitute our
immediate experiences, each of them has rejected
the independent reality which is postulated and explained by science, and each of them has substituted
for it a private reality of his own.   Where the
physicist, for example, assumes actual atoms and
motions and forces, Mill saw nothing but permanent
possibilities of sensation, and Mr. Spencer knows

[1] It is probably accurate to describe Mr. Spencer as an empiricist; though he has added to the accustomed first principles of empiricism certain doctrines of his own which, while they do not
strengthen his system, make it somewhat difficult to classify.   The
reader interested in such matters will find most of the relevant
points discussed in *Philosophic Doubt*, chaps. viii., ix., x.

nothing but 'the unknowable.' Without discussing the place which such entities may properly occupy in the general scheme of things, I content myself with observing, what I have elsewhere endeavoured to demonstrate at length, that they cannot occupy the place now filled by material Nature as conceived by science. That which is a 'permanent possibility,' but is nothing more, is permanent only in name. It represents no enduring reality, nothing which persists, nothing which has any being save during the brief intervals when, ceasing to be a mere 'possibility,' it blossoms into the actuality of sensation. Before sentient beings were, it was not. When they cease to exist, it will vanish away. If they change the character of their sensibility, it will sympathetically vary its nature. How unfit is this unsubstantial shadow of a phrase to take the place now occupied by that material universe, of which we are but fleeting accidents, whose attributes are for the most part absolutely independent of us, whose duration is incalculable!

A different but not a less conclusive criticism may be passed on Mr. Spencer's 'unknowable.' For anything I am here prepared to allege to the contrary, this may be real enough; but, unfortunately, it has not the kind of reality imperatively required by science. It is not in space. It is not in time. It possesses neither mass nor extension; nor is it capable of motion. Its very name implies that it eludes the grasp of thought, and cannot be caught up into formulæ. Whatever purpose, therefore, such an 'object' may subserve in the universe of things, it is as useless as a 'permanent possibility' itself to provide subject-matter for scientific treatment. If these be all that truly exist outside the circle of impressions and ideas, then is all science turned to foolishness, and evolution stands confessed as a mere figment of the imagination. Man, or rather 'I,' become not merely the centre of the world, but *am* the world. Beyond me and my ideas there is either nothing, or nothing that can be known. The problems about which we disquiet ourselves in vain, the origin of things and the modes of their development, the inner constitution of matter and its relations to mind, are questionings about nothing, interrogatories shouted into the void. The baseless fabric of the sciences, like the great globe itself, dissolves at the touch of theories like these, leaving not a wrack behind. Nor does there seem to be any other course open to the consistent agnostic, were such a being possible, than to contemplate in patience the long procession of his sensations, without disturbing himself with futile inquiries into what, if anything, may lie beyond.

VII

There remains but one problem further with which I need trouble the readers of this chapter. It is that raised by the only remaining proposition of

the three with which I promised just now to deal.
This asserts, it may be recollected, that the principle
of causation and, by parity of reasoning, any other
universal principle of sense-interpretation, may by
some process of logical alchemy be extracted, not
merely from experience in general,[1] but even from
the experience of a single individual.

But who, it may be asked, is unreasonable enough
to demand that it should be extracted from the experience of a single individual? What is there in
the empirical theory which requires us to impose so
arbitrary a limitation upon the sources of our knowledge? Have we not behind us the whole experience
of the race? Is it to count for nothing that for num-
berless generations mankind has been scrutinising
the face of Nature, and storing up for our guidance
innumerable observations of the laws which she
obeys? Yes, I reply, it *is* to count for nothing; and
for a most simple reason. In making this appeal to
the testimony of mankind with regard to the world
in which they live, we take for granted that there is
such a world, that mankind has had experiences of
it, and that, so far as is necessary for our purpose,
we know what those experiences have been. But
by what right do we take those things for granted?
They are not axiomatic or intuitive truths; they
must be proved by something; and that something
must, on the empirical theory, be in the last resort
experience, and experience alone. But whose ex-

[1] See *Philosophic Doubt*, ch. i.

perience? Plainly it cannot be *general* experience, for that is the very thing whose reality has to be established, and whose character is in question. It must, therefore, in every case and for each individual man be his own personal experience. This, and only this, can supply him with evidence for those fundamental beliefs, without whose guidance it is impossible for him either to reconstruct the past or to anticipate the future.

Consider, for example, the law of causation; one, but by no means the only one, of those general principles of interpretation which, as I am contending, are presupposed in any appeal to general experience, and cannot, therefore, be proved by it. If we endeavour to analyse the reasoning by which we arrive at the conviction that any particular event or any number of particular events have occurred outside the narrow ring of our own immediate perceptions, we shall find that not a step of this process can we take without assuming that the course of Nature is uniform[1]; or, if not absolutely uniform, at least sufficiently uniform to allow us to argue with tolerable security from effects to causes, or, if need be, from causes to effects, over great intervals of time and space. The whole of what is called historical evidence is, in its most essential parts, noth-

---

[1] The reader will find some observations on the meaning of the phrase, ' Uniformity of Nature,' on p. 289 et seq. In this chapter I have assumed (following empirical usage) that the Uniformity of Nature and the Law of Causation are different expressions for the same thing.

ing more than an argument or series of arguments of this kind. The fact that mankind have given their testimony to the general uniformity of Nature, or, indeed, to anything else, can be established by the aid of that principle itself, and by it alone; so that if we abandon it, we are in a moment deprived of all logical access to the outer world, of all cognisance of other minds, of all usufruct of their accumulated knowledge, of all share in the intellectual heritage of the race. While if we cling to it (as, to be sure, we must, whether we like it or not), we can do so only on condition that we forego every endeavour to prove it by the aid of general experience; for such a procedure would be nothing less than to compel what is intended to be the conclusion of our argument to figure also among the most important of its premises.

The problem, therefore, is reduced to this: Can we find in our personal experience adequate evidence of a law which, like the law of Causation, does, by the very terms in which it is stated, claim universal jurisdiction, as of right, to the utmost verge both of time and space. And surely, to enunciate such a question is to suggest the inevitable answer. The sequences familiar to us in the petty round of daily life, the accustomed recurrence of something resembling a former consequent, following on the heels of something resembling a former antecedent, are sufficient to generate the expectations and the habits by which we endeavour, with

9

what success we may, to accommodate our behaviour to the unyielding requirements of the world around us. But to throw upon experiences such as these[1] the whole burden of fixing our opinions as to the constitution of the universe is quite absurd. It would be absurd in any case. It would be absurd even if all the phenomena of which we have immediate knowledge succeeded each other according to some obvious and undeviating order; for the contrast between this microscopic range of observation and the gigantic induction which it is sought to rest thereon, would rob the argument of all plausibility. But it is doubly and trebly absurd when we reflect on what our experiences really are. So far are they from indicating, when taken strictly by themselves, the existence of a world where all things small and great follow with the most exquisite regularity and the most minute obedience the bidding of unchanging law, that they indicate precisely the reverse. In certain regions of experience, no doubt, orderly sequence appears to be the rule : day alternates with night, and summer follows upon spring; the sun moves through the zodiac, and unsupported bodies fall usually, though, to be sure, not always, to the ground. Even of such elementary astronomical and physical facts, however, it could hardly be maintained that any man would have a right, on the strength of his personal observation alone, confident-

---

[1] At least in the absence of any transcendental interpretation of them. See next chapter.

ly to assert their undeviating regularity. But when we come to the more complex phenomena with which we have to deal, the plain lesson taught by personal observation is not the regularity, but the irregularity, of Nature. A kind of ineffectual attempt at uniformity, no doubt, is commonly apparent, as of an ill-constructed machine that will run smoothly for a time, and then for no apparent reason begin to jerk and quiver; or of a drunken man who, though he succeeds in keeping to the high-road, yet pursues along it a most wavering and devious course. But of that perfect adjustment, that all-penetrating governance by law, which lies at the root of scientific inference we find not a trace. In many cases sensation follows sensation, and event hurries after event, to all appearances absolutely at random: no observed order of succession is ever repeated, nor is it pretended that there is any direct causal connection between the members of the series as they appear one after the other in the consciousness of the individual. But even when these conditions are reversed, perfect uniformity is never observed. The most careful series of experiments carried out by the most accomplished investigators never show identical results; and as for the general mass of mankind, so far are they from finding, either in their personal experiences or elsewhere, any sufficient reason for accepting in its perfected form the principle of Universal Causation, that, as a matter of fact, this doctrine has been steadily ignored by them up to the present hour.

This apparent irregularity of Nature, obvious enough when we turn our attention to it, escapes our habitual notice, of course, because we invariably attribute the want of observed uniformity to the errors of the observer. And without doubt we do well. But what does this imply? It implies that we bring to the interpretation of our sense-perception the principle of causation ready made. It implies that we do not believe the world to be governed by immutable law because our experiences appear to be regular; but that we believe that our experiences, in spite of their apparent irregularity, follow some (perhaps) unknown rule because we first believe the world to be governed by immutable law. But this is as much as to say that the principle is not proved by experience, but that experience is understood in the light of the principle. Here, again, empiricism fails us. As in the case of our judgments about particular matters of fact, so also in the case of these other judgments, whose scope is co-extensive with the whole realm of Nature, we find that any endeavour to formulate a rational justification for them based on experience alone breaks down, and, to all appearance, breaks down hopelessly.

VIII

But even if this reasoning be sound, may the reader exclaim, What is it that we gain by it? What harvest are we likely to reap from such broadcast sowing of scepticism as this? What does it profit us to show that a great many truths which every-body believes, and which no abstract speculations will induce us to doubt, are still waiting for a philo-sophic proof? Fair questions, it must be admitted; questions, nevertheless, to which I must reserve my full answer until a later stage of our inquiry. Yet even now something may be said, by way of conclu-sion to this chapter, on the relation which these crit-icisms bear to the scheme of thought whose practi-cal consequences we traced out in the first part of these Notes.

I begin by admitting that the criticisms them-selves are, from the nature of the case, incomplete. They contain but the concise and even meagre out-line of an argument which is itself but a portion only of the whole case. For want of space, or to avoid unsuitable technicalities, much has been omitted which would have been relevant to the issues raised, and have still further strengthened the position which has been taken up. Yet, though more might have been said, what has been said is, in my opinion, sufficient; and I shall, therefore, not scruple hence-forth to assume that a purely empirical theory of things, a philosophy which depends for its premises in the last resort upon the particulars revealed to us in perceptive experience alone, is one that can-not rationally be accepted.

Is this conclusion, then, adverse to Naturalism? And, if so, must it not tell with equal force against

Science, seeing that it is solely against that part of the naturalistic teaching which is taken over bodily from Science that it appears to be directed? Of these two questions, I answer the first in the affirmative, the second in the negative. Doubtless, if empiricism be shattered, it must drag down naturalism in its fall; for, after all, naturalism is nothing more than the assertion that empirical methods are valid, and that no others are so. But because any effectual criticism of empiricism is the destruction of naturalism, is it therefore the destruction of science also? Surely not. The adherent of naturalism is an empiricist from necessity; the man of science, if he be an empiricist, is so only from choice. The latter may, if he please, have no philosophy at all, or he may have a different one. He is not obliged, any more than other men, to justify his conclusions by an appeal to first principles; still less is he obliged to take his first principles from so poor a creed as the one we have been discussing. Science preceded the theory of science, and is independent of it. Science preceded naturalism, and will survive it. Though the convictions involved in our practical conception of the universe are not beyond the reach of theoretic doubts, though we habitually stake our all upon assumptions which we never attempt to justify, and which we could not justify if we would, yet is our scientific certitude unshaken; and if we still strive after some solution of our sceptical difficulties, it is because this is necessary for the satisfaction of an intellectual ideal, not because it is required to fortify our confidence either in the familiar teachings of experience or in their utmost scientific expansion.   And hence arises my principal complaint against naturalism.   With Empirical philosophy, considered as a tentative contribution to the theory of science, I have no desire to pick a quarrel.   That it should fail is nothing. Other philosophies have failed.   Such is, after all, the common lot.   That it should have been contrived to justify conclusions already accepted is, if a fault at all—which I doubt—at least a most venial one, and one, moreover, which it has committed in the best of philosophic company.   That it should derive some moderate degree of imputed credit from the universal acceptance of the scientific beliefs which it countersigns, may be borne with, though for the real interests of speculative inquiry this has been, I think, a misfortune.   But that it should develop into naturalism, and then, on the strength of labours which it has not endured, of victories which it has not won, and of scientific triumphs in which it has no right to share, presume, in despite of its speculative insufficiency, to dictate terms of surrender to every other system of belief, is altogether intolerable.   Who would pay the slightest attention to naturalism if it did not force itself into the retinue of science, assume her livery, and claim, as a kind of poor relation, in some sort to represent her authority and to speak with her voice?

Of itself it is nothing. It neither ministers to the needs of mankind, nor does it satisfy their reason. And if, in spite of this, its influence has increased, is increasing, and as yet shows no signs of diminution; if more and more the educated and the half-educated are acquiescing in its pretensions and, however reluctantly, submitting to its domination, this is, at least in part, because they have not learned to distinguish between the practical and inevitable claims which experience has on their allegiance, and the speculative but quite illusory title by which the empirical school have endeavoured to associate naturalism and science in a kind of joint supremacy over the thoughts and consciences of mankind.

CHAPTER II

IDEALISM ; AFTER SOME RECENT ENGLISH WRITINGS[1]

I

THE difficulties in the way of an empirical philosophy of science, with which we dealt in the last

[1] The reader who has no familiarity with philosophic literature is advised to omit this chapter. The philosophic reader will, I hope, regard it as provisional. Transcendental Idealism is, if I mistake not, at this moment in rather a singular position in this country. In the land of its birth (as I am informed) it is but little considered. In English-speaking countries it is, within the narrow circle of professed philosophers, perhaps the dominant mood of thought; while without that circle it is not so much objected to as totally ignored. This anomalous state of things is no doubt due in part to the inherent difficulty of the subject ; but even more, I think, to the fact that the energy of English Idealists has been consumed rather in the production of commentaries on other people's systems than in expositions of their own. The result of this is that we do not quite know where we are, that we are more or less in a condition of expectancy, and that both learners and critics are placed at a disadvantage. Pending the appearance of some original work which shall represent the constructive views of the younger school of thinkers, I have written the following chapter, with reference chiefly to the writings of the late Mr. T. H. Green, which at present contain the most important exposition, so far as I know, of this phase of English thought. Mr. Bradley's noteworthy work, *Appearance and Reality*, published some time after this chapter was finished, is written with characteristic independence ; but I know not whether it has yet commanded any large measure of assent from the few who are competent to pronounce a verdict upon its merits.

chapter, largely arise from the conflict which exists between two parts of a system, the scientific half of which requires us to regard experience as an effect of an external and independent world, while the philosophic or epistemological half offers this same experience to us as the sole groundwork and logical foundation on which any knowledge whatever of an external and independent world may be rationally based. These difficulties and the arguments founded on them require to be urged, in the first instance, in opposition to those who explicitly hold what I have called the 'naturalistic' creed; and then to that general body of educated opinion which, though reluctant to contract its beliefs within the narrow circuit of 'naturalism,' yet habitually assumes that there is presented to us in science a body of opinion, certified by reason, solid, certain, and impregnable, to which theology adds, as an edifying supplement, a certain number of dogmas, of which the well-disposed assimilate as many, but only as many, as their superior allegiance to 'positive' knowledge will permit them to digest.

These two classes, however, by no means exhaust the kinds of opinion with which it is necessary to deal. And in particular there is a metaphysical school, few indeed in numbers, but none the less important in matters speculative, whose general position is wholly distinct and independent; who would, indeed, not perhaps very widely, dissent from the negative conclusions already reached, but who have their own positive solution of the problem of the universe. In their opinion, all the embarrassments which may be shown to attend on the empirical philosophy are due to the fact that empirical philosophers wholly misunderstand the essential nature of that experience on which they profess to found their beliefs. The theory of perception evolved out of Locke, by Berkeley and Hume, which may be traced without radical modification through their modern successors, is, according to the school of which I speak, at the root of all the mischief. Of this theory they make short work. They press to the utmost the sceptical consequences to which it inevitably leads. They show, or profess to show, that it renders not only scientific knowledge, but any knowledge whatever, impossible; and they offer as a substitute a theory of experience, very remote indeed from ordinary modes of expression, by which these consequences may, in their judgment, be entirely avoided.

The dimensions and character of these Notes render it impossible, even were I adequately equipped for the task, to deal fully with so formidable a subject as TRANSCENDENTAL IDEALISM, either in its historical or in its metaphysical aspect. Remote though it be from ordinary modes of thought, some brief discussion of the theory with which, in some recent English works, it supplies us concerning Nature and God is, however, absolutely necessary; and I therefore here present the following observa-

tions to the philosophic reader with apologies for
their brevity, and to the unphilosophic reader with
apologies for their length.

From what I have already said it is clear that
the theory to which Transcendental Idealism may
be, from our point of view, considered as a reply, is
not the theory of experience which is taken for
granted in ordinary scientific statement, but the
closely allied 'psychological theory of perception'
evolved by thinkers usually classed rather as philosophers than as men of science. The difference is
not wholly immaterial, as will appear in the sequel.

What, then, is this 'psychological theory of perception'? Or, rather, where is the weak point in it
at which it is open to attack by the transcendental
idealists? It lies in the account given by that theory of the *real*. According to this account the
'real' in external experience, that which, because it
is not due to any mental manipulation by the percipient, such as abstraction or comparison, may be
considered as the *experienced fact*, is, in ultimate
analysis, either a sensation or a group of sensations.
These sensations and groups of sensations are subjected in the mind to a process of analysis and comparison. Discrimination is made between those
which are unlike. Those which have points of resemblance are called by a common name. The sequences and co-existences which obtain among
them are noted; the laws by which they are bound
together are discovered; and the order in which

they may be expected to recur is foreseen and understood.

Now, say the idealists, if everything of which external reality can be predicated is thus either a sensation or a group of sensations, if these and these only
are 'given' in external appearance, everything else, in
cluding relations, being mere fictions of the mind,
we are reduced to the absurd position of holding
that the real is not only unknown, but is also unknowable. For a brief examination of the nature of
experience is sufficient to prove that an unrelated
'thing' (be that 'thing' a sensation or a group of
sensations), which is not qualified by its resemblance
to other things, its difference from other things, and
its connection with other things, is really, so far as
we are concerned, no 'thing' at all. It is not an
object of possible experience; its true character
must be for ever hid from us; or, rather, as character consists simply in relations, it *has* no character, nor can it form part of that intelligible
world with which alone we have to deal.

Ideas of relation are, therefore, required to convert the supposed 'real' of external experience into
something of which experience can take note. But
such ideas themselves are unintelligible, except as the
results of the intellectual activity of some 'Self' or
'I'. They must be somebody's thought, somebody's
ideas; if only for the purpose of mutual comparison, there must be some bond of union between
them other than themselves. Here again, therefore,

the psychological analysis of experience breaks
down, and it becomes plain that just as the real in
external experience is real only in virtue of an intellectual element, namely, ideas of relation (categories), through which it was apprehended, so in
internal experience ideas and sensations presuppose
the existence of an 'I,' or self-conscious unity, which
is neither sensation nor idea, which ought not,
therefore, on the psychological theory to be considered as having any claim to reality at all, but
which, nevertheless, is presupposed in the very possibility of phenomena appearing as elements in a
single experience.

We are thus apparently left by the idealist theory
face to face with a mind (thinking subject) which is
the source of relations (categories), and a world which
is constituted by relations : with a mind which is
conscious of itself, and a world of which that mind
may without metaphor be described as the creator.
We have, in short, reached the central position of
transcendental idealism.   But before we proceed to
subject the system to any critical observations, let
us ask what it is we are supposed to gain by endeavouring thus to *rethink* the universe from so unaccustomed a point of view.

In the first place, then, it is claimed for this theory
that it frees us from the scepticism which, in matters
scientific as well as in matters theological, follows
inevitably upon the psychological doctrine of perception as just explained : a scepticism which not only

leaves no room for God and the soul, but destroys
the very possibility of framing any general proposition about the 'external' world, by destroying the
possibility of there being any world, 'external' or
otherwise, in which permanent relation shall exist.

In the second place, it makes Reason no mere
accidental excrescence on a universe of material
objects; an element to be added to, or subtracted
from, the sum of 'things' as the blind shock of unthinking causes may decide.   Rather does it make
Reason the very essence of all that is or can be: the
(immanent) cause of the world-process; its origin
and its goal.

In the third place, it professes to establish on a
firm foundation the moral freedom of self-conscious
agents.   That 'Self' which is the prior condition of
there being a natural world cannot be the creature
of that world.   It stands above and beyond the sphere
of causes and effects; it is no mere object among
other objects, driven along its predestined course by
external forces in obedience to alien laws.   On the
contrary, it is a free, autonomous Spirit, not only
bound, but able, to fulfil the moral commands which
are but the expression of its own most essential being.

II

I am reluctant to suggest objections to any theory
which promises results so admirable.   Yet I cannot
think that all the difficulties with which it is sur-

rounded have been fairly faced, or, at any rate, fully explained, by those who accept its main principles. Consider, for example, the crucial question of the analysis which reduces all experience to an experience of relations, or, in more technical language, which constitutes the universe out of categories. We may grant without difficulty that the contrasted theory, which proposes to reduce the universe to an unrelated chaos of impressions or sensations, is quite untenable. But must we not also grant that in all experience there is a refractory element which, though it cannot be presented in isolation, nevertheless refuses wholly to merge its being in a network of relations, necessary as these may be to give it 'significance for us as thinking beings'? If so, whence does this irreducible element arise? The mind, we are told, is the source of relation. What is the source of that which is related? A 'thing-in-itself' which, by impressing the percipient mind, shall furnish the 'matter' for which categories provide the 'form,' is a way out of the difficulty (if difficulty there be) which raises more doubts than it solves. The followers of Kant themselves make haste to point out that this hypothetical cause of that which is 'given' in experience cannot, since *ex hypothesi* it lies beyond experience, be known as a cause, or even as existing. Nay, it is not so much unknown and unknowable as indescribable and unintelligible; not so much a riddle whose meaning is obscure as mere absence and vacuity of any meaning whatever. Accordingly, from the speculations with

which we are here concerned it has been dismissed
with ignominy, and it need not, therefore, detain us
further.

But we do not get rid of the difficulty by getting
rid of Kant's solution of it. His dictum still seems
to me to remain true, that 'without matter categories
are empty.' And, indeed, it is hard to see how it is
possible to conceive a universe in which relations
shall be all in all, but in which nothing is to be permitted for the relations to subsist between. Relations surely imply a something which is related,
and if that something is, in the absence of relations,
'nothing for us as thinking beings,' so relations in
the absence of that something are mere symbols
emptied of their signification; they are, in short, an
'illegitimate abstraction.'

Those, moreover, who hold that these all-consti-
tuting relations are the 'work of the mind' would
seem bound also to hold that this concrete world of
ours, down to its minutest detail, must evolve itself
a priori out of the movement of 'pure thought.'
There is no room in it for the 'contingent'; there is
no room in it for the 'given'; experience itself would
seem to be a superfluity. And we are at a loss, therefore, to understand why that dialectical process which
moves, I will not say so convincingly, but at least so
smoothly, through the abstract categories of 'being,'
'not-being,' 'becoming,' and so forth, should stumble
and hesitate when it comes to deal with that world
of Nature which is, after all, one of the principal

10

subjects about which we desire information. No explanation which I remember to have seen makes it otherwise than strange that we should, as the idealists claim, be able so thoroughly to identify ourselves with those thoughts of God which are the necessary preliminary to creation, but should so little understand creation itself; that we should out of our unaided mental resources be competent to reproduce the whole ground-plan of the universe, and should yet lose ourselves so hopelessly in the humblest of its ante-rooms.

This difficulty at once requires us to ask on what ground it is alleged that these constitutive relations are the 'work of the mind.' It is true, no doubt, that ordinary usage would describe as mental products the more abstract thoughts (categories), such, for example, as 'being,' 'not-being,' 'causation,' 'reciprocity,' &c. But it must be recollected, in the first place, that transcendental idealism does not, as a rule, derive its inspiration from ordinary usage; and in the second place, that even ordinary usage alters its procedure when it comes to such more concrete cases of relation as, for instance, 'shape' and 'position,' which, rightly or wrongly, are always considered as belonging to the 'external' world, and presented by the external world to thought, not created by thought for itself.

Are the transcendental idealists, then, bound by their own most essential principles, in opposition both to their arguments against Kant's 'thing-in-itself' and to the ordinary beliefs of mankind, to invest the thinking ' self ' with this attribute of causal or *quasi-*causal activity ?   It certainly appears to me that they are *not*.   Starting, it will be recollected, from the analysis (criticism) of experience, they arrived at the conclusion that the world of objects exists and has a meaning only for the self-conscious ' I ' (subject), and that the self-conscious ' I ' only knows itself in contrast and in opposition to the world of objects. Each is necessary to the other; in the absence of the other neither has any significance.   How, then, can we venture to say of one that the other is its product? and if we say it of either, must we not in consistency insist on saying it of both?   Thus, though the presence of a self-conscious principle may be necessary to constitute the universe, it cannot be considered as the creator of that universe ; or if it be, then must we acknowledge that precisely in the same way and precisely to the same extent is the universe the creator of the self-conscious principle.

All, therefore, that the transcendental argument requires or even allows us to accept, is a ' manifold ' of relations on the one side, and a bare self-conscious principle of unity on the other, by which that manifold becomes inter-connected in the ' field of a single experience.'   We are not permitted, except by a process of abstraction which is purely temporary and provisional, to consider the ' manifold ' apart from the ' unity,' nor the ' unity ' apart from the ' manifold.' The thoughts do not make the thinker, nor the

thinker the thoughts; but together they constitute
that Whole or Absolute whose elements, as they are
mere no-sense apart from one another, cannot in
strictness be even said to contribute separately towards the total result.

III

Now let us consider what bearing this conclusion
has upon (1) Theology, (2) Ethics, and (3) Science.

1. As regards Theology, it might be supposed
that at least idealism provided us with a universe
which, if not created or controlled by Reason (creation and control implying causal action), may yet
properly be said to be throughout infused by Reason and to be in necessary harmony with it. But
on a closer examination difficulties arise which somewhat mar this satisfactory conclusion. In the first
place, if theology is to provide us with a groundwork
work for religion, the God of whom it speaks must
be something more than the bare 'principle of unity'
required to give coherence to the multiplicity of
Nature. Apart from Nature He is, on the theory
we are considering, a mere metaphysical abstraction,
the geometrical point through which pass all the
threads which make up the web of possible experience: no fitting object, surely, of either love, reverence, or devotion. In combination with Nature He
is no doubt 'the principle of unity,' and all the fulness of concrete reality besides; but every quality

with which He is thus associated belongs to that portion of the Absolute Whole from which, by hypothesis, He distinguishes Himself; and, were it otherwise, we cannot find in these qualities, compacted,
as they are, of good and bad, of noble and base, the
Perfect Goodness without which religious feelings
can never find an adequate object. Thus, neither
the combining principle alone, nor the combining
principle considered in its union with the multiplicity which it combines, can satisfy the requirements
of an effectual theology. Not the first, because it is
a barren abstraction; not the second, because in its
all-inclusive universality it holds in suspension, without preference and without repulsion, every element
alike of the knowable world. Of these none, whatever be its nature, be it good or bad, base or noble,
can be considered as alien to the Absolute: all are
necessary, and all are characteristic.

Of these two alternatives, I understand that it
is the first which is usually adopted by the school
of thought with which we are at present concerned.
It may therefore be desirable to reiterate that a
'unifying principle' can, as such, have no qualities,
moral or otherwise. Lovingkindness, for example,
and Equity are attributes which, like all attributes,
belong not to the unifying principle, but to the
world of objects which it constitutes. They are
conceptions which belong to the realm of empirical psychology. Nor can I see any method by
which they are to be hitched on to the 'pure spirit-

ual subject,' as elements making up its essential character.

2. But if this be so, what is the ethical value of that freedom which is attributed by the idealistic theory to the self-conscious 'I'? It is true that this 'I' as conceived by idealism is above all the 'categories,' including, of course, the category of causation. It is not in space nor in time. It is subject neither to mutation nor decay. The stress of material forces touches it not, nor is it in any servitude to chance or circumstance, to inherited tendencies or acquired habits. But all these immunities and privileges it possesses in virtue of its being, *not* an agent in a world of concrete fact, but a thinking 'subject,' for whom alone, as it is alleged, such a world exists. Its freedom is metaphysical, not moral; for moral freedom can only have a meaning at all in reference to a being who acts and who wills, and is only of real importance for us in relation to a being who not only acts, but is acted on, who not only wills, but who wills against the opposing influences of temptation. Such freedom cannot, it is plain, be predicated of a mere 'subject,' nor is the freedom proper to a 'subject' of any worth to man as 'object,' to man as known in experience, to man fighting his way with varying fortunes against the stream of adverse circumstances, in a world made up of causes and effects.[1]

---

[1] This proposition would, probably, not be widely dissented from by some of the ethical writers of the idealist school. The freedom

These observations bring into sufficiently clear relief the difficulty which exists, on the idealistic theory, in bringing together into any sort of intelligible association the 'I' as supreme principle of unity, and the 'I' of empirical psychology, which

which they postulate is not the freedom merely of the pure self-conscious subject. On the contrary, it is the individual, with all his qualities, passions, and emotions, who in their view possesses free will. But the ethical value of the freedom thus attributed to self-conscious agents seems on further examination to disappear. Mankind, it seems, are on this theory free, but their freedom does not exclude determinism, *but only that form of determinism which consists in external constraint.* Their actions are upon this view strictly prescribed by their antecedents, but these antecedents are nothing other than the characters of the agents themselves.

Now it may seem at first sight plausible to describe that man as free whose behaviour is due to 'himself' alone. But without quarrelling over words, it is, I think, plain that, whether it be proper to call him free or not, he at least lacks freedom in the sense in which freedom is necessary in order to constitute responsibility. It is impossible to say of him that he 'ought,' and therefore he 'can'. For at any given moment of his life his next action is by hypothesis strictly determined. This is also true of every previous moment, until we get back to that point in his life's history at which he cannot, in any intelligible sense of the term, be said to have a character at all. Antecedently to this, the causes which have produced him are in no special sense connected with his individuality, but form part of the general complex of phenomena which make up the world. It is evident, therefore, that every act which he performs may be traced to pre-natal, and possibly to purely material, antecedents, and that, even if it be true that what he does is the outcome of his character, his character itself is the outcome of causes over which he has not, and cannot by any possibility have, the smallest control. Such a theory destroys responsibility, and leaves our actions the inevitable outcome of external conditions not less completely than any doctrine of controlling fate, whether materialistic or theological.

has desires and fears, pleasures and pains, faculties and sensibilities; which *was not* a little time since, and which a little time hence will be no more. The 'I' as principle of unity is outside time; it can have, therefore, no history. The 'I' of experience, which learns and forgets, which suffers and which enjoys, unquestionably has a history. What is the relation between the two? We seem equally precluded from saying that they are the same, and from saying that they are different. We cannot say that they are the same, because they are, after all, divided by the whole chasm which distinguishes 'subject' from 'object.' We cannot say they are different, because our feelings and our desires seem a not less interesting and important part of ourselves than a mere unifying principle whose functions, after all, are of a purely metaphysical character. We cannot say they are 'two aspects of the same thing,' because there is no virtue in this useful phrase which shall empower it on the one hand to ear-mark a fragment of the world of objects, and say of it, 'this is I,' or, on the other, to take the 'pure subject' by which the world of objects is constituted, and say of it that it shall be itself an object in that world from which its essential nature requires it to be self-distinguished.

But as it thus seems difficult or impossible intelligibly to unite into a personal whole the 'pure' and the 'empirical' Self, so it is difficult or impossible to conceive the relations between the pure, though limited, self-consciousness which is 'I' and the uni-

versal and eternal Self-consciousness which is God.
The first has been described as a 'mode' or 'manifestation' of the second. But are we not, in using
such language, falling into the kind of error against
which, in other connections, the idealists are most
careful to warn us? Are we not importing a category which has its meaning and its use in the world
of objects into a transcendental region where it
really has neither meaning nor use at all? Grant, however, for the sake of argument, that it has a meaning;
grant that we may legitimately describe one 'pure
subject' as a 'mode' or 'manifestation' of another—
how is this partial identity to be established? How
can we, who start from the basis of our own limited
self-consciousness, rise to the knowledge of that
completed and divine self-consciousness of which,
according to the theory, we share the essential nature?

The difficulty is evaded but not solved in those
statements of the idealist theory which always speak
of Thought without specifying *whose* Thought. It
seems to be thus assumed that the thought is God's,
and that in rethinking it we share His being. But
no such assumption would seem to be justifiable.
For the basis, we know, of the whole theory is a
'criticism' or analysis of the essential elements of
experience. But the criticism must, for each of us,
be necessarily of *his own* experience, for of no other
experience can he know anything, except indirectly
and by way of inference from his own. What, then,

is this criticism supposed to establish (say) for me? Is it that experience depends upon the unification by *a* self-conscious 'I' of a world constituted by relations? In strictness, No. It can only establish that *my* experience depends upon a unification by *my* self-conscious 'I' of a world of relations present to *me*, and to me alone. To this 'I,' to this particular 'self-conscious subject,' all other 'I's,' including God, must be objects, constituted like all objects by relations, rendered possible or significant only by their unification in the 'content of a single experience'—namely, my own. In other words, that which (if it exists at all) is essentially 'subject' can only be known, or thought of, or spoken about, as 'object.' Surely a very paradoxical conclusion.

It may perhaps be said by way of reply, that in talking of particular 'I's' and particular experiences we are using language properly applicable only to the 'self' dealt with by the empirical psychologist, the 'self' which is not the 'subject,' but the 'object,' of experience. I will not dispute about terms; and the relations which exist between the 'pure ego' and the 'empirical ego' are, as I have already said, so obscure that it is not always easy to employ a perfectly accurate terminology in endeavouring to deal with them. Yet this much would seem to be certain. If the words 'self,' 'ego,' 'I,' are to be used intelligibly at all, they must mean, whatever else they do or do not mean, a 'somewhat' which is self-distinguished, not only from every other knowable

object, but also from every other possible 'self.'
What we are 'in ourselves,' apart from the flux of
thoughts and feelings which move in never-ending
pageant through the chambers of consciousness,
metaphysicians have, indeed, found it hard to say.
Some of them have said we are nothing. But if this
conclusion be, as I think it is, conformable neither
to our instinctive beliefs nor to a sound psychology;
if we are, as I believe, more than a mere series of
occurrences, yet it seems equally certain that the
very notion of Personality excludes the idea of any
one person being a 'mode' of any other, and forces
us to reject from philosophy a supposition which, if
it be tolerable at all, can find a place only in mysticism.

But the idealistic theory pressed to its furthest
conclusions requires of us to reject, as it appears to
me, even more than this. We are not only precluded
by it from identifying ourselves, even partially, with
the Eternal Consciousness: we are also precluded
from supposing that either the Eternal Consciousness or any other consciousness exists, save only our
own. For, as I have already said, the Eternal Consciousness, if it is to be known, can only be known
on the same conditions as any other object of knowledge. It must be constituted by relations; it must
form part of the 'content of experience' of the
knower; it must exist as part of the 'multiplicity'
reduced to 'unity' by his self-consciousness. But to
say that it can only be known on these terms, is to

say that it cannot be known as it exists; for if it exists at all, it exists by hypothesis as Eternal Subject, and as such it clearly is not constituted by relations, nor is it either a 'possible object of experience,' or 'anything for us as thinking beings.'

No consciousness, then, is a possible object of knowledge for any other consciousness: a statement which, on the idealistic theory of knowledge, is equivalent to saying that for any one consciousness all other consciousnesses are less than non-existent. For as that which is 'critically' shown to be an inevitable element in experience has thereby conferred on it the highest possible degree of reality, so that which cannot on any terms become an element in experience falls in the scale of reality far below mere not-being, and is reduced, as we have seen, to mere meaningless no-sense. By this kind of reasoning the idealists themselves demonstrate the 'I' to be necessary; the unrelated object and the thing-in-itself to be impossible. Not less, by this kind of reasoning, must each one of us severally be driven to the conclusion that in the infinite variety of the universe there is room for but one knowing subject, and that this subject is 'himself.'[1]

---

[1] Prof. Caird, in his most interesting and suggestive lecture on the Evolution of Religion, puts forward a theory essentially different from the one I have just been dealing with. In his view, a multiplicity of objects apprehended by a single self-conscious subject does not suffice to constitute an intelligible universe. The world of objects and the perceiving mind are themselves opposites which require a higher unity to hold them together. This higher unity is

IV

3. That the transcendental 'solipsism' which is the natural outcome of such speculations is not less inconsistent with science, morality, and common-sense than the psychological, or Berkeleian[1] form of the same creed, is obvious. But without attempting further to press idealism to results which, whether legitimate or not, all idealists would agree in

God; so that by the simplest of metaphysical demonstrations Prof. Caird lays deep the foundations of his theology, and proves not only that God exists, but that His Being is philosophically involved in the very simplest of our experiences.

I confess, with regret, that this reasoning appears to me inconclusive. Surely we must think of God as, on the transcendental theory, we think of ourselves; that is, as a Subject distinguishing itself from, but giving unity to, a world of phenomena. But if such a Subject and such a world cannot be conceived without also postulating some higher unity in which their differences shall vanish and be dissolved, then God Himself would require some yet higher deity to explain His existence. If, in short, a multiplicity of phenomena presented to and apprehended by a conscious 'I' form together an intelligible and self-sufficient whole, then it is hard to see by what logic we are to get beyond the solipsism which, as I have urged in the text, seems to be the necessary outcome of one form, at least, of the transcendental argument. If, on the other hand, subject and object cannot form such an intelligible and self-sufficient whole, then it seems impossible to imagine what is the nature of that Infinite One in which the multiplicity of things and persons find their ultimate unity. Of such a God we can have no knowledge, nor can we say that we are formed in His image, or share His essence.

[1] Of course I do not mean to suggest that Berkeley was a 'solipsist' On the scientific bearing of psychological idealism, see *Philosophic Doubt*, chap. ix.

repudiating, let me, in conclusion, point out how little assistance this theory is able under any circumstances to afford us in solving important problems connected with the Philosophy of Science.

The psychology of Hume, as we have seen, threw doubt upon the very possibility of legitimately framing general propositions about the world of objects. The observation of isolated and unrelated impressions of sense, which is in effect what experience became reduced to under his process of analysis, may generate habits of expectation, but never can justify rational beliefs. The law of universal causation, for example, can never be proved by a mere repetition, however prolonged, of similar sequences, though the repetition may, through the association of ideas, gradually compel us to expect the second term of the sequence whenever the first term comes within the field of our observation. So far Hume as interpreted by the transcendental idealists.

Now, how is this difficulty met on the idealistic theory? Somewhat in this way. These categories or general principles of relation have not, say the idealists, to be collected (so to speak) from individual and separate experiences (as the empirical philosophers believe, but as Hume, the chief among empiricists, showed to be impossible); neither are they, as the *a priori* philosophers supposed, part of the original furniture of the observing mind, intended by Providence to be applied as occasion arises to the world of experience with which by a beneficent, if unexplained, adaptation they find themselves in a pre-established harmony. On the contrary, they are the 'necessary *prius*,' the antecedent condition, of there being any experience at all; so that the difficulty of subsequently extracting them from experience does not arise. The world of phenomena is in truth their creation; so that the conformity between the two need not be any subject of surprise. Thus, at one and the same time does idealism vindicate experience and set the scepticism of the empiricist at rest.

I doubt, however, whether this solution of the problem will really stand the test of examination. Assuming for the sake of argument that the world is constituted by 'categories,' the old difficulty arises in a new shape when we ask on what principle those categories are in any given case to be applied. For they are admittedly not of universal application; and, as the idealists themselves are careful to remind us, there is no more fertile source of error than the importation of them into a sphere wherein they have no legitimate business. Take, for example, the category of causation, from a scientific point of view the most important of all. By what right does the existence of this 'principle of relation' enable us to assert that throughout the whole world every event must have a cause, and every cause must be invariably succeeded by the same event? Because we *can* apply the category, are we, therefore, *bound* to apply it? Does any absurdity or contradiction ensue from our supposing that the order of Nature is arbitrary and casual, and that, repeat the antecedent with what accuracy we may, there is no security that the accustomed consequent will follow? I must confess that I can perceive none. Of course, we should thus be deprived of one of our most useful 'principles of unification'; but this would by no means result in the universe resolving itself into that unthinkable chaos of unrelated atoms which is the idealist bugbear. There are plenty of categories left; and if the final aim of philosophy be, indeed, to find the Many in One and the One in Many, this end would be as completely, if not as satisfactorily, accomplished by conceiving the world to be presented to the thinking 'subject' in the haphazard multiplicity of unordered succession, as by any more elaborate method. Its various elements lying side by side in one Space and one Time would still be related together in the content of a single experience; they would still form an intelligible whole; their unification would thus be effectually accomplished without the aid of the higher categories. But it is evident that a universe so constituted, though it might not be inconsistent with Philosophy, could never be interpreted by Science.

As we saw in the earlier portion of this chapter, it is not very easy to understand why, if the universe be constituted by relations, and relations are the work of the mind, the mind should be dependent on experience for finding out anything about the universe. But granting the necessity of experience, it seems as hard to make that experience answer our questions on the idealist as on the empirical hypothesis. Neither on the one theory nor on the other does any method exist for extracting general truths out of particular observations, unless *some* general truths are first assumed. On the empirical hypothesis there are no such general truths. Pure empiricism has, therefore, no claim to be a philosophy. On the idealist hypothesis there appears to be only one general truth applicable to the whole intelligible world—a world which, be it recollected, includes everything in respect to which language can be significantly used; a world which, therefore, includes the negative as well as the positive, the false as well as the true, the imaginary as well as the real, the impossible as well as the possible. This single all-embracing truth is that the multiplicity of phenomena, whatever be its nature, must always be united, and only exists in virtue of being united, in the experience of a single self-conscious Subject. But this general proposition, whatever be its value, cannot, I conceive, effectually guide us in the application of subordinate categories. It supplies us with no method for applying one principle rather than another within the field of experience. It cannot give us information as to what portion of that field, if any, is subject to the law of causation, nor tell us which of our perceptions, if any, may be taken as evidence of the existence of a permanent world of objects such as is implied in all scientific doctrine. Though, therefore, the old questions come upon us

11

in a new form, clothed, I will not say shrouded, in a new terminology, they come upon us with all the old insistence. They are restated, but they are not solved ; and I am unable, therefore, to find in idealism any escape from the difficulties which, in the region of theology, ethics, and science, empiricism leaves upon our hands.[1]

[1] I have made in this chapter no reference to the idealistic theory of æsthetics. Holding the views I have indicated upon the general import of idealism, such a course seemed unnecessary. But I cannot help thinking that even those who find in that theory a more satisfactory basis for their convictions than I am able to do, must feel that there is something rather forced and arbitrary in the attempts that have been made to exhibit the artistic fancies of an insignificant fraction of the human race during a very brief period of its history as essential and important elements in the development and manifestation of the world-producing ' Idea.'

CHAPTER III

I

BRIEFLY, if not adequately, I have now endeavoured to indicate the weaknesses which seem to me to be inseparable from any empirical theory of the universe, and almost equally to beset the idealistic theory in the form given to it by its most systematic exponents in this country. The reader may perhaps feel tempted to ask whether I propose, in what purports to be an Introduction to Theology, to pass under similar review *all* the metaphysical systems which have from time to time held sway in the schools, or have affected the general course of speculative opinion. He need, however, be under no alarm. My object is strictly practical; and I have no concern with theories, however admirable, which can no longer pretend to any living philosophic power —which have no *de facto* claims to present us with a reasoned scheme of knowledge, and which cannot prove their importance by actually supplying grounds for the conviction of some fraction, at least, of those by whom these pages may conceivably be read.

In saying that this condition is not satisfied by

the great historic systems which mark with their imperishable ruins the devious course of European thought, I must not be understood as suggesting that on that account these lack either value or interest. All I say is, that their interest is not of a kind which brings them properly within the scope of these Notes. Whatever be the nature or amount of our debt to the great metaphysicians of the past, unless here and now we go to them not merely for stray arguments on this or that question, but for a reasoned scheme of knowledge which shall include as elements our own actual beliefs, their theories are not, for the purposes of the present discussion, any concern of ours.

Now, of how many systems, outside the two that have already been touched on, can this even plausibly be asserted? Run over in memory some of the most important. Men value Plato for his imagination, for the genius with which he hazarded solutions of the secular problems which perplex mankind, for the finished art of his dialogue, for the exquisite beauty of his style. But even if it could be said—which it cannot—that he left a system, could it be described as a system which, as such, has any effectual vitality? It would be difficult, perhaps impossible, to sum up our debts to Aristotle. But assuredly they do not include a tenable theory of the universe. The Stoic scheme of life may still touch our imagination; but who takes any interest in its metaphysics? Who cares for the Soul of the world, the periodic conflagrations, and the recurring cycles of mundane events? The Neo-Platonists were mystics; and mysticism is, as I suppose, an undying element in human thought. But who is concerned about their hierarchy of beings connecting through infinite gradations the Absolute at one end of the scale with Matter at the other?

These, however, it may be said, were systems belonging to the ancient world; and mankind have not busied themselves with speculation for these two thousand years and more without making some advance. I agree; but in the matter of providing us with a philosophy—with a reasoned system of knowledge—has this advance been as yet substantial? If the ancients fail us, do we, indeed, fare much better with the moderns? Are the metaphysics of Descartes more living than his physics? Do his two substances or kinds of substance, or the single substance of Spinoza, or the innumerable substances of Leibnitz, satisfy the searcher after truth? From the modern English form of the empiricism which dominated the eighteenth century, and the idealism which disputes its supremacy in the nineteenth, I have already ventured to express a reasoned dissent. Are we, then, to look to such schemes as Schopenhauer's philosophy of Will, and Hartmann's philosophy of the Unconscious, to supply us with the philosophical metaphysics of which we are in need? They have admirers in this country, but hardly convinced adherents. Of those who are quite prepared to accept their pessimism, how many are there who take seriously its metaphysical foundation?

In truth there are but three points of view from which it seems worth while to make ourselves acquainted with the growth, culmination, and decay of the various metaphysical dynasties which have successively struggled for supremacy in the world of ideas. The first is purely historical. Thus regarded, metaphysical systems are simply significant phenomena in the general history of man: symptoms of his spiritual condition, aids, it may be, to his spiritual growth. The historian of philosophy, as such, is therefore quite unconcerned with the truth or falsehood of the opinions whose evolution he is expounding. His business is merely to account for their existence, to exhibit them in their proper historical setting, and to explain their character and their consequences. But, so considered, I find it difficult to believe that these opinions have been elements of primary importance to the advancement of mankind. All ages, indeed, which have exhibited intellectual vigour have cultivated one or more characteristic systems of metaphysics; but rarely, as it seems to me, have these systems been in their turn important elements in determining the character of the periods in which they flourished. They have been effects rather than causes; indications of the mood in which, under the special stress of their time and circumstance, the most detached intellects have faced the eternal problems of humanity; proofs of the unresting desire of mankind to bring their beliefs into harmony with speculative reason. But the beliefs have almost always preceded the speculations; they have frequently survived them; and I cannot convince myself that among the just titles to our consideration sometimes put forward on behalf of metaphysics we may count her claim to rank as a powerful instrument of progress.

No doubt—and here we come to the second point of view alluded to above—the constant discussion of these high problems has not been barren merely because it has not as yet led to their solution. Philosophers have mined for truth in many directions, and the whole field of speculation seems cumbered with the dross and lumber of their abandoned workings. But though they have not found the ore they sought for, it does not therefore follow that their labours have been wholly vain. It is something to have realised what *not* to do. It is something to discover the causes of failure, even though we do not attain any positive knowledge of the conditions of success. It is an even more substantial gain to have done something towards disengaging the questions which require to be dealt with, and towards creating and perfecting the terminology without which they can scarcely be adequately stated, much less satisfactorily answered.

And there is yet a third point of view from

which past metaphysical speculations are seen to retain their value, a point of view which may be called (not, I admit, without some little violence to accustomed usage) the *æsthetic*. Because reasoning occupies so large a place in metaphysical treatises we are apt to forget that, as a rule, these are works of imagination at least as much as of reason. Metaphysicians are poets who deal with the abstract and the super-sensible instead of the concrete and the sensuous. To be sure they are poets with a difference. Their appropriate and characteristic gifts are not the vivid realisation of that which is given in experience ; their genius does not prolong, as it were, and echo through the remotest regions of feeling the shock of some definite emotion ; they create for us no new worlds of things and persons ; nor can it be often said that the product of their labours is a thing of beauty. Their style, it must be owned, has not always been their strong point ; and even when it is otherwise, mere graces of presentation are but unessential accidents of their work. Yet, in spite of all this, they can only be justly estimated by those who are prepared to apply to them a quasi-æsthetic standard ; some other standard, at all events, than that supplied by purely argumentative comment. It may perhaps be shown that their metaphysical constructions are faulty, that their demonstrations do not convince, that their most permanent dialectical triumphs have fallen to them in the paths of criticism and negation.

Yet even then the last word will not have been said. For claims to our admiration will still be found in their brilliant intuitions, in the subtlety of their occasional arguments, in their passion for the Universal and the Abiding, in their steadfast faith in the rationality of the world, in the devotion with which they are content to live and move in realms of abstract speculation too far removed from ordinary interests to excite the slightest genuine sympathy in the breasts even of the cultivated few. If, therefore, we are for a moment tempted, as surely may sometimes happen, to contemplate with respectful astonishment some of the arguments which the illustrious authors of the great historic systems have thought good enough to support their case, let it be remembered that for minds in which the critical intellect holds undisputed sway, the creation of any system whatever in the present state of our knowledge is, perhaps, impossible. Only those in whom powers of philosophical criticism are balanced, or more than balanced, by powers of metaphysical imagination can be fitted to undertake the task. Though even to them success may be impossible, at least the illusion of success is permitted; and but for them mankind would fall away in hopeless discouragement from its highest intellectual ideal, and speculation would be strangled at its birth.

To some, indeed, it may appear as if the loss would not, after all, be great. What use, they may exclaim, can be found for any system which will not. stand critical examination? What value has reasoning which does not satisfy the reason? How can we know that these abstruse investigations supply even a fragmentary contribution towards a final philosophy, until we are able to look back upon them from the perhaps inaccessible vantage ground to be supplied by this final philosophy itself? To such questionings I do not profess to find a completely satisfactory answer. Yet even those who feel inclined to rate extant speculations at the lowest value will perhaps admit that metaphysics, like art, give us something we could ill afford to spare. Art may not have provided us with any reflection of immortal beauty; nor metaphysics have brought us into communion with eternal truth. Yet both may have historic value. In speculation, as in art, we find a vivid expression of the changeful mind of man, and the interest of both, perhaps, is at its highest when they most clearly reflect the spirit of the age which gave them birth, when they are most racy of the soil from which they sprung.

II

To this point I may have to return. But my more immediate business is to bring home to the reader's mind the consequences which may be drawn from the admission—supposing him disposed

to make it—that we have at the present time neither
a satisfactory system of metaphysics nor a satisfactory theory of science.   Many persons—perhaps it
would not be too much to say most persons—are
prepared contentedly to accept the first of these
propositions; but it is on the truth of the second
that I desire to lay at least an equal stress.   The
first man one meets in the street thinks it quite natural to accept the opinion that sense-experience is
the only source of rational conviction; that everything to which it does not testify is untrue, or, if
true, falls within the domain, not of knowledge, but
of faith.   Yet the criticism of knowledge indicated
in the two preceding chapters shows how one-
sided is such a view.   If faith be provisionally defined as conviction apart from or in excess of proof,
then it is upon faith that the maxims of daily life,
not less than the loftiest creeds and the most far-
reaching discoveries, must ultimately lean.   The
ground on which constant habit and inherited predispositions enable us to tread with a step so easy
and so assured, is seen on examination to be not less
hollow beneath our feet than the dim and unfamiliar
regions which lie beyond.   Certitude is found to be
the child, not of Reason, but of Custom; and if we
are less perplexed about the beliefs on which we
are hourly called upon to act than about those
which do not touch so closely our obvious and immediate needs, it is not because the questions suggested by the former are easier to answer, but be-

cause as a matter of fact we are much less inclined
to ask them.

Now, if this be true, it is plainly a fact of capi-
tal importance. It must revolutionise our whole
attitude towards the problems presented to us by
science, ethics, and theology. It must destroy the
ordinary tests and standards whereby we measure
essential truth. In particular, it requires us to see
what is commonly, if rather absurdly, called the
conflict between religion and science in a wholly
new aspect.' We can no longer be content with the
simple view, once universally accepted, that whenever any discrepancy, real or supposed, occurs between the two, science must be rejected as hereti-
cal; nor with the equally simple view, to which the
former has long given place, that every theological
statement, if unsupported by science, is doubtful;
if inconsistent with science, is false.

Opinions like these are evidently tolerable only
on the hypothesis that we are in possession of a
body of doctrine which is not only itself philosophically established, but to whose canons of proof
all other doctrines are bound to conform. But if
there is no such body of doctrine, what then? Are
we arbitrarily to erect one department of belief into
a law-giver for all the others? Are we to say that
though no scheme of knowledge exists, certain in
its first principles, and coherent in its elaborated
conclusions, yet that from among the provisional
schemes which we are inclined practically to accept

one is to be selected at random, within whose limits, and there alone, the spirit of man may range in confident security?

Such a position is speculatively untenable. It involves a use of the Canon of Consistency not justified by any philosophy; and as it is indefensible in theory, so it is injurious in practice. For, in truth, though the contented acquiescence in inconsistency is the abandonment of the philosophic quest, the determination to obtain consistency at all costs has been the prolific parent of many intellectual narrownesses and many frigid bigotries. It has shown itself in various shapes; it has stifled and stunted the free movement of thought in different ages and diverse schools of speculation; its unhappy effects may be traced in much theology which professes to be orthodox, in much criticism which delights to be heterodox. It is, moreover, the characteristic note of a not inconsiderable class of intelligences who conceive themselves to be specially reasonable because they are constantly employed in reasoning, and who can find no better method of advancing the cause of knowledge than to press to their extreme logical conclusions principles of which, perhaps, the best that can be said is that they contain, as it were in solution, some element of truth which no reagents at our command will as yet permit us to isolate.

III

That I am here attacking no imaginary evil will, I think, be evident to any reader who recalls the general trend of educated opinion during the last three centuries. It is, of course, true that in dealing with so vague and loosely outlined an object as 'educated opinion' we must beware of attributing to large masses of men the acceptance of elaborate and definitely articulated systems. Systems are, and must be, for the few. The majority of mankind are content with a mood or temper of thought, an impulse not fully reasoned out, a habit guiding them to the acceptance and assimilation of some opinions and the rejection of others, which acts almost as automatically as the processes of physical digestion. Behind these half-realised motives, and in closest association with them, may sometimes, no doubt, be found a 'theory of things' which is their logical and explicit expression. But it is certainly not necessary, and perhaps not usual, that this theory should be clearly formulated by those who seem to obey it. Nor for our present purpose is there any important distinction to be made between the case of the few who find a reason for their habitual judgments, and that of the many who do not.

Keeping this caution in mind, we may consider without risk of misconception an illustration of the misuse of the Canon of Consistency provided for us by the theory corresponding to that tendency of thought which has played so large a part in the development of the modern mind, and which is commonly known as Rationalism.   Now what is Rationalism?   Some may be disposed to reply that it is the free and unfettered application of human intelligence to the problems of life and of the world; the unprejudiced examination of every question in the dry light of emancipated reason.   This may be a very good account of a particular intellectual ideal; an ideal which has been sought after at many periods of the world's history, although assuredly it has been attained in none.   Usage, however, permits and even encourages us to employ the word in a much more restricted sense: as indicating a special form of that reaction against dogmatic theology which became prominent at the end of the seventeenth century; which dominated so much of the best thought in the eighteenth century, and which has reached its most complete expression in the Naturalism which occupied our attention through the first portion of these Notes.[1]   A reaction of some sort was no doubt in-

[1 In spite of this explicit statement I have been supposed by some of my critics to have attacked Reason where I have only been attacking Rationalism.   I gather, for instance, that Professor Karl Pearson has fallen into this mistake in a pamphlet published in 1895 which purports to be a review of the present work.   It contains a most interesting and curious mixture of bad politics, bad philosophy, and bad temper, and is styled ' Reaction.'

I have modified in this edition the historic description of Rationalism in deference to a well-founded criticism of Professor Pringle Pattison (A. Seth)   See *Man's Place in the Cosmos*, p. 256.]

evitable. Men found themselves in a world where
Literature, Art, and Science were enormously ex-
tending the range of human interests; in which
Religion seemed approachable only through the
languishing controversies which had burnt with
so fierce a flame during the sixteenth and seventeenth centuries; in which accepted theological
methods had their roots in a very different period of
intellectual growth, and were ceasing to be appropriate to the new developments. At such a time
there was, undoubtedly, an important and even a
necessary work to be done. The mind of man cannot, any more than the body, vary in one direction
alone. The whole organism suffers or gains from
the change, and every faculty and every limb must
be somewhat modified in order successfully to meet
the new demands thrown upon it by the altered balance of the remainder. So is it also in matters intellectual. It is hopeless to expect that new truths and
new methods of investigation can be acquired without the old truths requiring to be in some respects
reconsidered and restated, surveyed under a new
aspect, measured, perhaps, by a different standard.
Much had, therefore, to be modified, and something
—let us admit it—had to be destroyed. The new
system could hardly produce its best results until
the refuse left by the old system had been removed;
until the waste products were eliminated which,
like those of a muscle too long exercised, poisoned

and clogged the tissues in which they had once played the part of living and effective elements.

The world, then, required enlightenment, and the rationalists proceeded after their own fashion to enlighten it.   Unfortunately, however, their whole procedure was tainted by an original vice of method which made it impossible to carry on the honourable, if comparatively humble, work of clearance and purification without, at the same time, destroying much that ought properly to have been preserved. They were not content with protesting against practical abuses, with vindicating the freedom of science from theological bondage, with criticising the defects and explaining the limitations of the somewhat cumbrous and antiquated apparatus of prevalent theological controversy—apparatus, no doubt, much better contrived for dealing with the points on which theologians differ than for defending against a common enemy the points on which theologians are for the most part agreed.   These things, no doubt, to the best of their power, they did; and to the doing of them no objection need be raised.   The objection is to the principle on which the things were done. That principle appeared under many disguises, and was called by many names.   Sometimes describing itself as Common-sense, sometimes as Science, sometimes as Enlightenment, with infinite varieties of application and great diversity of doctrine, Rationalism consisted essentially in the application, consciously or unconsciously, of one great method to the decision of every controversy, to the moulding of every creed. Did a belief square with a view of the universe based exclusively upon the prevalent mode of interpreting sense-perception? If so, it might survive. Did it clash with such mode, or lie beyond it? It was superstitious; it was unscientific; it was ridiculous; it was incredible. Was it neither in harmony with nor antagonistic to such a view, but simply beside it? It might live on until it became atrophied from lack of use, a mere survival of a dead past.

These judgments were not, as a rule, supported by any very profound arguments. Rationalists as such are not philosophers. They are not pantheists nor speculative materialists. They ignore, if they do not despise, metaphysics, and in practice eschew the search for first principles. But they judge as men of the world, reluctant either to criticise too closely methods which succeed so admirably in everyday affairs, or to admit that any other methods can possibly be required by men of sense.

Of course, a principle so loosely conceived has led at different times and in different stages of knowledge to very different results. Through the greater portion of the world's history the 'ordinary mode of interpreting sense-perception' has been perfectly consistent with so-called 'supernatural' phenomena. It may become so again. And if during the rationalising centuries this has not been the case, it is because the interpretation of sense-perceptions has during that period been more and more governed by that Naturalistic theory of the world to which it has been steadily gravitating. It is true that the process of eliminating incongruous beliefs has been gradual. The general body of rationalisers have been slow to see and reluctant to accept the full consequences of their own principles. The assumption that the kind of 'experience' which gave us natural science was the sole basis of knowledge did not at first, or necessarily, carry with it the further inference that nothing deserved to be called knowledge which did not come within the circle of the natural sciences. But the inference was practically, if not logically, inevitable. Theism, Deism, Design, Soul, Conscience, Morality, Immortality, Freedom, Beauty—these and cognate words associated with the memory of great controversies mark the points at which rationalists who are not also naturalists have sought to come to terms with the rationalising spirit, or to make a stand against its onward movement. It has been in vain. At some places the fortunes of battle hung long in the balance; at others the issues may yet seem doubtful. Those who have given up God can still make a fight for conscience; those who have abandoned moral responsibility may still console themselves with artistic beauty. But, to my thinking, at least, the struggle can have but one termination. Habit and education may delay the inevitable conclusion; they cannot in the end avert it. For these ideas are no native growth of a rationalist epoch, strong in their harmony with contemporary moods of thought. They are the products of a different age, survivals from, as some think, a decaying system. And howsoever stubbornly they may resist the influences of an alien environment, if this undergoes no change, in the end they must surely perish.

Naturalism, then, the naturalism whose practical consequences have already occupied us so long, is nothing more than the result of rationalising methods applied with pitiless consistency to the whole circuit of belief; it is the completed product of rationalism, the final outcome of using the 'current methods of interpreting sense-perception' as the universal instrument for determining the nature and fixing the limits of human knowledge. What wealth of spiritual possession this creed requires us to give up I have already explained. What, then, does it promise us in exchange? It promises us Consistency. Religion may perish at its touch, it may strip Virtue and Beauty of their most precious attributes; but in exchange it promises us Consistency. True, the promise is in any circumstances but imperfectly kept. This creed, which so arrogantly requires that everything is to be made consistent with it, is not, as we have seen, consistent with itself. The humblest attempts to co-ordinate and to justify the assumptions on which it proceeds with such unquestioning confidence bring to light speculative perplexities and contradictions whose very existence seems unsus-

pected, whose solution is not even attempted. But
even were it otherwise we should still be bound to
protest against the assumption that consistency is a
necessity of the intellectual life, to be purchased, if
need be, at famine prices. It is a valuable commod-
ity, but it may be bought too dear. No doubt a
principal function of Reason is to smooth away contradictions, to knock off corners, and to fit, as far as
may be, each separate belief into its proper place
within the framework of one harmonious creed. No
doubt, also, it is impossible to regard any theory
which lacks self-consistency as either satisfactory or
final. But principles going far beyond admissions
like these are required to compel us to acquiesce in
rationalising methods and naturalistic results, to the
destruction of every form of belief with which they
do not happen to agree. Before such terms of surrender are accepted, at least the victorious system
must show, not merely that its various parts are
consistent with each other, but that the whole is
authenticated by Reason. Until this task is accomplished (and how far at present it is from being accomplished in the case of naturalism the reader
knows) it would be an act of mere blundering Unreason to set up as the universal standard of belief a
theory of things which itself stands in so great need
of rational defence, or to make a reckless and unthinking application of the canon of consistency when
our knowledge of first principles is so manifestly
defective.

CHAPTER IV

RATIONALIST ORTHODOXY

AT this point, however, it may perhaps occur to the reader that I have somewhat too lightly assumed that Rationalism is the high-road to Naturalism. Why, it may be asked, is there any insuperable difficulty in framing another scheme of belief which shall permanently satisfy the requirements of consistency, and yet harmonise in its general procedure with the rationalising spirit? · Why are we to assume that the extreme type of this mode of thought is the only stable type? Such doubts would be the more legitimate because there is actually in existence a scheme of great historic importance, and some present interest, by which it has been sought to run Modern Science and Theology together into a single coherent and self-sufficient system of thought, by the simple process of making Science supply all the premises on which theological conclusions are afterwards based. If this device be really adequate, no doubt much of what was said in the last chapter, and much that will have to be said in future chapters, becomes superfluous. If 'our ordinary method of interpreting sense-perception,' which gives us Science, is able also to supply us

with Theology, then at least, whether it be philosophically valid or not, the majority of mankind may
very well rest content with it until philosophers
come to some agreement about a better. If it does
not satisfy the philosophic critic, it will probably
satisfy everyone else; and even the philosophic
critic need not quarrel with its practical outcome.

The system by which these results are thought
to be attained pursues the following method. It
divides Theology into Natural and Revealed. Natural Theology expounds the theological beliefs
which may be arrived at by a consideration of the
general course of Nature as this is explained to us
by Science. It dwells principally upon the number-
less examples of adaptation in the organic world,
which apparently display the most marvellous indications of ingenious contrivance, and the nicest adjustment of means to ends. From facts like these
it is inferred that Nature has an intelligent and a
powerful Creator. From the further fact that these
adjustments and contrivances are in a large number
of cases designed for the interests of beings capable
of pleasure and pain, it is inferred that the Creator
is not only intelligent and powerful, but also benevolent; and the inquiring mind is then supposed to be
sufficiently prepared to consider without prejudice
the evidence for there having been a special Revelation by which further truths may have been im-
parted, not otherwise accessible to our unassisted
powers of speculation.

The evidences of Revealed Religion are not drawn, like those of Natural Religion, from general laws and widely disseminated particulars; but they profess none the less to be solely based upon facts which, according to the classification I have adhered to throughout these Notes, belong to the scientific order. According to this theory, the logical burden of the entire theological structure is thrown upon the evidence for certain events which took place long ago, and principally in a small district to the east of the Mediterranean, the occurrence of which it is sought to prove by the ordinary methods of historical investigation, and by these alone—unless, indeed, we are to regard as an important ally the aforementioned presumption supplied by Natural Theology. It is true, of course, that the immediate reason for accepting the beliefs of Revealed Religion is that the religion *is* revealed. But it is thought to be revealed because it was promulgated by teachers who were inspired; the teachers are thought to have been inspired because they worked miracles; and they are thought to have worked miracles because there is historical evidence of the fact, which it is supposed would be more than sufficient to produce conviction in any unbiassed mind.

Now it must be conceded that if this general train of reasoning be assumed to cover the whole ground of 'Christian Evidences,' then, whether it be conclusive or inconclusive, it does at least attain the desideratum of connecting Science on the one hand, Religion—'Natural' and 'Revealed'—on the other, into one single scheme of interconnected propositions. But it attains it by making Theology in form a mere annex or appendix to Science; a mere footnote to history; a series of conclusions inferred from data which have been arrived at by precisely the same methods as those which enable us to pronounce upon the probability of any other events in the past history of man, or of the world in which he lives. We are no longer dealing with a creed whose real premises lie deep in the nature of things. It is no question of metaphysical speculation, moral intuition, or mystical ecstasy with which we are concerned. We are asked to believe the Universe to have been designed by a Deity for the same sort of reason that we believe Canterbury Cathedral to have been designed by an architect; and to believe in the events narrated in the Gospels for the same sort of reason that we believe in the murder of Thomas à Becket.

Now I am not concerned to maintain that these arguments are bad; on the contrary, my personal opinion is that, as far as they go, they are good. The argument, or perhaps I should say *an* argument, from design, in some shape or other, will always have value; while the argument from history must always form a part of the evidence for any historical religion. The first will, in my opinion, survive any presumptions based upon the doctrine

of natural selection; the second will survive the consequences of critical assaults. But more than this is
desirable; more than this is, indeed, necessary. For
however good arguments of this sort are, or may be
made, they are not equal by themselves to the task
of upsetting so massive an obstacle as developed
Naturalism. They have not, as it were, sufficient
intrinsic energy to effect so great a change. They
may not be ill directed, but they lack momentum.
They may not be technically defective, but they are
assuredly practically inadequate.

To many this may appear self-evident. Those
who doubt it will, I think, be convinced of its truth
if they put themselves for a moment in the position
of a man trained on the strictest principles of Naturalism; acquainted with the general methods and
results of Science; cognisant of the general course
of secular human history, and of the means by
which the critic and the scholar have endeavoured
to extort the truth from the records of the past. To
such a man the growth and decay of great religions,
the legends of wonders worked and suffering endured by holy men in many ages and in different
countries, are familiar facts—to be fitted somehow
into his general scheme of knowledge. They are
phenomena to be explained by anthropology and
sociology, instructive examples of the operation of
natural law at a particular stage of human development—this, and nothing more.

Now present to one whose mind has been so

prepared and disciplined, first this account of Natural Religion, and then this version of the evidences for Revelation. So far as Natural Religion is concerned he will probably content himself with saying, that to argue from the universality of causation within the world to the necessity of First Cause outside the world is a process of very doubtful validity: that to argue from the character of the world to the benevolence of its Author is a process more doubtful still: but that, in any case, we need not disturb ourselves about matters we so little understand, inasmuch as the Deity thus inferred, if He really exists, completed the only task which Natural Religion supposes Him to have undertaken when, in a past immeasurably remote, He set going the machinery of causes and effects, which has ever since been in undisturbed operation, and about which alone we have any real sources of information.

Supposing, however, you have induced your Naturalistic philosopher to accept, if only for the sake of argument, your version of Natural Religion, what will he say to your method of extracting the proofs of Revealed Religion from the Gospel history? Explain to him that there is good historic evidence of the usual sort for believing that for one brief interval during the history of the Universe, and in one small corner of this planet, the continuous chain of universal causation has been broken; that in an insignificant country inhabited by an unimportant branch of the Semitic peoples events are alleged to have taken place which, if they really occurred, at once turn into foolishness the whole theory in the light of which he has been accustomed to interpret human experience, and convey to us knowledge which no mere contemplation of the general order of Nature could enable us even dimly to anticipate. What would be his reply? His reply would be, nay, is (for our imaginary interlocutor has unnumbered prototypes in the world about us), that questions like these can scarcely be settled by the mere accumulation of historic proofs. Granting all that was asked, and more, perhaps, than ought to be conceded; granting that the evidence for these wonders was far stronger than any that could be produced in favour of the apocryphal miracles which crowd the annals of every people; granting even that the evidence seemed far more than sufficient to establish any incident, however strange, which does not run counter to the recognised course of Nature; what then? We were face to face with a difficulty, no doubt; but the interpretation of the past was necessarily full of difficulties. Conflicts of testimony with antecedent probability, conflicts of different testimonies with each other, were the familiar perplexities of the historic inquirer. In thousands of cases no absolutely satisfactory solution could be arrived at. Possibly the Gospel histories were among these. Neither the theory of myths, nor the theory of contemporary fraud, nor the theory of late invention, nor any other which the ingenuity of critics could devise, might provide a perfectly clean-cut explanation of the phenomena. But at least it might be said with confidence that no explanation could be less satisfactory than one which required us, on the strength of three or four ancient documents—at the best written by eye-witnesses of little education and no scientific knowledge, at the worst spurious and of no authority—to remodel and revolutionise every principle which governs us with an unquestioned jurisdiction in our judgments on the Universe at large.

Thus, slightly modifying Hume, might the disciple of Naturalism reply. And as against the rationalising theologian, is not his answer conclusive? The former has borrowed the premises, the methods, and all the positive conclusions of Naturalism. He advances on the same strategic principles, and from the same base of operations. And though he professes by these means to have overrun a whole continent of alien conclusions with which Naturalism will have nothing to do, can he permanently retain his conquests? Is it not certain that the huge expanse of his theology, attached by so slender a tie to the main system of which it is intended to be a dependency, will sooner or later have to be abandoned; and that the weak and artificial connection which has been so ingeniously contrived will snap at the first strain to which it shall be subjected by the forces either of criticism or sentiment?

PART III

SOME CAUSES OF BELIEF

CHAPTER I

CAUSES OF EXPERIENCE

I

So far the results at which we have arrived may be not unfairly described as purely negative. In the first part of these Notes I endeavoured to show that Naturalism was practically insufficient. In the first chapter of Part II. I indicated the view that it was speculatively incoherent. The obvious conclusion was therefore drawn, that under these circumstances it was in the highest degree absurd to employ with an unthinking rigour the canon of consistency as if Rationalism, which is Naturalism in embryo, or Naturalism, which is Rationalism developed, placed us in the secure possession of some unerring standard of truth to which all our beliefs must be made to conform. A brief criticism of one theological scheme, by which it has been sought to avoid the narrownesses of Naturalism without breaking with Rationalising methods, confirmed the conclusion that any such procedure is predestined to be ineffectual, and that no mere inferences of the ordinary pattern, based upon ordinary experience, will enable us to break out of the Naturalistic prison-house.

13

But if Naturalism by itself be practically insufficient, if no conclusion based on its affirmations will
enable us to escape from the cold grasp of its negations, and if, as I think, the contrasted system of
Idealism has not as yet got us out of the difficulty,
what remedy remains? One such remedy consists
in simply setting up side by side with the creed of
natural science another and supplementary set of
beliefs, which may minister to needs and aspirations
which science cannot meet, and may speak amid
silences which science is powerless to break. The
natural world and the spiritual world, the world
which is immediately subject to causation and the
world which is immediately subject to God, are, on
this view, each of them real, and each of them the
objects of real knowledge. But the laws of the
natural world are revealed to us by the discoveries
of science; while the laws of the spiritual world are
revealed to us through the authority of spiritual
intuitions, inspired witnesses, or divinely guided
institutions. And the two regions of knowledge lie
side by side, contiguous but not connected, like em-
pires of different race and language, which own no
common jurisdiction nor hold any intercourse with
each other, except along a disputed and wavering
frontier where no superior power exists to settle
their quarrels or determine their respective limits.

To thousands of persons this patchwork scheme
of belief, though it may be in a form less sharply
defined, has, in substance, commended itself; and if

and in so far as it really meets their needs I have nothing to say against it, and can hold out small hope of bettering it. It is much more satisfactory as regards its content than Naturalism; it is not much less philosophical as regards its method; and it has the practical merit of supplying a rough-and-ready expedient for avoiding the consequences which follow from a premature endeavour to force the general body of belief into the rigid limits of one too narrow system.

It has, however, obvious inconveniences. There are many persons, and they are increasing in number, who find it difficult or impossible to acquiesce in this unconsidered division of the 'Whole' of knowledge into two or more unconnected frag-ments. Naturalism may be practically unsatisfac-tory. But at least the positive teaching of Natural-ism has secured general assent; and it shocks their philosophic instinct for unity to be asked to patch and plaster this accepted creed with a number of heterogeneous propositions drawn from an entirely different source, and on behalf of which no such common agreement can be claimed.

What such persons ask for, and rightly, is a philosophy, a scheme of knowledge, which shall give rational unity to an adequate creed. But, as the reader knows, I have it not to give; nor does it even seem to me that we have any right to flatter ourselves that we are on the verge of discovering some all-reconciling theory by which each inevitable claim of our complex nature may be harmonised under the supremacy of Reason. Unity, then, if it is to be attained at all, must be sought for, so to speak, at some lower speculative level. We must either pursue the Rationalising and Naturalistic method already criticised, and compel the desired unification of belief by the summary rejection of everything which does not fit into some convenient niche in the scheme of things developed by empirical methods out of sense-perception; or if, either for the reasons given in the earlier chapters of these Notes, or for others, we reject this method, we must turn for assistance towards a new quarter, and apply ourselves to the problem by the aid of some more comprehensive, or at least more manageable, principle.

II

To this end let us temporarily divest ourselves of all philosophic preoccupation. Provisionally restricting ourselves to the scientific point of view, let us forbear to consider beliefs from the side of proof, and let us survey them for a season from the side of origin only, and in their relation to the causes which gave them birth. Thus considered they are, of course, mere products of natural conditions; psychological growths comparable to the flora and fauna of continents or oceans; objects of which we may say that they are useful or harmful, plentiful or rare, but not, except parenthetically and with a certain irrelevance, that they are true or untrue.

How, then, would these beliefs appear to an investigator from another planet who, applying the ordinary methods of science, and in a spirit of detached curiosity, should survey them from the outside, with no other object than to discover the place they occupied in the natural history of the earth and its inhabitants? He would note, I suppose, to begin with, that the vast majority of these beliefs were the short-lived offspring of sense-perception, instinctive judgments on observed matter-of-fact. 'The sun is shining,' 'there is somebody in the room,' 'I feel tired,' would be examples of this class; whose members, from the nature of the case, refer immediately only to the passing moment, and die as soon as they are born. If now our investigator turned his attention to the causes of these beliefs of perception, he would, of course, discover, in the first place, that, when normal, they were invariably due to the action of external objects upon the organism, and more particularly upon the nervous system, of the percipient; and in the second place, that though these beliefs were thus all due to a certain kind of neural change, the converse of the proposition is by no means true, since, taking the organic world at large, it was by no means the case that neural changes of this kind invariably, or even usually, issued in beliefs of perception, or, indeed, in any psychical result whatever.

For consider how the case must present itself to

our supposed observer.   He would see a series of organisms possessed of nervous systems ranging from
the most rudimentary type to the most complex.
He would observe that the action of the exterior
world upon those systems varied, in like manner,
from the simple irritation of the nerve-tissue to the
multitudinous correspondences and adjustments involved in some act of vision by man or one of the
higher mammals.   And he would conclude, and
rightly, that between the upper and the lower members of the scale there were differences of degree,
but not of kind; and that existing gaps might be
conceived as so filled in that each type might melt
into the one immediately below it by insensible gradations.

If, however, he endeavoured to draw up a scale
of psychical effects whose degrees should correspond
with this scale of physiological causes, two results
would make themselves apparent.   The first is, that
the lower part of the psychical scale would be a blank,
because in the case of the simple organisms nervous
changes carried with them no mental consequents.
The second is, that even when mental consequents
do appear, they form no continuous series like their
physiological antecedents ; but, on the contrary,
those at the top of the scale are found to differ in
something more than degree from those which appear
lower down.   We do not, for example, suppose that
protozoa can properly be said to feel, nor that every
animal which feels can properly be said to form

judgments or to possess immediate beliefs of perception.

One conclusion our observer would, I suppose, draw from facts like these is, that while neural sensibility to external influences is a widespread benefit to organic Nature, the feelings, and still more the beliefs, to which in certain cases it gives rise are relatively insignificant phenomena, useful supplements to the purely physiological apparatus, necessary, perhaps, to its highest developments, but still, if operative at all,[1] rather in the nature of final improvements to the machinery than of parts essential to its working.

A like result would attend his study of the next class of beliefs that might fall under his notice, those, namely, which, though they do not relate to things or events within the field of perception, like those we have just been considering, are yet not less immediate in their character. Memories of the past are examples of this type; I should be inclined to add, though I do not propose here to justify my opinion, certain instinctive and, so to speak, automatic expectations about the future or that part of the present which does not come within the reach of direct experience. Like the beliefs of perception of which we have been speaking, they would seem to be the psychical side of neural changes which, at least in their simpler forms, need be accompanied by no psychical manifestation.

[1] See Note on Chapter V., page 285.

Physiological co-ordination is sufficient by itself to perform services for the lower animals similar in kind to those which, in the case of man, are usefully, or even necessarily, supplemented by their beliefs of memory and of expectation.

These two classes of belief, relating respectively to the present and the absent, cover the whole ground of what is commonly called experience, and something more. They include, therefore, at least in rudimentary form, all particulars which, on any theory, are required for scientific induction; and, according to empiricism in its older forms, they supply not this only, but also the whole of the raw material, without any exception, out of which reason must subsequently fashion whatever stock of additional beliefs it is needful for mankind to entertain.

Our Imaginary Observer, however, quite indifferent to mundane theories as to what ought to produce conviction, and intent only on discovering how convictions are actually produced, would soon find out that there were other influences besides reasoning required to supplement the relatively simple physiological and psychological causes which originate the immediate beliefs of perception, memory, and expectation. These immediate beliefs belong to man as an individual. They involve no commerce between mind and mind. They might equally exist, and would equally be necessary, if each man stood face to face with material Nature in friendless isolation. But they neither provide, nor by any merely logical extension can be made to provide, the apparatus of beliefs which we find actually connected with the higher scientific social and spiritual life of the race. These also are, without doubt, the product of antecedent causes — causes many in number and most diverse in character. They presuppose, to begin with, the beliefs of perception, memory, and expectation in their elementary shape; and they also imply the existence of an organism fitted for their hospitable reception by ages of ancestral preparation. But these conditions, though necessary, are clearly not enough; the appropriate environment has also to be provided. And though I shall not attempt to analyse with the least approach to completeness the elements of which that environment consists, yet it contains one group of causes so important in their collective operation, and yet in popular discourse so often misrepresented, that a detailed notice of it seems desirable.

CHAPTER II

AUTHORITY AND REASON

I

THIS group is perhaps best described by the term Authority, a word which by a sharp transition transports us at once into a stormier tract of speculation than we have been traversing in the last few pages, though, as my readers may be disposed to think, for that reason, perhaps, among others, a tract more nearly adjacent to theology and the proper subject-matter of these Notes. However this may be, it is, I am afraid, the fact that the discussion on which I am about to enter must bring us face to face with one problem, at least, of which, so far as I am aware, no entirely satisfactory solution has yet been reached; which certainly I cannot pretend to solve; which can, therefore, for the present only be treated in a manner provisional, and therefore unsatisfactory. Nor are these perennial and inherent difficulties the only obstacles we have to contend with. For the subject is, unfortunately, one familiar to discussion, and, like all topics which have been the occasion of passionate debate, it is one where party watchwords have exercised their perturbing and embittering influence.

It would be, perhaps, an exaggeration to assert that the theory of authority has been for three centuries the main battlefield whereon have met the opposing forces of new thoughts and old. But if so, it is only because, at this point at least, victory is commonly supposed long ago to have declared itself decisively in favour of the new. The very statement that the rival and opponent of authority is reason[1] seems to most persons equivalent to a declaration that the latter must be in the right, and the former in the wrong; while popular discussion and speculation have driven deep the general opinion that authority serves no other purpose in the economy of Nature than to supply a refuge for all that is most bigoted and absurd.

The current theory by which these views are supported appears to be something of this kind. Everyone has a 'right' to adopt any opinions he pleases. It is his 'duty,' before exercising this 'right,' critically to sift the reasons by which such opinions may be supported, and so to adjust the degree of his convictions that they shall accurately correspond with the evidences adduced in their favour. Authority, therefore, has no place among the legitimate causes of belief. If it appears among them, it is as an in-

---

[1] It is, perhaps, hardly necessary to note that throughout this chapter I use Reason in its ordinary and popular, not in its transcendental, sense. There is no question here of the Logos or Absolute Reason.

truder, to be jealously hunted down and mercilessly
expelled. Reason, and reason only, can be safely
permitted to mould the convictions of mankind. By
its inward counsels alone should beings who boast
that they are rational submit to be controlled.

Sentiments like these are among the common-
places of political and social philosophy. Yet, looked
at scientifically, they seem to me to be, not merely
erroneous, but absurd. Suppose for a moment a community of which each member should deliberately
set himself to the task of throwing off so far as possible all prejudices due to education; where each
should consider it his duty critically to examine the
grounds whereon rest every positive enactment and
every moral precept which he has been accustomed
to obey; to dissect all the great loyalties which make
social life possible, and all the minor conventions
which help to make it easy; and to weigh out with
scrupulous precision the exact degree of assent
which in each particular case the results of this process might seem to justify. To say that such a community, if it acted upon the opinions thus arrived
at, would stand but a poor chance in the struggle
for existence is to say far too little. It could never
even begin to be; and if by a miracle it was created,
it would without doubt immediately resolve itself
into its constituent elements.

For consider by way of illustration the case of
Morality. If the right and the duty of private
judgment be universal, it must be both the privilege

and the business of every man to subject the maxims of current morality to a critical examination; and unless the examination is to be a farce, every man should bring to it a mind as little warped as possible by habit and education, or the unconscious bias of foregone conclusions. Picture, then, the condition of a society in which the successive generations would thus in turn devote their energies to an impartial criticism of the 'traditional' view. What qualifications, natural or acquired, for such a task we are to attribute to the members of this emancipated community I know not. But let us put them at the highest. Let us suppose that every man and woman, or rather every boy and girl (for ought Reason to be ousted from her rights in persons under twenty-one years of age?), is endowed with the aptitude and training required to deal with problems like these. Arm them with the most recent methods of criticism, and set them down to the task of estimating with open minds the claims which charity, temperance and honesty, murder, theft and adultery respectively have upon the approval or disapproval of mankind. What the result of such an experiment would be, what wild chaos of opinions would result from this fiat of the Uncreating Word, I know not. But it might well happen that even before our youthful critics got so far as a re-arrangement of the Ten Commandments, they might find themselves entangled in the preliminary question whether judgments conveying moral approba-

tion and disapprobation were of a kind which reasonable beings should be asked to entertain at all;
whether 'right' and 'wrong' were words representing anything more permanent and important
than certain likes and dislikes which happen to be
rather widely disseminated, and more or less arbitrarily associated with social and legal sanctions. I
conceive it to be highly probable that the conclusions at which on this point they would arrive
would be of a purely negative character. The ethical systems competing for acceptance would by
their very numbers and variety suggest suspicions
as to their character and origin. Here, would our
students explain, is a clear presumption to be found
on the very face of these moralisings that they were
contrived, not in the interests of truth, but in the interests of traditional dogma. How else explain the
fact, that while there is no great difference of opinion as to what things are right or wrong, there is no
semblance of agreement as to why they are right
or why they are wrong. All authorities concur, for
instance, in holding that it is wrong to commit murder. But one philosopher tells us that it is wrong
because it is inconsistent with the happiness of mankind, and that to do anything inconsistent with the
happiness of mankind is wrong. Another tells us
that it is contrary to the dictates of conscience, and
that everything which is contrary to the dictates of
conscience is wrong. A third tells us that it is
against the commandments of God, and that every-

thing which is against the commandments of God is
wrong. A fourth tells me that it leads to the gal-
lows, and that, inasmuch as being hanged involves
a sensible diminution of personal happiness, creatures who, like man, are by nature incapable of
doing otherwise than seek to increase the sum of
their personal pleasures and diminish the sum of
their personal pains cannot, if they really comprehend the situation, do anything which may bring
their existence to so distressing a termination.

Now whence, it would be asked, this curious mixture of agreement and disagreement? How account
for the strange variety exhibited in the premises of
these various systems, and the not less strange uniformity exhibited in their conclusions? Why does
not as great a divergence manifest itself in the
results arrived at as we undoubtedly find in the
methods employed? How comes it that all these
explorers reach the same goal, when their points of
departure are so widely dispersed? Plainly but one
plausible method of solving the difficulty exists.
The conclusions were in every case determined before the argument began, the goal was in every case
settled before the travellers set out. There is here
no surrender of belief to the inward guidance of unfettered reason. Rather is reason coerced to a fore-
ordained issue by the external operation of prejudice
and education, or by the rougher machinery of social
ostracism and legal penalty. The framers of ethical
systems are either philosophers who are unable to

free themselves from the unfelt bondage of customary opinion, or advocates who find it safer to exercise their liberty of speculation in respect to premises about which nobody cares, than in respect to
conclusions which might bring them into conflict
with the police.

So might we imagine the members of our emancipated community discussing the principles on
which morality is founded. But, in truth, it were
a vain task to work out in further detail the results
of an experiment which, human nature being what
it is, can never be seriously attempted. That it can
never be seriously attempted is not, be it observed,
because it is of so dangerous a character that the
community in its wisdom would refuse to embark
upon it. This would be a frail protection indeed.
Not the danger of the adventure, but its impossi-
bility, is our security. To reject all convictions
which are not the products of free speculative investigation is, fortunately, an exercise of which humanity is in the strictest sense incapable. Some
societies and some individuals may show more inclination to indulge in it than others. But in no condition of society and in no individual will the inclination be more than very partially satisfied. Always
and everywhere our Imaginary Observer, contem-
plating from some external coign of vantage the
course of human history, would note the immense,
the inevitable, and on the whole the beneficent, part
which Authority plays in the production of belief.

II

This truth finds expression, and at first sight we might feel inclined to say recognition also, in such familiar commonplaces as that every man is the 'product of the society in which he lives,' and that 'it is vain to expect him to rise much above the level of his age.' But aphorisms like these, however useful as aids to a correct historical perspective, do not, as ordinarily employed, show any real apprehension of the verity on which I desire to insist. They belong to a theory which regards these social influences as clogs and hindrances, hampering the free movements of those who might under happier circumstances have struggled successfully towards the truth; or as perturbing forces which drive mankind from the even orbit marked out for it by reason. Reason, according to this view, is a kind of Ormuzd doing constant battle against the Ahriman of tradition and authority. Its gradual triumph over the opposing powers of darkness is what we mean by Progress. Everything which shall hasten the hour of that triumph is a gain; and if by some magic stroke we could extirpate, as it were in a moment, every cause of belief which was not also a reason, we should, it appears, be the fortunate authors of a reform in the moral world only to be paralleled by the abolition of pain and disease in the physical. I have already indicated some of the grounds which induce me to form a very different estimate of the part which reason plays in human affairs. Our ancestors, whose errors we palliate on account of their environment with a feeling of satisfaction, due partly to our keen appreciation of our own happier position and greater breadth of view, were not to be pitied because they reasoned little and believed much; nor should we necessarily have any particular cause for self-gratulation if it were true that we reasoned more and, it may be, believed less. Not thus has the world been fashioned. But, nevertheless, this identification of reason with all that is good among the causes of belief, and authority with all that is bad, is a delusion so gross and yet so prevalent that a moment's examination into the exaggerations and confusions which lie at the root of it may not be thrown away.

The first of these confusions may be dismissed almost in a sentence. It arises out of the tacit assumption that reason means *right* reason. Such an assumption, it need hardly be said, begs half the point at issue. Reason, for purposes of this discussion, can no more be made to mean right reason than authority can be made to mean legitimate authority. True, we might accept the first of these definitions, and yet deny that all right belief was the fruit of reason. But we could hardly deny the converse proposition, that reason thus defined must always issue in right belief. Nor need we be concerned to deny a statement at once so obvious and so barren.

The source of error which has next to be noted presents points of much greater interest. Though it be true, as I am contending, that the importance of reason among the causes which produce and maintain the beliefs, customs, and ideals which form the groundwork of life has been much exaggerated, there can yet be no doubt that reason is, or appears to be, the cause over which we have the most direct control, or rather the one which we most readily identify with our own free and personal action. We are acted on by authority. It moulds our ways of thought in spite of ourselves, and usually unknown to ourselves. But when we reason we are the authors of the effect produced. We have ourselves set the machine in motion. For its proper working we are ourselves immediately responsible; so that it is both natural and desirable that we should concentrate our attention on this particular class of causes, even though we should thus be led unduly to magnify their importance in the general scheme of things.

I have somewhere seen it stated that the steam-engine in its primitive form required a boy to work the valve by which steam was admitted to the cylinder. It was his business at the proper period of each stroke to perform this necessary operation by pulling a string; and though the same object has long since been attained by mechanical methods far simpler and more trustworthy, yet I have little doubt that until the advent of that revolutionary

youth who so tied the string to one of the moving
parts of the engine that his personal supervision was
no longer necessary, the boy in office greatly magni-
fied his functions, and regarded himself with pardonable pride as the most important, because the
only rational, link in the chain of causes and effects
by which the energy developed in the furnace was
ultimately converted into the motion of the fly-
wheel. So do we stand as reasoning beings in the
presence of the complex processes, physiological
and psychical, out of which are manufactured the
convictions necessary to the conduct of life. To the
results attained by their co-operation reason makes
its slender contribution; but in order that it may do
so effectively, it is beneficently decreed that, pending the evolution of some better device, reason
should appear to the reasoner the most admirable
and important contrivance in the whole mechanism.

The manner in which attention and interest are
thus unduly directed towards the operations, vital
and social, which are under our direct control,
rather than those which we are unable to modify, or
can only modify by a very indirect and circuitous
procedure, may be illustrated by countless examples. Take one from physiology. Of all the complex causes which co-operate for the healthy nourishment of the body, no doubt the conscious choice
of the most wholesome rather than the less wholesome forms of ordinary food is far from being the
least important. Yet, as it is within our immedi-

ate competence, we attend to it, moralise about it, and generally make much of it. But no man can by taking thought directly regulate his digestive secretions. We never, therefore, think of them at all until they go wrong, and then, unfortunately, to very little purpose. So it is with the body politic. A certain proportion (probably a small one) of the changes and adaptations required by altered surroundings can only be effected through the solvent action of criticism and discussion. How such discussion shall be conducted, what are the arguments on either side, how a decision shall be arrived at, and how it shall be carried out, are matters which we seem able to regulate by conscious effort and the deliberate adaptation of means to ends. We therefore unduly magnify the part they play in the furtherance of our interests. We perceive that they supply business to the practical politician, raw material to the political theorist; and we forget amid the buzzing of debate the multitude of incomparably more important processes, by whose undesigned co-operation alone the life and growth of the State are rendered possible.

III

There is, however, a third source of illusion, respecting the importance of reason in the actual conduct of human affairs, which well deserves the attentive study of those who, like our Imaginary Observer, are interested in the purely external and scientific in-

vestigation of the causes which produce belief. I
have already in this chapter made reference to the
'spirit of the age' as one form in which authority most
potently manifests itself; and undoubtedly it is so.
Dogmatic education in early years may do much.[1]
The immediate pressure of domestic, social, scientific,
ecclesiastical surroundings in the direction of specific beliefs may do even more. But the power of
authority is never more subtle and effective than
when it produces a psychological 'atmosphere' or
'climate' favourable to the life of certain modes of
belief, unfavourable, and even fatal, to the life of
others. Such 'climates' may be widely diffused, or
the reverse. Their range may cover a generation,
an epoch, a whole civilisation, or it may be narrowed down to a sect, a family, even an individual.
And as they may vary infinitely in respect to the
extent of their influence, so also they may vary in
respect to its intensity and quality. But whatever
be their limits and whatever their character, their
importance to the conduct of life, social and individual, cannot easily be overstated.

Consider, for instance, their effect on great
classes of belief with which reasoning, were it only
on account of their mass, is quite incompetent to
deal. If all credible propositions, all propositions
which somebody at some time had been able to believe, were only to be rejected after their claims had

[1] I may again remind the reader that the word 'dogmatic' as
used in these Notes has no special theological reference.

been impartially tested by a strictly logical investigation, the intellectual machine would be over-
burdened, and its movements hopelessly choked by
mere excess ·of material.   Even such products as it
could turn out would, as I conjecture (for the experiment has never been tried), prove but a mot-
ley collection, so diverse in design, so incongruous
and ill-assorted, that they could scarcely contribute
the fitting furniture of a well-ordered mind.   What
actually happens in the vast majority of cases is
something very different.   To begin with, external
circumstances, mere conditions of time and place,
limit the number of opinions about which anything
is known, and on which, therefore, it is (so to speak)
materially possible that reason can be called upon
to pronounce a judgment.   But there are internal
limitations not less universal and not less necessary.
Few indeed are the beliefs, even among those which
come under his observation, which any individual
for a moment thinks himself called upon seriously
to consider with a view to their possible adoption.
The residue he summarily disposes of, rejects without a hearing, or, rather, treats as if they had not
even that *primâ facie* claim to be adjudicated on
which formal rejection seems to imply.

Now, can this process be described as a rational
one?   That it is not the immediate result of reasoning is, I think, evident enough.   All would admit,
for example, that when the mind is closed against
the reception of any truth by ' bigotry ' or 'inveterate

prejudice,' the effectual cause of the victory of error is not so much bad reasoning as something which, in its essential nature, is not reasoning at all. But there is really no ground for drawing a distinction as regards their mode of operation between the 'psychological climates' which we happen to like and those of which we happen to disapprove. However various their character, all, I take it, work out their results very much in the same kind of way. For good or for evil, in ancient times and in modern, among savage folk and among civilised, it is ever by an identic process that they have sifted and selected the candidates for credence, on which reason has been afterwards called upon to pass judgment; and that process is one with which ratiocination has little or nothing directly to do.

But though these 'psychological climates' do not work through reasoning, may they not themselves, in many cases, be the products of reasoning? May they not, therefore, be causes of belief which belong, though it be only at the second remove, to the domain of reason rather than to that of authority? To the first of these questions the answer must doubtless be in the affirmative. Reasoning has unquestionably a great deal to do with the production of psychological climates. As 'climates' are among the causes which produce beliefs, so are beliefs among the causes which produce 'climates,' and all reasoning, therefore, which culminates in belief may be, and indeed must be, at least indirectly concerned in the effects which

belief develops.   But are these results rational ?   Do
they follow, I mean, on reason *quâ* reason ; or are
they, like a schoolboy's tears over a proposition of
Euclid, consequences of reasoning, but not conclusions from it?

In order to answer this question it may be worth
while to consider it in the light of an example which
I have already used in another connection and under
a different aspect.   It will be recollected that in a
preceding chapter I considered Rationalism, not as
a psychological climate, a well-characterised mood of
mind, but as an explicit principle of judgment, in
which the rationalising temper may for purposes of
argument find definite expression.   To Rationalism
in the first of these senses—to Rationalism, in other
words, considered as a form of Authority—I now
revert ; taking it as an incident specially suited to
our purpose, not only because its meaning is well
understood, but because it is found at our own level
of intellectual development, and we can therefore
study its origin and character with a kind of insight
quite impossible when we are dealing with the
' climates ' which govern in so singular a fashion the
beliefs of primitive races.   These, too, may be, and I
suppose are, to some extent, the products of reasoning.   But the reasoning appears to us as arbitrary
as the resulting ' climates ' are repugnant; and
though we can note and classify the facts, we can
hardly comprehend them with sympathetic understanding.

With Rationalism it is different. How the discoveries of science, the growth of criticism, and the
diffusion of learning should have fostered the rationalising temper seems intelligible to all, because all,
in their different degrees, have been subject to these
very influences. Not everyone is a rationalist; but.
everyone, educated or uneducated, is prepared to
reject without further examination certain kinds of
statement which, before the rationalising era set in,
would have been accepted without difficulty by the
wisest among mankind.

Now this modern mood, whether in its qualified
or unqualified (*i.e.* naturalistic) form, is plainly no
mere product of non-rational conditions, as the enumeration I have just given of its most conspicuous
causes is sufficient to prove. Natural science and
historical criticism have not been built up without a
vast expenditure of reasoning, and (though for present
purposes this is immaterial) very good reasoning,
too. But are we on that account to say that the
results of the rationalising temper are the work of
reason? Surely not. The rationalist rejects miracles;
and if you force him to a discussion, he may no doubt
produce from the ample stores of past controversy
plenty of argument in support of his belief. But do
not therefore assume that his belief is the result of
his argument. The odds are strongly in favour of
argument and belief having both grown up under
the fostering influence of his 'psychological climate.'
For observe that precisely in the way in which he

rejects miracles he also rejects witchcraft.   Here there has been no controversy worth mentioning. The general belief in witchcraft has died a natural death, and it has not been worth anybody's while to devise arguments against it.   Perhaps there are none. But, whether there be or not, no logical axe was required to cut down a plant which had not the least chance of flourishing in a mental atmosphere so rigorous and uncongenial as that of rationalism ; and accordingly no logical axe has been provided.

The belief in mesmerism, however, supplies in some ways a more instructive case than the belief either in miracles or witchcraft.   Like these, it found in rationalism a hostile influence.   But, unlike these, it could call in almost at will the assistance of what would now be regarded as ocular demonstration.   For two generations, however, this was found insufficient.   For two generations the rationalistic bias proved sufficiently strong to pervert the judgment of the most distinguished observers, and to incapacitate them from accepting what under more favourable circumstances they would have called the 'plain evidence of their senses.'   So that we are here presented with the curious spectacle of an intellectual mood or temper, whose origin was largely due to the growth of the experimental sciences, making it impossible for those affected to draw the simplest inference, even from the most conclusive experiments.

This is an interesting case of the conflict between authority and reason, because it illustrates the general truth for which I have been contending, with an emphasis that would be impossible if we took as our example some worn-out vesture of thought, threadbare from use, and strange to eyes accustomed to newer fashions. Rationalism, in its turn, may be predestined to suffer a like decay; but in the meanwhile it forcibly exemplifies the part played by authority in the formation of beliefs. If rationalism be regarded as a non-rational effect of reason and a non-rational cause of belief, the same admission will readily be made about all other intellectual climates; and that rationalism should be so regarded is now, I trust, plain to the reader. The only results which reason can claim as hers by an exclusive title are of the nature of logical conclusions; and rationalism, in the sense in which I am now using the word, is not a logical conclusion, but an intellectual temper. The only instruments which reason, as such, can employ are arguments; and rationalism is not an argument, but an impulse towards belief, or disbelief. So that, though rationalism, like other 'psychological climates,' is doubtless due, among other causes, to reason, it is not on that account a rational product; and though in its turn it produces beliefs, it is not on that account a rational cause.

From the preceding considerations it may, I think, be fairly concluded, firstly, that reason is not necessarily, nor perhaps usually, dominant among the im

mediate causes which produce a particular 'psychological climate.' Secondly, that the efficiency of such
a 'climate' in promoting or destroying beliefs is quite
independent of the degree to which reason has contributed to its production ; and, thirdly, that however
much the existence of the 'climate' may be due to
reason, its action on beliefs, be it favourable or hostile,
is in its essential nature wholly non-rational.

IV

The most important source of error on this subject remains, however, to be dealt with ; and it arises
directly out of that jurisdiction which in matters of
belief we can hardly do otherwise than recognise as
belonging to Reason by a natural and indefeasible
title. No one finds (if my observations in this matter
are correct) any serious difficulty in attributing the
origin of other people's beliefs, especially if he disa-
agree with them, to causes which are not reasons.
That interior assent should be produced in countless
cases by custom, education, public opinion, the contagious convictions of countrymen, family, party, or
Church, seems natural, and even obvious. That but
a small number, at least of the most important and
fundamental beliefs, are held by persons who could
give reasons for them, and that of this small number
only an inconsiderable fraction are held in consequence of the reasons by which they are nominally

supported, may perhaps be admitted with no very great difficulty. But it is harder to recognise that this law is not merely, on the whole, beneficial, but that without it the business of the world could not possibly be carried on; nor do we allow, without reluctance and a sense of shortcoming, that in our own persons we supply illustrations of its operation quite as striking as any presented to us by the rest of the world.

Now this reluctance is not the result of vanity, nor of any fancied immunity from weaknesses common to the rest of mankind. It is, rather, a direct consequence of the view we find ourselves compelled to take of the essential character of reason and of our relations to it. Looked at from the outside, as one among the complex conditions which produce belief, reason appears relatively insignificant and ineffectual; not only appears so, but *must* be so, if human society is to be made possible. Looked at from the inside, it claims by an inalienable title to be supreme. Measured by its results it may be little; measured by its rights it is everything. There is no problem it may not investigate, no belief which it may not assail, no principle which it may not test. It cannot, even by its own voluntary act, deprive itself of universal jurisdiction, as, according to a once fashionable theory, primitive man, on entering the social state, contracted himself out of his natural rights and liberties. On the contrary, though its claims may be ignored, they cannot be repudiated; and even those who shrink from the criticism of dogma as a sin, would probably admit that they do so because it is an act forbidden by those they are bound to obey; do so, that is to say, nominally at least, for a reason which, at any moment, if it should think fit, reason itself may reverse.

Why, under these circumstances, we are moved to regard ourselves as free intelligences, forming our opinions solely in obedience to reason; why we come to regard reason itself, not only as the sole legitimate source of belief—which, perhaps, it may be—but the sole source of legitimate beliefs—which it assuredly is not, must now, I hope, be tolerably obvious, and needs not to be further emphasised. It is more instructive for our present purpose to consider for a moment certain consequences of this antinomy between the equities of Reason and the expediencies of Authority which rise into prominence whenever, under the changing conditions of society, the forces of the latter are being diverted into new and unaccustomed channels.

It is true, no doubt, that the full extent and difficulty of the problems involved have not commonly been realised by the advocates either of authority or reason, though each has usually had a sufficient sense of the strength of the other's position to induce him to borrow from it, even at the cost of some little inconsistency. The supporter of authority, for in-

stance, may point out some of the more obvious evils
by which any decrease in its influence is usually accompanied: the comminution of sects, the divisions
of opinion, the weakened powers of co-operation, the
increase of strife, the waste of power.   Yet, so far as
I am aware, no nation, party, or Church has ever
courted controversial disaster by admitting that, if
its claims were impartially tried at the bar of Reason,
the verdict would go against it.   In the same way,
those who have most clamorously upheld the pre-
rogatives of individual reason have always been
forced to recognise by their practice, if not by their
theory, that the right of every man to judge on every
question for himself is like the right of every man
who possesses a balance at his bankers to require its
immediate payment in sovereigns.   The right may
be undoubted; but it can only be safely enjoyed on
condition that too many persons do not take it into
their heads to exercise it together.   Perhaps, however, the most striking evidence, both of the powers
of authority and the rights of reason, may be found
in the fact already alluded to, that beliefs which are
really the offspring of the first, when challenged, invariably claim to trace their descent from the second,
although this improvised pedigree may be as imaginary as if it were the work of a college of heralds.
To be sure, when this contrivance has served its
purpose it is usually laid silently aside, while the
belief it was intended to support remains quietly in

possession, until, in the course of time, some other, and perhaps not less illusory, title has to be devised to rebut the pleas of a new claimant.

If the reader desires an illustration of this procedure, here is one taken at random from English political history. Among the results of the movement which culminated in the Great Rebellion was of necessity a marked diminution in the universality and efficacy of that mixture of feelings and beliefs which constitutes loyalty to national government. Now loyalty, in some shape or other, is necessary for the stability of any form of polity. It is one of the most valuable products of authority, and, whether in any particular case conformable to reason or not, is essentially unreasoning. Its theoretical basis therefore excites but little interest, and is of very subordinate importance so long as it controls the hearts of men with undisputed sway. But as soon as its supremacy is challenged, men begin to cast about anxiously for reasons why it should continue to be obeyed.

Thus, to those who lived through the troubles which preceded and accompanied the Great Rebellion, it became suddenly apparent that it was above all things necessary to bolster up by argument the creed which authority had been found temporarily insufficient to sustain; and of the arguments thus called into existence two, both of extraordinary absurdity, have become historically famous—that contained in Hobbes's ' Leviathan,' and that taught for a period with much vigour by the Anglican clergy under the name of Divine right. These theories may have done their work; in any case they had their day. It was discovered that, as is the way of abstract arguments dragged in to meet a concrete difficulty, they led logically to a great many conclu. sions much less convenient than the one in whose defence they had been originally invoked. The crisis which called them forth passed gradually away. They were repugnant to the taste of a different age; 'Leviathan' and 'passive obedience' were handed over to the judgment of the historian.

This is an example of how an ancient principle, broadly based though it be on the needs and feelings of human nature, may be thought now and again to require external support to enable it to meet some special stress of circumstances. But often the stress is found to be brief; a few internal alterations meet all the necessities of the case; to a new generation the added buttresses seem useless and unsightly. They are soon demolished, to make way in due time, no doubt, for others as temporary as themselves. Noth. ing so quickly waxes old as apologetics, unless, per. haps, it be criticism.

A precisely analogous process commonly goes on in the case of new principles struggling into recognition. As those of older growth are driven by the instincts of self-preservation to call reasoning to their assistance, so these claim the aid of the same ally for purposes of attack and aggression; and the incongruity between the causes by which beliefs are sustained, and the official reasons by which they are from time to time justified, is usually as glaring in the case of the last novelty in doctrine as in that of some long descended and venerable prejudice. Witness the ostentatious futility of the theories—'rights of man,' and so forth—by the aid of which the modern democratic movement was nursed through its infant maladies.

Now these things are true, not alone in politics, but in every field of human activity where authority and reason co-operate to serve the needs of mankind at large. And thus may we account for the singular fact that in many cases conclusions are more permanent than premises, and that the successive growths of apologetic and critical literature do often not more seriously affect the enduring outline of the beliefs by which they are occasioned than the successive forests of beech and fir determine the shape of the everlasting hills from which they spring.

V

Here, perhaps, I might fitly conclude this portion of my task, were it not that one particular mode in which Authority endeavours to call in reasoning to its assistance is so important in itself, and has led to so much confusion both of thought and of lan-

guage, that a few paragraphs devoted to its consideration may help the reader to a clearer understanding of the general subject.   Authority, as I have
been using the term, is in all cases contrasted with
Reason, and stands for that group of non-rational
causes, moral, social, and educational, which produces its results by psychic processes other than
reasoning.   But there is a simple operation, a mere
turn of phrase, by which many of these non-rational
causes can, so to speak, be converted into reasons
without seeming at first sight thereby to change
their function as channels of Authority ; and so convenient is this method of bringing these two sources
of conviction on to the same plane, so perfectly does
it minister to our instinctive desire to produce a
reason for every challenged belief, that it is constantly resorted to (without apparently any clear
idea of its real import), both by those who regard themselves as upholders and those who regard
themselves as opponents of Authority in matters of
opinion.   To say that I believe a statement because
I have been taught it, or because my father believed
it before me, or because everybody in the village
believes it, is to announce what everyday experience informs us is a quite adequate *cause* of belief—
it is not, however, *per se*, to give a *reason* for belief
at all.   But such statements can be turned at once
into reasons by no process more elaborate than that
of explicitly recognising that my teachers, my family,

or my neighbours, are truthful persons, happy in the possession of adequate means of information—propositions which in their turn, of course, require argumentative support. Such a procedure may, I need hardly say, be quite legitimate ; and reasons of this kind are probably the principal ground on which in mature life we accept the great mass of our subordinate scientific and historical convictions. I believe, for instance, that the moon falls in towards the earth with the exact velocity required by the force of gravitation, for no other reason than that I believe in the competence and trustworthiness of the persons who have made the necessary calculations. In this case the reason for my belief and the immediate cause of it are identical ; the cause, indeed, is a cause only in virtue of its being first a reason. But in the former case this is not so. *Mere* early training, paternal authority, or public opinion, were causes of belief before they were reasons ; they continued to act as non-rational causes after they became reasons ; and it is not improbable that to the very end they contributed less to the resultant conviction in their capacity as reasons than they did in their capacity as non-rational causes.

Now the temptation thus to convert causes into reasons seems under certain circumstances to be almost irresistible, even when it is illegitimate. Authority, as such, is from the nature of the case dumb in the presence of argument. It is only by reasoning that reasoning can be answered.   It can be, and has often been, thrust silently aside by that instinctive feeling of repulsion which we call prejudice when we happen to disagree with it.   But it can only be replied to by its own kind.   And so it comes about. that whenever any system of belief is seriously questioned, a method of defence which is almost certain to find favour is to select one of the causes by which the belief has been produced, and forthwith to erect it into a reason why the system should continue to be accepted.   Authority, as I have been using the term, is thus converted into 'an authority,' or into 'authorities.'   It ceases to be the opposite or correlative of reason.   It can no longer be contrasted with reason.   It becomes a species of reason, and as a species of reason it must be judged.

So judged, it appears to me that two things pertinent to the present discussion may be said of it. In the first place, it is evidently an argument of immense utility and of very wide application.   As I have just noted, it is the proximate reason for an enormous proportion of our beliefs as to matters of fact, past and present, and for that very large body of scientific knowledge which even experts in science can have no opportunity of personally verifying. But, in the second place, it seems not less clear that the argument from 'an authority' or 'authorities' is almost always useless as a *foundation* for a system of belief.   The deep-lying principles which alone deserve this name may be, and frequently are, the product of authority. But the attempt to ground them dialectically upon *an* authority can scarcely be attempted, except at the risk of logical disaster.

· Take as an example the general system of our beliefs about the material universe. The greater number of these are, as we have seen, quite legitimately based upon the argument from 'authorities'; not so those few which lie at the root of the system. These also are largely due to Authority. But they cannot be rationally derived from 'authorities'; though the attempt so to derive them is almost certain to be made. The ' universal experience,' or the ' general consent of mankind,' will be adduced as an authoritative sanction of certain fundamental presuppositions of physical science; and of these, at least, it will be said, *securus judicat orbis terrarum.* But a very little consideration is sufficient to show that this procedure is illegitimate, and that, as I have pointed out, we can neither know that the verdict of mankind has been given, nor, if it has, that anything can properly be inferred from it, unless we first assume the truth of the very principles which that verdict was invoked to establish.[1]

The state of things is not materially different in the case of ethics and theology. There also the argument from ' an authority ' or ' authorities ' has

[1] Cf. for a development of this statement, *Philosophic Doubt*, chap. vii.

a legitimate and most important place; there also there is a constant inclination to extend the use of the argument so as to cover the fundamental portions of the system; and there also this endeavour, when made, seems predestined to end in a piece of circular reasoning. I can hardly illustrate this statement without mentioning dogma; though, as the reader will readily understand, I have not the slightest desire to do anything so little relevant to the purposes of this Introduction in order to argue either for or against it. As to the reality of an infallible guide, in whatever shape this has been accepted by various sections of Christians, I have not a word to say. As part of a creed it is quite outside the scope of my inquiry. I have to do with it only if, and in so far as, it is represented, not as part of the thing to be believed, but as one of the fundamental reasons for believing it; and in that position I think it inadmissible.

Merely as an illustration, then, let us consider for a moment the particular case of Papal Infallibility, an example which may be regarded with the greater impartiality as I am not, I suppose, likely to have among the readers of these Notes many by whom it is accepted. If I rightly understand the teaching of the Roman Catholic theologians upon this subject, the following propositions, at *least*, must be accepted before the doctrine of Infallibility can be regarded as satisfactorily proved or adequately held:—(1) That

the words 'Thou art Peter, and upon this rock,' &c.,
and, again, ' Feed my sheep,' were uttered by Christ;
and that, being so uttered, were of Divine authorship,
and cannot fail. (2) That the meaning of these words
is—(*a*) that St. Peter was endowed with a primacy
of jurisdiction over the other Apostles; (*b*) that he
was to have a perpetual line of successors, similarly
endowed with a primacy of jurisdiction; (*c*) that
these successors were to be Bishops of Rome; (*d*)
that the primacy of jurisdiction carries with it the
certainty of Divine ' assistance'; (*e*) that though this
' assistance' does not ensure either the morality, or,
the wisdom, or the general accuracy of the Pontiff
to whom it is given, it does ensure his absolute
inerrancy whenever he shall, *ex cathedrâ*, define a
doctrine of faith or morals; (*f*) that no pronouncement can be regarded as *ex cathedrâ* unless it relates
to some matter already thoroughly sifted and considered by competent divines.

Now it is no part of my business to ask how the
six sub-heads constituting the second of these con-
tentions can by any legitimate process of exegesis be
extracted from the texts mentioned in the first; nor
how, if they be accepted to the full, they can obviate
the necessity for the complicated exercise of private
judgment required to determine whether any particular decision has or has not been made under the conditions necessary to constitute it a pronouncement
ex cathedrâ. These are questions to be discussed

between Roman Catholic and non-Roman Catholic controversialists, and with them I have nothing here to do. My point is, that the first proposition alone is so absolutely subversive of any purely naturalistic view of the universe, involves so many fundamental elements of Christianity (*e.g.* the supernatural character of Christ and the trustworthiness of the first and fourth Gospels, with all that this carries with it), that if it does not require the argument from an infallible authority for its support, it seems hard to understand where the necessity for that argument can come in at any fundamental stage of apologetic demonstration. And that this proposition does not require infallible authority for its support seems plain from the fact that it does itself supply the main ground on which the existence of infallible authority is believed.

This is not, and is not intended to be, an objection to the doctrine of Papal Infallibility; it is not, and is not intended to be, a criticism by means of example directed against other doctrines involving the existence of an unerring guide. But if the reader will attentively consider the matter he will, I think, see that whatever be the truth or the value of such doctrines, they can never be used to supply any fundamental support to the systems of which they form a part without being open to a reply like that which I have supposed in the case of Papal Infallibility. Indeed, when we reflect upon the character

of the religious books and of the religious organisations through which Christianity has been built up;
when we consider the variety in date, in occasion,
in authorship, in context, in spiritual development,
which mark the first; the stormy history and the inevitable division which mark the second; when we,
further, reflect on the astonishing number of the
problems, linguistic, critical, metaphysical, and historical, which must be settled, at least in some preliminary fashion, before either the books or the organisations can be supposed entitled by right of
rational proof to the position of infallible guides, we
can hardly suppose that we were intended to find in
these the *logical* foundations of our system of religious beliefs, however important be the part (and
can it be exaggerated?) which they were destined
to play in producing, fostering, and directing it.

VI

Enough has now, perhaps, been said to indicate
the relative positions of Reason and Authority in the
production of belief. To Reason is largely due the
growth of new and the sifting of old knowledge;
the ordering, and in part the discovery, of that vast
body of systematised conclusions which constitute
so large a portion of scientific, philosophical, ethical,
political, and theological learning. To Reason we
are in some measure beholden, though not, perhaps,

so much as we suppose, for hourly aid in managing
so much of the trifling portion of our personal affairs entrusted to our care by Nature as we do not
happen to have already surrendered to the control
of habit.   By Reason also is directed, or misdirected,
the public policy of communities within the narrow limits of deviation permitted by accepted custom and tradition.   Of its immense indirect consequences, of the part it has played in the evolution
of human affairs by the disintegration of ancient
creeds, by the alteration of the external conditions
of human life, by the production of new moods of
thought, or, as I have termed them, psychological
climates, we can in this connection say nothing.
For these are no rational effects of reason; the
causal nexus by which they are bound to reason has
no logical aspect; and if reason produces them, as
in part it certainly does, it is in a manner indistinguishable from that in which similar consequences
are blindly produced by the distribution of continent and ocean, the varying fertility of different regions, and the other material surroundings by which
the destinies of the race are modified.

When we turn, however, from the conscious
work of Reason to that which is unconsciously performed for us by Authority, a very different spectacle arrests our attention.   The effects of the first,
prominent as they are through the dignity of their
origin, are trifling compared with the all-pervading

influences which flow from the second. At every moment of our lives, as individuals, as members of a family, of a party, of a nation, of a Church, of a universal brotherhood, the silent, continuous, unnoticed influence of Authority moulds our feelings, our aspirations, and, what we are more immediately concerned with, our beliefs. It is from Authority that Reason itself draws its most important premises. It is in unloosing or directing the forces of Authority that its most important conclusions find their principal function. And even in those cases where we may most truly say that our beliefs are the rational product of strictly intellectual processes, we have, in all probability, only got to trace back the thread of our inferences to its beginnings in order to perceive that it finally loses itself in some general principle which, describe it as we may, is in fact due to no more defensible origin than the influence of Authority.

Nor is the comparative pettiness of the *rôle* thus played by reasoning in human affairs a matter for regret. Not merely because we are ignorant of the data required for the solution, even of very simple problems in organic and social life, are we called on to acquiesce in an arrangement which, to be sure, we have no power to disturb; nor yet because these data, did we possess them, are too complex to be dealt with by any rational calculus we possess or are ever likely to acquire; but because, in addition to

these difficulties, reasoning is a force most apt to divide and disintegrate; and though division and disintegration may often be the necessary preliminaries
of social development, still more necessary are the
forces which bind and stiffen, without which there
would be no society to develop.

It is true, no doubt, that we can, without any
great expenditure of research, accumulate instances
in which Authority has perpetuated error and re-
tarded progress; for, unluckily, none of the influences, Reason least of all, by which the history of
the race has been moulded have been productive of
unmixed good. The springs at which we quench
our thirst are always turbid. Yet, if we are to
judge with equity between these rival claimants, we
must not forget that it is Authority rather than
Reason to which, in the main, we owe, not religion
only, but ethics and politics; that it is Authority
which supplies us with essential elements in the
premises of science; that it is Authority rather than
Reason which lays deep the foundations of social
life; that it is Authority rather than Reason which
cements its superstructure. And though it may
seem to savour of paradox, it is yet no exaggeration
to say, that if we would find the quality in which
we most notably excel the brute creation, we should
look for it, not so much in our faculty of convincing
and being convinced by the exercise of reasoning, as

in our capacity for influencing and being influenced through the action of Authority.

[NOTE

ON THE USE OF THE WORDS 'AUTHORITY' AND 'REASON'

Much criticism has been directed against the use to which the word 'Authority' has been put in this chapter. And there can be no doubt that a terminology which draws so sharp a distinction between phrases so nearly identical as 'authority' and 'an authority' must be open to objection.

Yet it still seems to me difficult to find a more suitable expression. There is no word in the English language which describes what I want to describe, and yet describes nothing else. Every alternative term seems at least as much open to misconception as the one I have employed, and I do not observe that those who have most severely criticised it, have suggested an unobjectionable substitute. Professor Pringle Pattison (Seth) in a most interesting and sympathetic review of this work,[1] goes the length of saying that my use of the word is a 'complete departure from ordinary usage.'[2] But I can hardly think that this is so. However else the word may be employed in common parlance, it is surely often employed exactly as it is in this chapter—namely, to describe those causes of belief which are not reasons and yet are due to the influence of mind on mind. Parental influence is typical of the species: and it would certainly be in conformity with accepted usage to describe this as 'Authority.' A child does not accept its mother's teaching because it regards its mother as 'an authority' whom it is reasonable to believe. The process is one of non-rational (not *ir*rational) causation. Again I do not think it would be regarded as forced to talk of the 'authority of public opinion' or the 'authority of custom' exactly with the meaning which such expression would bear in the preceding chapter. 'He submitted to the *authority* of a

[1] Since republished in *Man's Place in the Cosmos.*
[2] *Op. cit.* p. 265.

stronger will.' ' He never asked on what basis the claims of his Church rested ; he simply bowed, as from his childhood he ha'd always bowed, to her unchallenged *authority.*' ' No doubts were ever entertained, no inconvenient questions were ever asked, about the propriety of a practice which was enforced by the *authority* of unbroken custom.' I think it will be admitted that in all these examples the word ' authority ' is used in the sense I have attributed to it, that this sense is a natural sense, and that no other single word could advantageously be substituted for it. If so, the reasons for its employment seem not inadequate.

I feel on even stronger ground in replying to the criticisms passed on my use here of the word ' reason.' Professor Pattison, though he does not like it, admits that it is in accordance with the practice of the older English thinkers. I submit that it is also in accordance with the usage prevalent in ordinary discourse. But I go further and say that I am employing the word in the sense in which it is always employed when ' reason ' is contrasted with ' authority.' If a man boasts that all his opinions have been arrived at by ' following reason,' he is referring not to the Universal Reason or Logos, but to his own faculty of discursive reason: and what he wishes the world to understand is that his beliefs are based on reasoning, not on authority or prejudice. Now this is the very individual whom I had in my mind when writing this chapter : and if I had been debarred from using the words ' reason ' and ' reasoning ' in their ordinary everyday meaning, I really do not see in what language I could have addressed myself to him at all.]

PART IV

SUGGESTIONS TOWARDS
A PROVISIONAL PHILOSOPHY

CHAPTER I

THE GROUNDWORK

I

WE have now considered beliefs, or certain important classes of them, under three aspects. We have considered them from the point of view of their practical necessity; from that of their philosophic proof; and from that of their scientific origin. Inquiries relating to the same subject-matter more distinct in their character it would be difficult to conceive. It remains for us to consider whether it is possible to extract from their combined results any general view which may command at least a provisional assent.

It is evident, of course, that this general view, if we are fortunate enough to reach it, will not be of the nature of a complete or adequate philosophy. The unification of all belief into an ordered whole, compacted into one coherent structure under the stress of reason, is an ideal which we can never abandon; but it is also one which, in the present condition of our knowledge, perhaps even of our faculties, we seem incapable of attaining. For the moment we must content ourselves with something less than this. The best system we can hope to construct will suffer from gaps and rents, from loose ends and ragged edges. It does not, however, follow from this that it will be without a high degree of value; and, whether valuable or worthless, it may at least represent the best within our reach.

By the best I, of course, mean best in relation to reflective reason. If we have to submit, as I think we must, to an incomplete rationalisation of belief, this ought not to be because in a fit of intellectual despair we are driven to treat reason as an illusion; nor yet because we have deliberately resolved to transfer our allegiance to irrational or non-rational inclination; but because reason itself assures us that such a course is, at the lowest, the least irrational one open to us. If we have to find our way over difficult seas and under murky skies without compass or chronometer, we need not on that account allow the ship to drive at random. Rather ought we to weigh with the more anxious care every indication, be it negative or positive, and from whatever quarter it may come, which can help us to guess at our position and to lay out the course which it behoves us to steer.

Now, the first and most elementary principle which ought to guide us in framing any provisional scheme of unification, is to decline to draw any distinction between different classes of belief where no relevant distinction can as a matter of fact be discovered. To pursue the opposite course would be gratuitously to irrationalise (to coin a convenient word) our scheme from the very start; to destroy, by a quite arbitrary treatment, any hope of its symmetrical and healthy development. And yet, if there be any value in the criticisms contained in the Second Part of these Notes, this is precisely the mistake into which the advocates of naturalism have invariably blundered. Without any preliminary analysis, nay, without any apparent suspicion that a preliminary analysis was necessary or desirable, they have chosen to assume that scientific beliefs stand not only upon a different, but upon a much more solid, platform than any others; that scientific standards supply the sole test of truth, and scientific methods the sole instruments of discovery.

The reader is already in possession of some of the arguments which are, as it seems to me, fatal to such claims, and it is not necessary here to repeat them. What is more to our present purpose is to find out whether, in the absence of philosophic proof, judgments about the phenomenal, and more particularly about the material, world possess any other characteristics which, in our attempt at a provisional unification of knowledge, forbid us to place them on a level with other classes of belief. That there are differences of some sort no one, I imagine, will attempt to deny. But are they of a kind which require us either to give any special precedence to science, or to exclude other beliefs altogether from our general scheme?

One peculiarity there is which seems at first sight effectually to distinguish certain scientific beliefs from any which belong, say, to ethics or theology; a peculiarity which may, perhaps, be best expressed by the word 'inevitableness.' Everybody has, and everybody is obliged to have, some convictions about the world in which he lives—convictions which in their narrow and particular form (as what I have before called beliefs of perception, memory, and expectation) guide us all, children, savages, and philosophers alike, in the ordinary conduct of day-to-day existence; which, when generalised and extended, supply us with some of the leading presuppositions on which the whole fabric of science appears logically to depend. No convictions quite answering to this description can, I think, be found either in ethics, æsthetics, or theology. Some kind of morality is, no doubt, required for the stability even of the rudest form of social life. Some sense of beauty, some kind of religion, is, perhaps, to be discovered (though this is disputed) in every human community. But certainly there is nothing in any of these great departments of thought quite corresponding to our habitual judgments about the things we see and handle; judgments which, with reason or without it, all mankind are practically compelled to entertain.

Compare, for example, the central truth of theology—'There is a God'—with one of the fundamental presuppositions of science (itself a generalised statement of what is given in ordinary judgments of perception)—'There is an independent material world.' I am myself disposed to doubt whether so good a case can be made out for accepting the second of these propositions as can be made out for accepting the first. But while it has been found by many, not only possible, but easy, to doubt the existence of God, doubts as to the independent existence of matter have assuredly been confined to the rarest moments of subjective reflection, and have dissolved like summer mists at the first touch of what we are pleased to call reality.

Now, what are we to make of this fact? In the opinion of many persons, perhaps of most, it affords a conclusive ground for elevating science to a different plane of certitude from that on which other systems of belief must be content to dwell. The evidence of the senses, as we loosely describe these judgments of perception, is for such persons the best of all evidence: it is inevitable, so it is true; seeing, as the proverb has it, is indeed believing. This somewhat crude view, however, is not one which we can accept. The coercion exercised in the production of these beliefs is not, as has been already shown, a rational coercion. Even while we submit to it we may judge it; and in the very act of believing we may be conscious that the strength of our belief is far in excess of anything which mere reasoning can justify.

I am making no complaint of this disparity between belief and its reasons. On the contrary, I have already noted my dissent from the popular view that it is our business to take care that, as far as possible, these two shall in every case be nicely adjusted. It cannot, I contend, be our duty to do that in the name of reason which, if it were done, would bring any kind of rational life to an immediate standstill. And even if we could suppose it to be our duty, it is not one which, as was shown in the last chapter, we are practically competent to perform. If this be true in the case of those beliefs which owe their origin largely to Authority, or the non-rational action of mind on mind, not less is it true in the case of those elementary judgments which arise out of sense-stimulation. Whether there be an independent material universe or not may be open to philosophic doubt. But that, if it exists, it is expedient that the belief in it should be accepted with a credence which for all practical purposes is immediate and unwavering, admits, I think, of no doubt whatever. If we could suppose a community to be called into being who, in its dealings with the 'external world,' should permit action to wait upon speculation, and require all its metaphysical difficulties to be solved before reposing full belief in some such material surroundings as those which we habitually postulate, its members would be overwhelmed by a ruin more rapid and more complete than that which, in a preceding chapter, was prophesied for those who should succeed in ousting authority from its natural position among the causes of belief.

But supposing this be so, it follows necessarily, on accepted biological principles,[1] that a kind of credulity so essential to the welfare, not merely of the race as a whole, but of every single member of it, will be bred by elimination and selection into its inmost organisation. If we consider what must have happened[2] at that critical moment in the history of organic development when first conscious judgments of sense-perception made themselves felt as important links in the chain connecting nervous irritability with muscular action, is it not plain that any individual in whom such judgments were habitually qualified and enfeebled by even the most legitimate scepticism would incontinently perish, and that those only would survive who possessed, and could presumably transmit to their descendants, a stubborn assurance which was beyond the power of reasoning either to fortify or to undermine?

No such process would come to the assistance of

[1] At the first glance, the reader may be disposed to think that to bring in science to show why no peculiar certainty should attach to scientific premises is logically inadmissible. But this is not so: though the converse procedure, by which scientific conclusions would be made to *establish* scientific premises, would, no doubt, involve an argument in a circle.

[2] Cf. Note, p. 285.

other faiths, however true, which were the growth of higher and later stages of civilised development. For, in the first place, such faiths are not necessarily, nor perhaps at all, an advantage in the struggle for existence. In the second place, even where they are an 'advantage, it is rather to the community as a whole in its struggles with other communities, than to each particular individual in his struggle with other individuals, or with the inanimate forces of Nature. In the third place, the whole machinery of selection and elimination has been weakened, if not paralysed, by civilisation itself. And, in the fourth place, were it still in full operation, it could not, through the mere absence of time and opportunity, have produced any sensible effect in moulding the organism for the reception of beliefs which, by hypothesis, are the recent acquisition of a small and advanced minority.

II

We are now in a position to answer the question put a few pages back. What, I then asked, if any, is the import, from our present point of view, of the universality and inevitableness which unquestionably attach to certain judgments about the world of phenomena, and to these judgments alone? The answer must be, that these peculiarities have no import. They exist, but they are irrelevant. Faith or assurance, which, if not in excess of reason, is at least independent of it, seems to be a necessity in every great department of knowledge which touches on action; and what great department is there which does not? The analysis of sense-experience teaches us that we require it in our ordinary dealings with the material world. The most cursory examination into the springs of moral action shows that it is an indispensable supplement to ethical speculation. Theologians are for the most part agreed that without it religion is but the ineffectual profession of a barren creed. The comparative value, however, of these faiths is not to be measured either by their intensity or by the degree of their diffusion. It is true that all men, whatever their speculative opinions, enjoy a practical assurance with regard to what they see and touch. It is also true that few men have an assurance equally strong about matters of which their senses tell them nothing immediately; and that many men have on such subjects no assurance at all. But as this is precisely what we should expect if, in the progress of evolution, the need for other faiths had arisen under conditions very different from those which produced our innate and long-descended confidence in sense-perception, how can we regard it as a distinction in favour of the latter? We can scarcely reckon universality and necessity as badges of pre-eminence, at the same moment that we recognise them as marks of the elementary and primitive character of the beliefs to which they give their all-powerful, but none the less irrational, sanction. The time has passed for believing that the further we go back towards the 'state of nature,' the nearer we get to Virtue and to Truth.

We cannot, then, extract out of the coercive character of certain unreasoned beliefs any principle of classification which shall help us to the provisional philosophy of which we are in search. What such a principle would require us to include in our system of beliefs contents us not. What it would require us to exclude we may not willingly part with. And if, dissatisfied with this double deficiency, we examine more closely into its character and origin, we find, not only that it is without rational justification—of which at this stage of our inquiry we have no right to complain—but that the very account which it gives of itself precludes us from finding in it even a temporary place of intellectual repose.

I do not, be it observed, make it a matter of complaint that those who erect the inevitable judgments of sense-perception into a norm or standard of right belief have thereby substituted (however unconsciously) psychological compulsion for rational necessity; for, as rational necessity does not, so far as I can see, carry us at the best beyond a system of mere 'solipsism,' it must, somehow or other, be supplemented if we are to force an entrance into any larger and worthier inheritance. My complaint rather is, that having asked us to acquiesce in the guidance of non-rational impulse, they should then require us arbitrarily to narrow down the impulses which we may follow to the almost animal instincts lying at the root of our judgments about material phenomena. It is surely better—less repugnant, I mean, to reflective reason —to frame for ourselves some wider scheme which, though it be founded in the last resort upon our needs, shall at least take account of other needs than those we share with our brute progenitors.

And here, if not elsewhere, I may claim the support of the most famous masters of speculation. Though they have not, it may be, succeeded in supplying us with a satisfactory explanation of the Universe, at least the Universe which they have sought to explain has been something more than a mere collection of hypostatised sense-perceptions, packed side by side in space, and following each other with blind uniformity in time. All the great architects of systems have striven to provide accommodation within their schemes for ideas of wider sweep and richer content; and whether they desired to support, to modify, or to oppose the popular theology of their day, they have at least given hospitable welcome to some of its most important conceptions.

In the case of such men as Leibnitz, Kant, Hegel, this is obvious enough. It is true, I think, even in such a case as that of Spinoza. Philosophers, indeed, may find but small satisfaction in his methods or conclusions. They may see but little to admire in his elaborate but illusory show of quasi-mathe-matical demonstration; in the Nature which is so unlike the Nature of the physicist that we feel no surprise at its being also called God; in the God Who is so unlike the God of the theologian that we feel no surprise at His also being called Nature; in the *a priori* metaphysic which evolves the universe from definitions; in the freedom which is indistin-guishable from necessity; in the volition which is indistinguishable from intellect; in the love which is indistinguishable from reasoned acquiescence; in the universe from which have been expelled pur-pose, morality, beauty, and causation, and which contains, therefore, but scant room for theology, ethics, æsthetics, or science. In the two hundred years and more which have elapsed since the pub-lication of his system, it may be doubted whether two hundred persons have been convinced by his reasoning. Yet he continues to interest the world; and why? Not, surely, as a guide through the mazes of metaphysics. Not as a pioneer of 'higher' criti-cism. Least of all because he was anything so com-monplace as a heretic or an atheist. The true rea-son appears to me to be very different. It is partly, at least, because in despite of his positive teaching he was endowed with a religious imagination which, in however abstract and metaphysical a fashion, illumined the whole profitless bulk of inconclusive demonstration; which enabled him to find in notions most remote from sense-experience the only abiding realities; and to convert a purely rational adhesion to the conclusions supposed to flow from the nature of an inactive, impersonal, and unmoral substance, into something not quite inaptly termed the Love of God.

It will, perhaps, be objected that we have no right to claim support from the example of system-makers with whose systems we do not happen to agree. How, it may be asked, can it concern us that Spinoza extracted something like a religion out of his philosophy, if we do not accept his philosophy? Or that Hegel found it possible to hitch large fragments of Christian dogma into the development of the 'Idea,' if we are not convinced by his dialectic? It concerns us, I reply, inasmuch as facts like these furnish fresh confirmation of a truth reached before by another method. The naturalistic creed, which merely systematises and expands the ordinary judgments of sense-perception, we found by direct examination to be quite inadequate. We now note that its inadequacy has been commonly assumed by men whose speculative genius is admitted, who have seldom been content to allow that the world of which they had to give an account could be narrowed down to the naturalistic pattern.

III

But a more serious objection to the point of view here adopted remains to be considered. Is not, it will be asked, the whole method followed throughout the course of these Notes intrinsically unsound? Is it not substantially identical with the attempt, not made now for the first time, to rest superstition upon scepticism, and to frame our creed, not in accordance with the rules of logic, but with the promptings of desire? It begins (may it not be said?) by discrediting reason; and having thus guaranteed its results against inconvenient criticism, it proceeds to make the needs of man the measure of 'objective' reality, to erect his convenience into the touchstone of Eternal Truth, and to mete out the Universe on a plan authenticated only by his wishes.

Now, on this criticism I have, in the first place, to observe that it errs in assuming, either that the object aimed at in the preceding discussion is to discredit reason, or that as a matter of fact this has been its effect. On the contrary, be the character of our conclusions what it may, they have at least been arrived at by allowing the fullest play to free, rational investigation. If one consequence of this investigation has been to diminish the importance commonly attributed to reason among the causes by which belief is produced, it is by the action of reason itself that this result has been brought about. If another consequence has been that doubts have been expressed as to the theoretic validity of certain universally accepted beliefs, this is because the right of reason to deal with every province of knowledge, untrammelled by arbitrary restrictions or customary immunities, has been assumed and acted upon. If, in addition to all this, we have been incidentally compelled to admit that as yet we are without a satisfactory philosophy, the admission has not been asked for in the interests either of scepticism or of superstition. Reason is not honoured by pretending that she has done what as a matter of fact is still undone; nor need we be driven into a universal license of credulity by recognising that we must for the present put up with some working hypothesis which falls far short of speculative perfection.

But, further, is it true to say that, in the absence of reason, we have contentedly accepted mere desire for our guide? No doubt the theory here advocated requires us to take account, not merely of premises and their conclusions, but of needs and their satisfaction. But this is only asking us to do explicitly and on system what on the naturalistic theory is done unconsciously and at random. By the very constitution of our being we seem practically driven to assume a real world in correspondence with our ordinary judgments of perception. A harmony of some kind between our inner selves and the universe of which we form a part is thus the tacit postulate at the root of every belief we entertain about 'phe-nomena'; and all that I now contend for is, that a like harmony should provisionally be assumed between that universe and other elements in our nature which are of a later, of a more uncertain, but of no ignobler, growth.

Whether this correspondence is best described as that which obtains between a 'need' and its 'satisfaction,' may be open to question. But, at all events, let it be understood that if the relation so described is, on the one side, something different from that between a premise and its conclusion, so, on the other, it is intended to be equally remote from that between a desire and its fulfilment. That it has not the logical validity of the first I have already admitted, or rather asserted. That it has not the casual, wavering, and purely 'subjective' character of the second is not less true. For the correspondence postulated is not between the fleeting fancies of the individual and the immutable verities of an unseen world, but between these characteristics of our nature, which we recognise as that in us which, though not necessarily the strongest, is the highest; which, though not always the most universal, is nevertheless the best.

But because this theory may seem alike remote from familiar forms both of dogmatism and scepticism, and because I am on that account the more anxious that no unmerited plausibility should be attributed to it through any obscurity in my way of presenting it, let me draw out, even at the cost of some repetition, a brief catalogue of certain things which may, and of certain other things which may not, be legitimately said concerning it.

We may say of it, then, that it furnishes us with no adequate philosophy of religion. But we may not say of it that it leaves religion worse, or, indeed, otherwise provided for in this respect than science.

We may say of it that it assumes without proof a certain consonance between the 'subjective' and the 'objective'; between what we are moved to believe and what in fact *is*. We may not say that the presuppositions of science depend upon any more solid, or, indeed, upon any different, foundation.

We may say of it, if we please, that it gives us a practical, but not a theoretic, assurance of the truths with which it is concerned. But, if so, we must describe in the same technical language our assurance respecting the truths of the material world.

We may say of it that it accepts provisionally the theory, based on scientific methods, which traces back the origin of all beliefs to causes which, for the most part, are non-rational, and which carry with them no warranty that they will issue in right opinion. But we may not say of it that the distinction thus drawn between the non-rational causes which produce the immediate judgments of sense-perception, and those which produce judgments in

17

the sphere of ethics or theology, implies any superior certitude in the case of the former.

We may say of it that it admits judgments of
sense-perception to be the most inevitable, but denies
them to be the most worthy.

We may say of it generally, that as it assumes
the Whole, of which we desire a reasoned knowledge, to include human consciousness as an element,
it refuses to regard any system as other than irrational which, like Naturalism, leaves large tracts and
aspects of that consciousness unaccounted for and
derelict; and that it utterly declines to circumscribe
the Knowable by frontiers whose delimitation Reason itself assures us can be justified on no rational
principle whatsoever.

CHAPTER II

IF, as is not unlikely, there are readers who are unwilling to acknowledge this kind of equality between the different branches of knowledge—who are disposed to represent Science as a Land of Goshen, bright beneath the unclouded splendours of the midday sun, while Religion lies beyond, wrapped in the impenetrable darkness of the Egyptian plague—I would suggest for their further consideration certain arguments, not drawn like those in an earlier portion of this Essay from the deficiencies which may be detected in scientific proof, but based exclusively upon an examination of fundamental scientific ideas considered in themselves. For these ideas possess a quality, exhibited no doubt equally by ideas in other departments of knowledge, which admirably illustrates our ignorance of what we know best, our blindness to what we see most clearly. This quality, indeed, is not very easy to describe in a sentence; but perhaps it may be provisionally indicated by saying that, although these ideas seem quite simple so long as we only have to handle them for the practical purposes of daily life, yet, when they are subjected to critical investigation, they appear to crumble under the process; to lose all precision of outline; to vanish like the magician in the story, leaving only an elusive mist in the grasp of those who would arrest them.

Nothing, for instance, seems simpler than the idea involved in the statement that we are, each of us, situated at any given moment in some particular portion of space, surrounded by a multitude of material things, which are constantly acting upon us and upon each other. A proposition of this kind is merely a generalised form of the judgments which we make every minute of our waking lives, about whose meaning we entertain no manner of doubt, which, indeed, provide us with our familiar examples of all that is most lucid and most certain. Yet the purport of the sentence which expresses it is clear only till it is examined, is certain only till it is questioned; while almost every word in it suggests, and has long suggested, perplexing problems to all who are prepared to consider them.

What are 'we'? What is space? Can 'we' be in space, or is it only our bodies about which any such statement can be made? What is a 'thing'? and, in particular, what is a 'material thing'? What is meant by saying that one 'material thing' acts upon another? What is meant by saying that 'material things' act upon 'us'? Here are six questions all directly and obviously arising out of our most familiar acts of judgment. Yet, direct and obvious as they are, it is hardly too much to say that they involve all the leading problems of modern philosophy, and that the man who has found an answer to them is the fortunate possessor of a tolerably complete system of metaphysic.

Consider, for example, the simplest of the six questions enumerated above, namely, What is a 'material thing'? Nothing could be plainer till you consider it. Nothing can be obscurer when you do. A 'thing' has qualities—hardness, weight, shape, and so forth. Is it merely the sum of these qualities, or is it something more? If it is merely the sum of its qualities, have these any independent existence? Nay, is such an independent existence even conceivable? If it is something more than the sum of its qualities, what is the relation of the 'qualities' to the 'something more'? Again, can we on reflection regard a 'thing' as an isolated 'somewhat,' an entity self-sufficient and potentially solitary? Or must we not rather regard it as being what it is in virtue of its relation to other 'somewhats,' which, again, are what they are in virtue of their relation to it, and to each other? And if we take, as I think we must, the latter alternative, are we not driven by it into a profitless progression through parts which are unintelligible by themselves, but which yet obstinately refuse to coalesce into any fully intelligible whole?

Now, I do not serve up these cold fragments of ancient though unsolved controversies for no better purpose than to weary the reader who is familiar with metaphysical discussion, and to puzzle the reader who is not. I rather desire to direct attention to the universality of a difficulty which many persons seem glad enough to acknowledge when they come across it in Theology, though they admit it only with reluctance in the case of Ethics and Æsthetics, and for the most part completely ignore it when they are dealing with our knowledge of 'phenomena.' Yet in this respect, at least, all these branches of knowledge would appear to stand very much upon an equality. In all of them conclusions seem more certain than premises, the superstructure more stable than the foundation. In all of them we move with full assurance and a practical security only among ideas which are relative and dependent. In all of them these ideas, so clear and so sufficient for purposes of everyday thought and action, become confused and but dimly intelligible when examined in the unsparing light of critical analysis.

We need not, therefore, be surprised if we find it hard to isolate the permanent element in Beauty, seeing that it eludes us in material objects; that the ground of Moral Law should not be wholly clear, seeing that the ground of Natural Law is so obscure; that we do not adequately comprehend God, seeing that we can give no very satisfactory account of what we mean by 'a thing.' Yet I think a more profitable lesson is to be learnt from admissions like these than the general inadequacy of our existing metaphysic. And it is the more necessary to consider carefully what that lesson is, inasmuch as a very perverted version of it forms the basis of the only modern system of English growth which, professing to provide us with a general philosophy, has received any appreciable amount of popular support.

Mr. Spencer's theory admits, nay, insists, that what it calls 'ultimate scientific ideas' are inconsistent and, to use his own phrase, 'unthinkable.' Space, time, matter, motion, force, and so forth, are each in turn shown to involve contradictions which it is beyond our power to solve, and obscurities which it is beyond our power to penetrate; while the once famous dialectic of Hamilton and Mansel is invoked for the purpose of enforcing the same lesson with regard to the Absolute and the Unconditioned, which those thinkers identified with God, but which Mr. Spencer prefers to describe as the Unknowable.

So far, so good. Though the details of the demonstration may not be altogether to our liking, I, at least, have no particular quarrel with its general tenor, which is in obvious harmony with much that I have just been insisting on. But when we have to consider the conclusion which Mr. Spencer contrives to extract from these premises, our differences become irreconcilable. He has proved, or supposes himself to have proved, that the 'ultimate ideas' of science and the 'ultimate ideas' of theology are alike 'unthinkable.' What is the proper inference to be drawn from these statements? Why, clearly, that science and theology are so far on an equality that every proposition which con. siderations like these oblige us to assert about the one, we are bound to assert also about the other; and that our general theory of knowledge must take account of the fact that both these great departments of it are infected by the same weakness.

This, however, is not the inference drawn by Mr. Spencer. The idea that the conclusions of science should be profaned by speculative questionings is to him intolerable. He shrinks from an admission which seems to him to carry universal scepticism in its train. And he has, accordingly, hit upon a device for 'reconciling' the differences between science and religion by which so lamentable a catastrophe may be avoided. His method is a simple one. He divides the verities which have to be believed into those which relate to the Knowable and those which relate to the Unknowable. What is knowable he appropriates, without exception, for science. What is unknowable he abandons, without reserve, to religion. With the results of this arbitration both contending parties should, in his opinion, be satisfied. It is true that religion may complain that by this arrangement it is made the residuary legatee of all that is 'unthinkable'; but then, it should remember that it obtains in exchange an indefeasible title to all that is 'real.' Science, again, may complain that its activities are confined to the 'relative' and the 'dependent'; but then, it should remember that it has a monopoly of the 'intelligible.' The one possesses all that can be known; the other, all that seems worth knowing. With so equal a partition of the spoils both disputants should be content.

Without contesting the fairness of this curious arrangement, I am compelled to question its validity. Science cannot thus transfer the burden of its own obscurities and contradictions to the shoulders of religion; and Mr. Spencer is only, perhaps, misled into supposing such a procedure to be possible by his use of the word 'ultimate.' 'Ultimate' scientific ideas may, in his opinion, be 'unthinkable' without prejudice to the 'thinkableness' of 'proximate' scientific ideas. The one may dwell for ever in the penumbra of what he calls 'nascent consciousness,' in the dim twilight where religion and science are indistinguishable; while the other stands out, definite and certain, in the full light of experience and verification. Such a view is not, I think, philosophically tenable. As soon as the 'unthinkableness' of 'ultimate' scientific ideas is speculatively recognised, the fact must react upon our speculative attitudes towards 'proximate' scientific ideas. That which in the order of reason is dependent cannot be unaffected by the weaknesses and the obscurities of that on which it depends. If the one is unintelligible, the other can hardly be rationally established.

In order to prove this—if proof be required—we need not travel beyond the ample limits of Mr. Spencer's own philosophy. To be sure he obstinately shuts his ears against speculative doubts respecting the conclusions of science. 'To ask whether science is substantially true is [he observes] much like asking whether the sun gives light.'[1] It is, I admit, very much like it. But then, on Mr. Spencer's principles, *does* the sun give light? After due consideration we shall have to admit, I think, that it does not. For the question, if intelligently asked, not only involves the comprehension of matter, space, time, and force, which are, according to Mr. Spencer, all incomprehensible, but there is the further difficulty that, if his system is to be believed, 'what we are conscious of as properties of matter, even down to weight and resistance, are but subjective affections produced by objective agencies, which are unknown and unknowable.'[2] It would seem, therefore, either that the sun is a 'subjective affection,' in which case it can hardly be said to 'give light'; or it is 'unknown' and 'unknowable,' in which case no assertion respecting it can be regarded as supplying us with any very flattering specimen of scientific certitude.

The truth is that Mr. Spencer, like many of his

[1] *First Principles*, p. 19. [2] *Principles of Psychology*, ii. 493.

predecessors, has impaired the value of his speculations by the hesitating timidity with which he has
pursued them. Nobody is required to investigate
first principles ; but those who voluntarily undertake
the task should not shrink from its results. And if
among these we have to count a theoretical scepticism about scientific knowledge, we make matters,
not better, but worse, by attempting to ignore it. In
Mr. Spencer's case this procedure has, among other
ill consequences, caused him to miss the moral which
at one moment lay ready to his hand. He has had
the acuteness to see that our beliefs cannot be limited
to the sequences and the co-existences of phenomena ;
that the ideas on which science relies, and in terms
of which all science has to be expressed, break down
under the stress of criticism ; that beyond what we
think we know, and in closest relationship with it,
lies an infinite field which we do not know, and which
with our present faculties we can never know, yet
which cannot be ignored without making what we
do know unintelligible and meaningless. But he
has failed to see whither such speculations must inevitably lead him. He has failed to see that if the
certitudes of science lose themselves in depths of un-
fathomable mystery, it may well be that out of these
same depths there should emerge the certitudes of
religion ; and that if the dependence of the ' knowable ' upon the ' unknowable ' embarrasses us not in
the one case, no reason can be assigned why it should
embarrass us in the other.

Mr. Spencer, in short, has avoided the error of dividing all reality into a Perceivable which concerns us, and an Unperceivable which, if it exists at all, concerns us not.   Agnosticism so understood he explicitly repudiates by his theory, if not by his practice. But he has not seen that, if this simple-minded creed be once abandoned, there is no convenient halting-place till we have swung round to a theory of things which is almost its precise opposite : a theory which, though it shrinks on its speculative side from no severity of critical analysis, yet on its practical side finds the source of its constructive energy in the deepest needs of man, and thus recognises, alike in science, in ethics, in beauty, in religion, the halting expression of a reality beyond our reach, the half-seen vision of transcendent Truth.

CHAPTER III

SCIENCE AND THEOLOGY

I

THE point of view we have thus reached is obviously the precise opposite of that which is adopted by those who either accept the naturalistic view of things in its simplicity, or who agree with naturalism in taking our knowledge of Nature as the core and substance of their creed, while gladly adding to it such supernatural supplements as are permitted them by the canons of their rationalising philosophy. Of these last there are two varieties. There are those who refuse to add anything to the teaching of science proper, except such theological doctrines as they persuade themselves may be deduced from scientific premises. And there are those who, being less fastidious in the matter of proof, are prepared, tentatively and provisionally, to admit so much of theology as they think their naturalistic premises do not positively contradict.

It must, I think, be admitted that the members of these two classes are at some disadvantage compared with the naturalistic philosophers proper. To be sure, the scheme of belief so confidently propounded by the latter is, as we have seen, both incoherent and inadequate. But its incoherence is hid from them by the inevitableness of its positive teaching; while its inadequacy is covered by the, as yet, unsquandered heritage of sentiments and ideals which has come down to us from other ages inspired by other faiths. On the other hand, as a set-off against this, they may justly claim that their principles, such as they are, have been worked out to their legitimate conclusion. They have reached their journey's end, and there they may at least rest, if it is not given them to be thankful. Far different is the fate of those who are reluctantly travelling the road to naturalism, driven thither by a false philosophy honestly entertained. To them each new discovery in geology, morphology, anthropology, or the 'higher criticism,' arouses as much theological anxiety as it does scientific interest. They are perpetually occupied in the task of 'reconciling,' as the phrase goes, 'religion and science.' This is to them, not an intellectual luxury, but a pressing and overmastering necessity. For their theology exists only on sufferance. It rules over its hereditary territories as a tributary vassal dependent on the forbearance of some encroaching overlord. Province after province which once acknowledged its sovereignty has been torn from its grasp; and it depends no longer upon its own action, but upon the uncontrolled policy of its too powerful neighbour, how long it shall preserve a precarious authority over the remainder.

Now, my reasons for entirely dissenting from this melancholy view of the relations between the various departments of belief have been one of the chief themes of these Notes. But it must not be supposed that I intend either to deny that it is our business to 'reconcile' all beliefs, so far as possible, into a self-consistent whole, or to assert that, because a perfectly coherent philosophy cannot as yet be attained, it is, in the meanwhile, a matter of complete indifference how many contradictions and obscurities we admit into our provisional system. Some contradictions and obscurities there needs must be. That we should not be able completely to harmonise the detached hints and isolated fragments in which alone Reality comes into relation with us; that we should but imperfectly co-ordinate what we so imperfectly comprehend, is what we might expect, and what for the present we have no choice but to submit to. Yet it will, I think, be found on examination that the discrepancies which exist between different departments of belief are less in number and importance than those which exist within the various departments themselves; that the difficulties which science, ethics, or theology have to solve in common are more formidable by far than any which divide them from each other; and that, in particular, the supposed 'conflict between science and religion,' which occupies so large a space in contemporary literature, is the theme of so much vigorous debate, and seems to so many earnest souls the one question worth resolving, is either concerned for the most part with matters in themselves comparatively trifling, or touches interests lying far beyond the limits of pure theology.

Of course, it must be remembered that I am now talking of science, not of naturalism. The differences between naturalism and theology are, no doubt, irreconcilable, since naturalism is by definition the negation of all theology. But science must not be dragged into every one of the many quarrels which naturalism has taken upon its shoulders. Science is in no way concerned, for instance, to deny the reality of a world unrevealed to us in sense-perception, nor the existence of a God who, however imperfectly, may be known by those who diligently seek Him. All it says, or ought to say, is that these are matters beyond its jurisdiction; to be tried, therefore, in other courts, and before judges administering different laws.

But we may go further. The being of God may be beyond the province of science, and yet it may be from a consideration of the general body of scientific knowledge that philosophy draws some important motives for accepting the doctrine. Any complete survey of the 'proofs of theism' would, I need not say, be here quite out of place; yet, in order to make clear where I think the real difficulty lies in framing any system which shall include both theology and science, I may be permitted to say enough about theism to show where I think the difficulty does *not* lie. It does not lie in the doctrine that there is a supernatural or, let us say, a metaphysical ground, on which the whole system of natural phenomena depend; nor in the attribution to this ground of the quality of reason, or, it may be, of something higher than reason, in which reason is, so to speak, included. This belief, with all its inherent obscurities, is, no doubt, necessary to theology, but it is at the same time so far, in my judgment, from being repugnant to science that, without it, the scientific view of the natural world would not be less, but more, beset with difficulties than it is at present.

This fact has been in part obscured by certain infelicities in the popular statements of what is known as the 'Argument from Design.' In a famous answer to that argument it has been pointed out that the inference from the adaptation of means to ends, which rightly convinces us in the case of manufactured articles that they are produced by intelligent contrivance, can scarcely be legitimately applied to the case of the universe as a whole. An induction which may be perfectly valid within the circle of phenomena, may be quite meaningless when it is employed to account for the circle itself. You cannot infer a God from the existence of the world as you infer an architect from the existence of a house, or a mechanic from the existence of a watch.

Without discussing the merits of this answer at length, so much may, I think, be conceded to it—that it suggests a doubt whether the theologians who thus rely upon an inductive proof of the being of God are not in a position somewhat similar to that of the empirical philosophers who rely upon an inductive proof of the uniformity of Nature. The uniformity of Nature, as I have before explained, cannot be proved by experience, for it is what makes proof from experience possible.[1] We must bring it, or something like it, to the facts in order to infer anything from them at all. Assume it, and we shall no doubt find that, broadly speaking and in the rough, what we call the facts conform to it. But this conformity is not inductive proof, and must not be confounded with inductive proof. In the same way, I do not contend that, if we start from Nature without God, we shall be logically driven to believe in Him by a mere consideration of the examples of adaptation which Nature undoubtedly contains. It is enough that when we bring this belief with us to the study of phenomena, we can say of

---

[1] This phrase has a Kantian ring about it; but I need not say that it is not here used in the Kantian sense. The argument is touched on, as the reader may recollect, at the end of Chapter I., Part II. See, however, below, a further discussion as to what the uniformity of Nature means, and as to what may be properly inferred from it.

it, what we have just said of the principle of uniformity, namely, that, ' broadly speaking and in the
rough,' the facts harmonise with it, and that it gives
a unity and a coherence to our apprehension of the
natural world which it would not otherwise possess.

II

But the argument from design, in whatever
shape it is accepted, is not the only one in favour of
theism with which scientific knowledge furnishes
us. Nor is it, to my mind, the most important.
The argument from design rests upon the world as
known. But something also may be inferred from
the mere fact that we know—a fact which, like
every other, has to be accounted for. And how is
it to be accounted for? I need not repeat again
what I have already said about Authority and Reason; for it is evident that, whatever be the part
played by reason among the proximate causes of
belief, among the ultimate causes it plays, according to science, no part at all. On the naturalistic
hypothesis, the whole premises of knowledge are
clearly due to the blind operation of material causes,
and in the last resort to these alone. On that hypothesis we no more possess free reason than we
possess free will. As all our volitions are the inevitable product of forces which are quite alien to
morality, so all our conclusions are the inevitable
product of forces which are quite alien to reason.

As the casual introduction of conscience, or a 'good will,' into the chain of causes which ends in a 'virtuous action' ought not to suggest any idea of merit, so the casual introduction of a little ratiocination as a stray link in the chain of causes which ends in what we are pleased to describe as a 'demonstrated conclusion,' ought not to be taken as implying that the conclusion is in harmony with fact. Morality and reason are august names, which give an air of respectability to certain actions and certain arguments; but it is quite obvious on examination that, if the naturalistic hypothesis be correct, they are but unconscious tools in the hands of their unmoral and non-rational antecedents, and that the real responsibility for all they do lies in the distribution of matter and energy which happened to prevail far back in the incalculable past.

These conclusions are, no doubt, as we saw at the beginning of this Essay, embarrassing enough to Morality. But they are absolutely ruinous to Knowledge. For they require us to accept a system as rational, one of whose doctrines is that the system itself is the product of causes which have no tendency to truth rather than falsehood, or to falsehood rather than truth. Forget, if you please, that reason itself is the result, like nerves or muscles, of physical antecedents. Assume (a tolerably violent assumption) that in dealing with her premises she obeys only her own laws. Of what value is this autonomy if those premises are settled for her by purely irrational forces, which she is powerless to control, or even to comprehend? The professor of naturalism rejoicing in the display of his dialectical resources, is like a voyager, pacing at his own pleasure up and down the ship's deck, who should suppose that his movements had some important share in determining his position on the illimitable ocean. And the parallel would be complete if we can conceive such a voyager pointing to the alertness of his step and the vigour of his limbs as auguring well for the successful prosecution of his journey, while assuring you in the very same breath that the vessel, within whose narrow bounds he displays all this meaningless activity, is drifting he knows not whence nor whither, without pilot or captain, at the bidding of shifting winds and undiscovered currents.

Consider the following propositions, selected from the naturalistic creed or deduced from it :—

(i.) My beliefs, in so far as they are the result of reasoning at all, are founded on premises produced in the last resort by the ' collision of atoms.'

(ii.) Atoms, having no prejudices in favour of truth, are as likely to turn out wrong premises as right ones ; nay, more likely, inasmuch as truth is single and error manifold.

(iii.) My premises, therefore, in the first place, and my conclusions in the second, are certainly untrustworthy, and probably false. Their falsity, moreover, is of a kind which cannot be remedied ; since any attempt to correct it must start from

premises not suffering under the same defect. But
no such premises exist.

(iv.) Therefore, again, my opinion about the
original causes which produced my premises, as it
is an inference from them, partakes of their weakness; so that I cannot either securely doubt my
own certainties or be certain about my own doubts.

This is scepticism indeed; scepticism which is
forced by its own inner nature to be sceptical even
about itself; which neither kills belief nor lets it
live. But it may perhaps be suggested in reply to
this argument, that whatever force it may have
against the old-fashioned naturalism, its edge is
blunted when turned against the evolutionary agnosticism of more recent growth; since the latter
establishes the existence of a machinery which, irrational though it be, does really tend gradually, and
in the long run, to produce true opinions rather
than false. That machinery is, I need not say, Selection, and the other forces (if other forces there be)
which bring the ' organism ' into more and more
perfect harmony with its ' environment.' Some harmony is necessary—so runs the argument—in order
that any form of life may be possible; and as life develops, the harmony necessarily becomes more and
more complete. But since there is no more important form in which this harmony can show itself than
truth of belief, which is, indeed, only another name
for the perfect correspondence between belief and
fact, Nature, herein acting as a kind of cosmic In-

quisition, will repress by judicious persecution any lapses from the standard of naturalistic orthodoxy. Sound doctrine will be fostered; error will be discouraged or destroyed; until at last, by methods which are neither rational themselves nor of rational origin, the cause of reason will be fully vindicated.

Arguments like these are, however, quite insufficient to justify the conclusion which is drawn from them. In the first place, they take no account of any causes which were in operation before life appeared upon the planet. Until there occurred the unexplained leap from the Inorganic to the Organic, Selection, of course, had no place among the evolutionary processes; while even after that date it was, from the nature of the case, only concerned to foster and perpetuate those chance-borne beliefs which minister to the continuance of the species. But what an utterly inadequate basis for speculation is here! We are to suppose that powers which were evolved in primitive man and his animal progenitors in order that they might kill with success and marry in security, are on that account fitted to explore the secrets of the universe. We are to suppose that the fundamental beliefs on which these powers of reasoning are to be exercised reflect with sufficient precision remote aspects of reality, though they were produced in the main by physiological processes which date from a stage of development when the only curiosities which had to be satisfied were those of fear and those of hunger. To say that instruments of research constructed solely for uses like these cannot be expected to supply us with a metaphysic or a theology, is to say far too little. They cannot be expected to give us any general view even of the phenomenal world, or to do more than guide us in comparative safety from the satisfaction of one useful appetite to the satisfaction of another. On this theory, therefore, we are again driven back to the same sceptical position in which we found ourselves left by the older forms of the 'positive,' or naturalistic creed. On this theory, as on the other, reason has to recognise that her rights of independent judgment and review are merely titular dignities, carrying with them no effective powers; and that, whatever her pretensions, she is, for the most part, the mere editor and interpreter of the utterances of unreason.

I do not believe that any escape from these perplexities is possible, unless we are prepared to bring to the study of the world the presupposition that it was the work of a rational Being, who made *it* intelligible, and at the same time made *us*, in however feeble a fashion, able to understand it. This conception does not solve all difficulties; far from it.[1] But,

---

[1] According to a once prevalent theory, 'innate ideas' were true because they were implanted in us by God. According to my way of putting it, there must be a God to justify our confidence in (what used to be called) innate ideas. I have given the argument in a form which avoids all discussion as to the nature of the relation between mind and body. Whatever be the mode of describing this which ultimately commends itself to naturalistic psychologists,

at least, it is not on the face of it incoherent. It does
not attempt the impossible task of extracting reason
from unreason; nor does it require us to accept
among scientific conclusions any which effectually
shatter the credibility of scientific premises.

III

Theism, then, whether or not it can in the strict
meaning of the word be described as proved by science, is a principle which science, for a double reason, requires for its own completion. The ordered
system of phenomena asks for a cause; our knowledge of that system is inexplicable unless we assume
for it a rational Author. Under this head, at least,
there should be no 'conflict between science and religion.'

It is true, of course, that if theism smoothes away
some of the difficulties which atheism raises, it is not
on that account without difficulties of its own. We
cannot, for example, form, I will not say any adequate, but even any tolerable, idea of the mode in
which God is related to, and acts on, the world of
phenomena. That He created it, that He sustains
it, we are driven to believe. How He created it,
how He sustains it, is impossible for us to imagine.
But let it be observed that the difficulties which thus
arise are no peculiar heritage of theology, or of a

the reasoning in the text holds good. *Cf.* the purely sceptical
presentation of the argument contained in *Philosophic Doubt*,
chap. xiii.

science which accepts among its presuppositions the central truth which theology teaches. Naturalism itself has to face them in a yet more embarrassing form. For they meet us not only in connection with the doctrine of God, but in connection with the doctrine of man. Not Divinity alone intervenes in the world of things. Each living soul, in its measure and degree, does the same. Each living soul which acts on its surroundings raises questions analogous to, and in some ways more perplexing than, those suggested by the action of a God immanent in a universe of phenomena.

Of course I am aware that, in thus speaking of the connection between man and his material surroundings, I am assuming the truth of a theory which some men of science (in this, however, travelling a little beyond their province) would most energetically deny. But their denial really only serves to emphasise the extreme difficulty of the problem raised by the relation of the Self to phenomena. So hardly pressed are they by these difficulties that, in order to evade them, they attempt an impossible act of suicide; and because the Self refuses to figure as a phenomenon among phenomena, or complacently to fit in to a purely scientific view of the world, they set about the hopeless task of suppressing it altogether. Enough has already been said on this point to permit me to pass it by. I will, therefore, only observe that those who ask us to reject the conviction entertained by each one of us, that he does actually and effectually intervene in the material world, may have many grounds of objection to theology, but should certainly not include among them the reproach that it asks us to believe the incredible.

But, in truth, without going into the metaphysics of the Self, our previous discussions [1] contain ample

[1] Cf. *ante*, Part II., Chaps. I. and II.   It may be worth while reminding the reader of one set of difficulties to which I have made little reference in the text.   Every theory of the relation between Will, or, more strictly, the Willing Self and Matter, must come under one of two heads :—(1) Either Will acts on Matter, or (2) it does not.   If it does act on Matter, it must be either as Free Will or as Determined Will.   If it is as Free Will, it upsets the uniformity of Nature, and our most fundamental scientific conceptions must be recast.   If it is as Determined Will, that is to say, if volition be interpolated as a necessary link between one set of material movements and another, then, indeed, it leaves the uniformity of Nature untouched; but it violates mechanical principles.   According to the mechanical view of the world, the condition of any material system at one moment is absolutely determined by its condition at the preceding moment.   In a world so conceived there is no room for the interpolation even of Determined Will among the causes of material change.   It is mere surplusage.

(2.) If the Will does not act on Matter, then we must suppose either that volition belongs to a psychic series running in a parallel stream to the physiological changes of the brain, though neither influenced by it nor influencing it—which is, of course, the ancient theory of pre-established harmony; or else we must suppose that it is a kind of superfluous consequence of certain physiological changes, produced presumably without the exhaustion of any form of energy, and having no effect whatever, either upon the material world or, I suppose, upon other psychic conditions.   This reduces us to automata, and automata of a kind very difficult to find proper accommodation for in a world scientifically conceived.

None of these alternatives seem very attractive, but one of them would seem to be inevitable.

material for showing how impenetrable are the mists
which obscure the relation of mind to matter, of
things to the perception of things. Neither can be
eliminated from our system. Both must perforce
form elements in every adequate representation of
reality. Yet the philosophic artist has still to arise
who shall combine the two into a single picture,
without doing serious violence to essential features,
either of the one or the other. I am myself, indeed,
disposed to doubt whether any concession made by
the 'subjective' to the 'objective,' or by the 'objective' to the 'subjective,' short of the total destruction of one or the other, will avail to produce
a harmonious scheme. And certainly no discord
could be so barren, so unsatisfying, so practically
impossible, as a harmony attained at such a cost.
We must acquiesce, then, in the existence of an unsolved difficulty. But it is a difficulty which meets
us, in an even more intractable form, when we strive
to realise the nature of our own relations to the little
world in which we move, than when we are dealing
with a like problem in respect to the Divine Spirit,
Who is the Ground of all being and the Source of
all change.

IV

But though there should thus be no conflict
between theology and science, either as to the existence of God or as to the possibility of His acting
on phenomena, it by no means follows that the idea

of God which is suggested by science is compatible with the idea of God which is developed by theology. Identical, of course, they need not be. Theology would be unnecessary if all we are capable of learning about God could be inferred from a study of Nature. Compatible, however, they seemingly must be, if science and religion are to be at one.

And yet I know not whether those who are most persuaded that the claims of these two powers are irreconcilable rest their case willingly upon the most striking incongruity between them which can be produced—I mean the existence of misery and the triumphs of wrong. Yet no one is, or, indeed, could be, blind to the difficulty which thence arises. From the world as presented to us by science we might conjecture a God of power and a God of reason; but we never could infer a God who was wholly loving and wholly just. So that what religion proclaims aloud to be His most essential attributes are precisely those respecting which the oracles of science are doubtful or are dumb.

One reason, I suppose, why this insistent thought does not, so far as my observation goes, supply a favourite weapon of controversial attack, is that ethics is obviously as much interested in the moral attributes of God as theology can ever be (a point to which I shall presently return). But another reason, no doubt, may be found in the fact that the difficulty is one which has been profoundly realised by religious minds ages before organised science can

be said to have existed ; while, on the other hand,
the growth of scientific knowledge has neither increased nor diminished the burden of it by a feather-
weight. The question, therefore, seems, though not,
I think, quite correctly, to be one which is wholly,
as it were, within the frontiers of theology, and
which theologians may, therefore, be left to deal
with as best they may, undisturbed by any arguments supplied by science. If this be not in theory
strictly true, it is in practice but little wide of the
mark. The facts which raise the problem in its
acutest form belong, indeed, to that portion of the
experience of life which is the common property of
science and theology ; but theology is much more
deeply concerned in them than science can ever be,
and has long faced the unsolved problem which they
present. The weight which it has thus borne for
all these centuries is not likely now to crush it; and,
paradoxical though it seems, it is yet surely true,
that what is a theological stumbling-block may also
be a religious aid ; and that it is in part the thought
of 'all creation groaning and travailing in pain together, waiting for redemption,' which creates in
man the deepest need for faith in the love of God.

v

I conceive, then, that those who talk of the 'conflict between science and religion ' do not, as a rule,
refer to the difficulty presented by the existence of

Evil. Where, then, in their opinion, is the point of irreconcilable difference to be found? It will, I suppose, at once be replied, in Miracles. But though the answer has in it a measure of truth, though, without doubt, it is possible to approach the real kernel of the problem from the side of miracles, I confess this seems to me to be in fact but seldom accomplished; while the very term is more suggestive of controversy, wearisome, unprofitable, and unending, than any other in the language, Free Will alone being excepted. Into this Serbonian bog I scarcely dare ask the reader to follow me, though the adventure must, I am afraid, be undertaken if the purpose of this chapter is to be accomplished.

In the first place, then, it seems to me unfortunate that the principle of the Uniformity of Nature should so often be dragged into a controversy with which its connection is so dubious and obscure. For what do we mean by saying that Nature is uniform? We may mean, perhaps we ought to mean, that (leaving Free Will out of account) the condition of the world at one moment is so connected with its condition at the next, that if we could imagine it brought twice into exactly the same position, its subsequent history would in each case be exactly the same. Now no one, I suppose, imagines that uniformity in this sense has any quarrel with miracles. If a miracle is a wonder wrought by God to meet the needs arising out of the special circumstances of a particular moment, then, supposing the circumstances were to recur, as they would if the world were twice to pass through the same phase, the miracle, we cannot doubt, would recur also. It is not possible to suppose that the uniformity of Nature thus broadly interpreted would be marred by Him on Whom Nature depends, and Who is immanent in all its changes.

But it will be replied that the uniformity with which miracles are thus said to be consistent carries with it no important consequences whatever. Its truth or untruth is a matter of equal indifference to the practical man, the man of science, and the philosopher. It asserts in reality (it may be said) no more than this, that if history once began repeating itself, it would go on doing so, like a recurring decimal. But as history in fact never does exactly repeat itself, as the universe never is twice over precisely in the same condition, we should no more be able to judge the future from the past, or to detect the operation of particular laws of Nature in a world where only this kind of theoretic uniformity prevailed, than we should under the misrule of chaos and blind chance.

There is force in these observations, which are, however, much more embarrassing to the philosophy of science than to that of theology. Without doubt all experimental inference, as well as the ordinary conduct of life, depends on supplementing this general view of the uniformity of Nature with certain working hypotheses which are not, though

they always ought to be, most carefully distinguished from it. One of these is, that Nature is
not merely uniform as a whole, but is made up of a
bundle of smaller uniformities; or, in other words,
that there is a determinate relation, not only between the successive phases of the whole universe,
but between successive phases of certain fragments
of it; which successive phases we commonly describe as 'causes' and 'effects.' Another of these
working hypotheses is, that though the universe as
a whole never repeats itself, these isolated fragments
of it do. And a third is, that we have means at our
disposal whereby these fragments can be accurately
divided off from the rest of Nature, and confidently
recognised when they recur. Now I doubt whether
any one of these three presuppositions—which, be it
noted, lie at the very root of the collection of empirical maxims which we dignify with the name of
inductive logic—can, from the point of view of philosophy, be regarded as more than an approximation.
It is hard to believe that the concrete Whole of
things can be thus cut up into independent portions.
It is still harder to believe that any such portion is
ever repeated absolutely unaltered; since its character must surely in part depend upon its relation
to all the other portions, which (by hypothesis) are
not repeated with it. And it is quite impossible to
believe that inductive logic has succeeded by any
of its methods in providing a sure criterion for determining, when any such portion is apparently re-

peated, whether all the elements, and not more than all, are again present which on previous occasions did really constitute it a case of 'cause' and 'effect.'[1]

If this seems paradoxical, it is chiefly because we habitually use phraseology which, strictly interpreted, seems to imply that a 'law of Nature,' as it is called, is a sort of self-subsisting entity, to whose charge is confided some department in the world of phenomena, over which it rules with undisputed sway. Of course this is not so. In the world of phenomena, Reality is exhausted by what is and what happens. Beyond this there is nothing. These 'laws' are merely abstractions devised by us for our own guidance through the complexities of fact. They possess neither independent powers nor actual existence. And if we would use language with perfect accuracy, we ought, it would seem, either to say that the same cause would always be followed by precisely the same effect, if it recurred—which it never does; *or* that, in certain regions of Nature, though only in certain regions, we can detect subordinate uniformities of repetition which, though not exact, enable us without sensible insecurity or error to anticipate the future or reconstruct the past.

This hurried glance which I have asked the reader to take into some obscure corners of inductive theory is by no means intended to suggest that

---

[1] See some of these points more fully worked out in *Philosophic Doubt*, Part I., Chap. II.

it is as easy to believe in a miracle as not; or even that on other grounds, presently to be referred to, miracles ought not to be regarded as incredible. But it does show, in my judgment, that no profit can yet be extracted from controversies as to the precise relation in which they stand to the Order of the world. Those engaged in these controversies have not uncommonly committed a double error. They have, in the first place, chosen to assume that we have a perfectly clear and generally accepted theory as to what is meant by the Uniformity of Nature, as to what is meant by particular Laws of Nature, as to the relation in which the particular Laws stand to the general Uniformity, and as to the kind of proof by which each is to be established. And, having committed this philosophic error, they proceed to add to it the historical error of crediting primitive theology with a knowledge of this theory, and with a desire to improve upon it. They seem to suppose that apostles and prophets were in the habit of looking at the natural world in its ordinary course, with the eyes of an eighteenth-century deist, as if it were a bundle of uniformities which, once set going, went on for ever automatically repeating themselves; and that their message to mankind consisted in announcing the existence of another, or supernatural world, which occasionally upset one or two of these natural uniformities by means of a miracle. No such theory can be extracted from their writings, and no such theory should be read into them; and this not merely because such an attribution is unhistorical, nor yet because there is any ground for doubting the interaction of the 'spiritual' and the 'natural'; but because this account of the 'natural' itself is one which, if interpreted strictly, seems open to grave philosophical objection, and is certainly deficient in philosophic proof.

The real difficulties connected with theological miracles lie elsewhere. Two qualities seem to be of their essence: they must be wonders, and they must be wonders due to the special action of Divine power; and each of these qualities raises a special problem of its own. That raised by the first is the question of evidence. What amount of evidence, if any, is sufficient to render a miracle credible? And on this, which is apart from the main track of my argument, I may perhaps content myself with pointing out, that if by evidence is meant, as it usually is, historical testimony, this is not a fixed quantity, the same for every reasonable man, no matter what may be his other opinions. It varies, and must necessarily vary, with the general views, the 'psychological climate,' which he brings to its consideration. It is possible to get twelve plain men to agree on the evidence which requires them to announce from the jury box a verdict of guilty or not guilty, because they start with a common stock of presuppositions, in the light of which the evidence submitted to them may, without preliminary discussion, be interpreted. But

when, as in the case of theological miracles, there is
no such common stock, any agreement on a verdict
can scarcely be looked for.   One of the jury may
hold the naturalistic view of the world.   To him, of
course, the occurrence of a miracle involves the
abandonment of the whole philosophy in terms of
which he is accustomed to interpret the universe.
Argument, custom, prejudice, authority—every con-
viction-making machine, rational and non-rational,
by which his scheme of belief has been fashioned—
conspire to make this vast intellectual revolution
difficult.   And we need not be surprised that even
the most excellent evidence for a few isolated inci-
dents is quite insufficient to effect his conversion;
nor that he occasionally shows a disposition to go
very extraordinary lengths in contriving historical
or critical theories for the purpose of explaining
such evidence away.

Another may believe in 'verbal inspiration.'   To
him, the discussion of evidence in the ordinary sense
is quite superfluous.   Every miracle, whatever its
character, whatever the circumstances in which it
occurred, whatever its relation, whether essential
or accidental, to the general scheme of religion, is
to be accepted with equal confidence, provided it
be narrated in the works of inspired authors.   It is
written: it is therefore true.   And in the light of
this presupposition alone must the results of any
merely critical or historical discussion be finally
judged.

A third of our supposed jurymen may reject both naturalism and verbal inspiration. He may appraise the evidence alleged in favour of ' Wonders due to the special action of Divine power' by the light of an altogether different theory of the world and of God's action therein. He may consider religion to be as necessary an element in any adequate scheme of belief as science itself. Every event, therefore, whether wonderful or not, a belief in whose occurrence is involved in that religion, every event by whose disproof the religion would be seriously impoverished or altogether destroyed, has behind it the whole combined strength of the system to which it belongs. It is not, indeed, believed independently of external evidence, any more than the most ordinary occurrences in history are believed independently of external evidence. But it does not require, as some people appear to suppose, the impossible accumulation of proof on proof, of testimony on testimony, before the presumption against it can be neutralised. For, in truth, no such presumption may exist at all. Strange as the miracle must seem, and inharmonious when considered as an alien element in an otherwise naturalistic setting, it may assume a character of inevitableness, it may almost proclaim aloud that thus it has occurred, and not otherwise, to those who consider it in its relation, not to the natural world alone, but to the spiritual, and to the needs of man as a citizen of both.

VI

Many other varieties of ' psychological climate '
might be described; but what I have said is, perhaps,
enough to show how absurd it is to expect any
unanimity as to the value of historical evidence until
some better agreement has been arrived at respecting the presuppositions in the light of which alone
such evidence can be estimated. I pass, therefore,
to the difficulty raised by the *second*, and much more
fundamental, attribute of theological miracles to
which I have adverted, namely, that they are due to
the ' special action of God.' But this, be it observed, is, from a religious point of view, no peculiarity of miracles. Few schemes of thought which
have any religious flavour about them at all, wholly
exclude the idea of what I will venture to call the
' preferential exercise of Divine power,' whatever
differences of opinion may exist as to the manner in
which it is manifested. There are those who reject
miracles but who, at least in those fateful moments
when they imaginatively realise their own helpless-
ness, will admit what in a certain literature is called
a ' special Providence.' There are those who reject
the notion of ' special Providence,' but who admit a
sort of Divine superintendence over the general
course of history. There are those, again, who reject in its ordinary shape the idea of Divine superintendence, but who conceive that they can escape

from philosophic reproach by beating out the idea
yet a little thinner, and admitting that there does
exist somewhere a 'Power which makes for righteousness.'

For my own part, I think all these various
opinions are equally open to the only form of attack
which it is worth while to bring against any one of
them. And if we allow, as (supposing religion in
any shape to be true) we must allow, that the 'preferential action' of Divine power is possible, nothing
is gained by qualifying the admission with all those
fanciful limitations and distinctions with which different schools of thought have seen fit to encumber
it. The admission itself, however, is one which, in
whatever shape it may be made, no doubt suggests
questions of great difficulty. How can the Divine
Being Who is the Ground and Source of everything
that is, Who sustains all, directs all, produces all, be
connected more closely with one part of that which
He has created than with another? If every event
be wholly due to Him, how can we say that any single
event, such as a miracle, or any tendency of events,
such as 'making for righteousness,' is specially His?
What room for difference or distinction is there
within the circuit of His universal power? Since
the relation between His creation and Him is
throughout and in every particular one of absolute
dependence, what meaning can we attach to the
metaphor which represents Him as taking part with
one fragment of it, or as hostile to another?

Now it has, in the first place, to be observed that ethics is as much concerned with this difficulty as theology itself.   For if we cannot believe in 'preferential action,' neither can we believe in the moral qualities of which 'preferential action' is the sign; and with the moral qualities of God is bound up the fate of anything which deserves to be called morality at all.   I am not now arguing that ethics cannot exist unsupported by theism.   On this theme I have already said something, and shall have to say more.   My present contention is, that though history may show plenty of examples in heathendom of ethical theory being far in advance of the recognised religion, it is yet impossible to suppose that morality would not ultimately be destroyed by the clearly realised belief in a God Who was either indifferent to good or inclined to evil.

For a universe in which all the power was on the side of the Creator, and all the morality on the side of creation, would be one compared with which the universe of naturalism would shine out a paradise indeed.   Even the poet has not dared to represent Jupiter torturing Prometheus without the dim figure of Avenging Fate waiting silently in the background.   But if the idea of an immoral Creator governing a world peopled with moral, or even with sentient, creatures, is a speculative nightmare, the case is not materially mended by substituting for an immoral Creator an indifferent one.   Once assume a God, and we shall be obliged, sooner or later, to introduce harmony into our system by making obedience to His will coincident with the established rules of conduct. We cannot frame our advice to mankind on the hypothesis that to defy Omnipotence is the beginning of wisdom. But if this process of adjustment is to be done consistently with the maintenance of any eternal and absolute distinction between right and wrong, then must His will be a 'good will,' and we must suppose Him to look with favour upon some parts of this mixed world of good and evil, and with disfavour upon others. If, on the other hand, this distinction seems to us metaphysically impossible; if we cannot do otherwise than regard Him as related in precisely the same way to every portion of His creation, looking with indifferent eyes upon misery and happiness, truth and error, vice and virtue, then our theology must surely drive us, under whatever disguise, to empty ethics of all ethical significance, and to reduce virtue to a colourless acquiescence in the Appointed Order.

Systems there are which do not shrink from these speculative conclusions. But their authors will, I think, be found rather among those who approach the problem of the world from the side of a particular metaphysic, than those who approach it from the side of science. He who sees in God no more than the Infinite Substance of which the world of phenomena constitutes the accidents, or who requires Him for no other purpose than as Infinite Subject, to supply the 'unity' without which the world of phenomena would be an 'unmeaning flux of unconnected particulars,' may naturally suppose Him to be equally related to everything, good or bad, that has been, is, or can be. But I do not think that the man of science is similarly situated; for the doctrine of evolution has in this respect made a change in his position which, curiously enough, brings it closer to that occupied in this matter by theology and ethics than it was in the days when 'special creation' was the fashionable view.

I am not contending, be it observed, that evolution strengthens the evidence for theism. My point rather is, that if the existence of God be assumed, evolution does, to a certain extent, harmonise with that belief in His 'preferential action' which religion and morality alike require us to attribute to Him. For whereas the material and organic world was once supposed to have been created 'all of a piece,' and to show contrivance on the part of its Author merely by the machine-like adjustment of its parts, so now science has adopted an idea which has always been an essential part of the Christian view of the Divine economy, has given to that idea an undreamed-of extension, has applied it to the whole universe of phenomena, organic and inorganic, and has returned it again to theology enriched, strengthened, and developed. Can we, then, think of evolution in a God-created world without attributing to its Author the notion of purpose slowly worked out; the striving towards something which is not, but which gradually becomes, and in the fulness of time will be? Surely not. But, if not, can it be denied that evolution—the evolution, I mean, which takes place in time,·the natural evolution of science, as distinguished from the dialectical evolution of metaphysics—does involve something in the nature of that 'preferential action' which it is so difficult to understand, yet so impossible to abandon?

CHAPTER IV

SUGGESTIONS TOWARDS A PROVISIONAL UNIFICATION

I

BUT if I confined myself to saying that the belief
in a God who is not merely 'substance,' or 'subject,' but is, in Biblical language, 'a living God,' affords no ground of quarrel between theology and
science, I should much understate my thought. I
hold, on the contrary, that some such presupposition is not only tolerated, but is actually required,
by science; that if it be accepted in the case of
science, it can hardly be refused in the case of
ethics, æsthetics, or theology ; and that if it be thus
accepted as a general principle, applicable to the
whole circuit of belief, it will be found to provide
us with a working solution of some, at least, of the
difficulties with which naturalism is incompetent to
deal.

For what was it that lay at the bottom of those
difficulties? Speaking broadly, it may be described
as the perpetual collision, the ineffaceable incongruity, between the origin of our beliefs, in so far
as these can be revealed to us by science, and the
beliefs themselves. This it was that, as I showed

in the first part of this Essay, touched with the frost of scepticism our ideals of conduct and our ideals of beauty. This it was that, as I showed in the Second Part, cut down scientific philosophy to the root. And all the later discussions with which I have occupied the attention of the reader serve but to emphasise afresh the inextricable confusion which the naturalistic hypothesis introduces into every department of practice and of speculation, by refusing to allow us to penetrate beyond the phenomenal causes by which, in the order of Nature, our beliefs are produced.

Review each of these departments in turn, and, in the light of the preceding discussion, compare its position in a theological setting with that which it necessarily occupies in a naturalistic one. Let the case of science be taken first, for it is a crucial one. Here, if anywhere, we might suppose ourselves independent of theology. Here, if anywhere, we might expect to be able to acquiesce without embarrassment in the negations of naturalism. But when once we have realised the scientific truth that at the root of every rational process lies an irrational one; that reason, from a scientific point of view, is itself a natural product; and that the whole material on which it works is due to causes, physical, physiological, and social, which it neither creates nor controls, we shall (as I showed just now) be driven in mere self-defence to hold that, behind these non-rational forces, and above them, guiding

them by slow degrees, and, as it were, with difficulty, to a rational issue, stands that Supreme Reason in whom we must thus believe, if we are to believe in anything.

Here, then, we are plunged at once into the
middle of theology. The belief in God, the attribution to Him of reason, and of what I have called
'preferential action' in relation to the world which
He has created, all seem forced upon us by the single assumption that science is not an illusion, and
that, with the rest of its teaching, we must accept
what it has to say to us about itself as a natural
product. At no smaller cost can we reconcile the
origins of science with its pretensions, or relieve
ourselves of the embarrassments in which we are
involved by a naturalistic theory of Nature. But
evidently the admission, if once made, cannot stand
alone. It is impossible to refuse to ethical beliefs
what we have already conceded to scientific beliefs.
For the analogy between them is complete. Both
are natural products. Neither rank among their remoter causes any which share their essence. And
as it is easy to trace back our scientific beliefs to
sources which have about them nothing which is
rational, so it is easy to trace back our ethical beliefs to sources which have about them nothing
which is ethical. Both require us, therefore, to seek
behind these phenomenal sources for some ultimate
ground with which they shall be congruous; and as
we have been moved to postulate a rational God in

the interests of science, so we can scarcely decline
to postulate a moral God in the interests of morality.

But, manifestly, those who have gone thus far
cannot rest here. If we are to assign a 'providen-
tial' origin to the long and complex train of events
which have resulted in the recognition of a moral
law, we must embrace within the same theory those
sentiments and influences, without which a moral
law would tend to become a mere catalogue of commandments, possessed, it may be, of an undisputed
authority, but obtaining on that account but little
obedience. This was the point on which I dwelt at
length in the first portion of this Essay. I then
showed, that if the pedigrees of conscience, of our
ethical ideals, of our capacity for admiration, for
sympathy, for repentance, for righteous indignation,
were finally to lose themselves among the accidental
variations on which Selection does its work, it was
inconceivable that they should retain their virtue
when once the creed of naturalism had thoroughly
penetrated and discoloured every mood of thought
and belief. But if, deserting naturalism, we regard
the evolutionary process issuing in these ethical results as an instrument for carrying out a Divine
purpose, the natural history of the higher sentiments
is seen under a wholly different light. They may
be due, doubtless they are in fact due, to the same
selective mechanism which produces the most cruel
and the most disgusting of Nature's contrivances for

protecting the species of some loathsome parasite. Between the two cases science cannot, and naturalism will not, draw any valid distinction. But here theology steps in, and by the conception of design revolutionises our point of view. The most unlovely germ of instinct or of appetite to which we trace back the origin of all that is most noble and of good report, no longer throws discredit upon its developed offshoots. Rather is it consecrated by them. For if, in the region of Causation, it is wholly by the earlier stages that the later are determined, in the region of Design it is only through the later stages that the earlier can be understood.

But if these be the consequences which flow from substituting a theological for a naturalistic interpretation of science, of ethics, and of ethical sentiments, what changes will the same process effect in our conception of æsthetics? Naturalism, as we saw, destroys the possibility of objective beauty—of beauty as a real, persistent quality of objects; and leaves nothing but feelings of beauty on the one side, and on the other a miscellaneous assortment of objects, called beautiful in their moments of favour, by which, through the chance operation of obscure associations, at some period, and in some persons, these feelings of beauty are aroused. A conclusion of this kind no doubt leaves us chilled and depressed spectators of our own æsthetic enthusiasms. And it may be that to put the scientific theory in a theological setting, instead of in a naturalistic one, will not wholly remove the unsatisfactory effect which the theory itself may leave upon the mind. And yet it surely does something. If we cannot say that Beauty is in any particular case an 'objective' fact, in the sense in which science requires us to believe that 'mass,' for example, and 'configuration,' are 'objective' facts, we are not precluded on that account from referring our feeling of it to God, nor from supposing that in the thrill of some deep emotion we have for an instant caught a far-off reflection of Divine beauty. This is, indeed, my faith; and in it the differences of taste which divide mankind lose all their harshness. For we may liken ourselves to the members of some endless procession winding along the borders of a sunlit lake. Towards each individual there will shine along its surface a moving lane of splendour, where the ripples catch and deflect the light in his direction; while on either hand the waters, which to his neighbour's eyes are brilliant in the sun, for him lie dull and undistinguished. So may all possess a like enjoyment of loveliness. So do all owe it to one unchanging Source. And if there be an endless variety in the immediate objects from which we severally derive it, I know not, after all, that this should furnish any matter for regret.

II

And, lastly, we come to theology, denied by naturalism to be a branch of knowledge at all, but whose truth we have been obliged to assume in order to find a basis for the only knowledge which naturalism allows.

Those who are prepared to admit that, in dealing with the causes of scientific and ethical belief, the theory which offers least difficulty is that which assumes them to have been 'providentially' guided, are not likely to raise objections to a similar theory in the case of religion. For here, at least, might we expect preferential Divine intervention, supposing such intervention were anywhere possible. Much more, then, if it be accepted as actual in other regions of belief. And this is, in fact, the ordinary view of mankind. They have almost always claimed for their beliefs about God that they were due to God. The belief in religion has almost always carried with it, in some shape or other, the belief in Inspiration.

To this rule there is, no doubt, to be found an apparent exception in what is known as *natural* religion—natural religion being defined as the religion to which unassisted reason may attain, in contrast to that which can be reached only by the aid of revelation. But, for my own part, I object altogether to the theory underlying this distinction. I do not believe that, strictly speaking, there is any such thing as 'unassisted reason.' And I am sure that if there be, the conclusions of 'natural religion' are not among its products. The attentive reader does not require to be told that, according to the views here advocated, every idea involved in such a proposition as that 'There is a moral Creator and Ruler of the world' (which I may assume, for purposes of illustration, to constitute the substance of natural religion) is due to a complex of causes, of which human reason was not the most important; and that this natural religion never would have been heard of, much less have been received with approval, had it not been for that traditional religion of which it vainly supposes itself to be independent.

But if this way of considering the matter be accepted; if we are to apply unaltered, in the case of religious beliefs, the procedure already adopted in the case of scientific, ethical, and æsthetic beliefs, and assume for them a Cause harmonious with their essential nature, we must evidently in so doing transcend the common division between 'natural' and 'supernatural.' We cannot consent to see the 'preferential working of Divine power' only in those religious manifestations which refuse to accommodate themselves to our conception (whatever that may be) of the strictly 'natural' order of the world; nor can we deny a Divine origin to those aspects of religious development which natural laws seem competent to explain. The familiar distinction, indeed, between 'natural' and 'supernatural' coincides

neither with that between natural and spiritual, nor
with that between 'preferential action' and 'non-
preferential,' nor with that between 'phenomenal'
and 'noumenal.' It is, perhaps, less important than
is sometimes supposed; and in this particular connection, at all events, is, as it seems to me, merely
irrelevant and confusing—a burden, not an aid, to
religious speculation.

For, whatever difference there may be between
the growth of theological knowledge and of other
knowledge, their resemblances are both numerous
and instructive. In both we note that movement
has been sometimes so rapid as to be revolutionary,
sometimes so slow as to be imperceptible. In both,
that it has been sometimes an advance, sometimes
a retrogression. In both, that it has been sometimes on lines permitting a long, perhaps an indefinite, development, sometimes in directions where farther progress seems barred for ever. In both, that
the higher is, from the point of view of science,
largely produced by the lower. In both, that, from
the point of view of our provisional philosophy, the
lower is only to be explained by the higher. In
both, that the final product counts among its causes
a vast multitude of physiological, psychological,
political, and social antecedents with which it has no
direct rational or spiritual affiliation.

How, then, can we most completely absorb these
facts into our theory of Inspiration? It would, no
doubt, be inaccurate to say that inspiration is that,

seen from its Divine side, which we call discovery
when seen from the human side. But it is not, I
think, inaccurate to say that every addition to knowledge, whether in the individual or the community,
whether scientific, ethical, or theological, is due to a
co-operation between the human soul which assimi-
lates and the Divine power which inspires. Neither
acts, or, as far as we can pronounce upon such matters, could act, in independent isolation. For 'unassisted reason' is, as I have already said, a fiction;
and pure receptivity it is impossible to conceive.
Even the emptiest vessel must limit the quantity
and determine the configuration of any liquid with
which it may be filled.

But because this view involves a use of the term
'inspiration' which, ignoring all minor distinctions,
extends it to every case in which the production of
belief is due to the 'preferential action' of Divine
power, it does not, of course, follow that minor distinctions do not exist. All I wish here to insist on
is, that the sphere of Divine influence in matters of
belief exists as a whole, and may therefore be studied
as a whole; and that, not improbably, to study it as
a whole would prove no unprofitable preliminary to
any examination into the character of its more important parts.

So studied, it becomes evident that Inspiration, if
this use of the word is to be allowed, is limited to no
age, to no country, to no people. It is required by
those who learn not less than by those who teach.

Wherever an approach has been made to truth, wherever any individual soul has assimilated some old discovery, or has forced the secret of a new one, there is its co-operation to be discovered. Its workings are to be traced not merely in the later development of beliefs, but far back among their unhonoured beginnings. Its aid has been granted not merely along the main line of religious progress, but in the side-alleys to which there seems no issue. Are we, for example, to find a full measure of inspiration in the highest utterances of Hebrew prophet or psalmist, and to suppose that the primitive religious conceptions common to the Semitic race had in them no touch of the Divine? Hardly, if we also believe that it was these primitive conceptions which the 'Chosen People' were divinely ordained to purify, to elevate, and to expand until they became fitting elements in a religion adequate to the necessities of a world. Are we, again, to deny any measure of inspiration to the ethico-religious teaching of the great Oriental reformers, because there was that in their general systems of doctrine which prevented, and still prevents, these from merging as a whole in the main stream of religious advance? Hardly, unless we are prepared to admit that men may gather grapes from thorns or figs from thistles. These things assuredly are of God; and whatever be the terms in which we choose to express our faith, let us not give colour to the opinion that His assistance to mankind has been narrowed down to

the sources, however unique, from which we immediately, and consciously, draw our own spiritual
nourishment.

If a preference is shown by any for a more
limited conception of the Divine intervention in
matters of belief, it must, I suppose, be on one of
two grounds. It may, in the first place, arise out
of a natural reluctance to force into the same category the transcendent intuitions of prophet or
apostle and the stammering utterances of earlier
faiths, clouded as these are by human ignorance
and marred by human sin. Things spiritually so far
asunder ought not, it may be thought, by any system of classification, to be brought together. They
belong to separate worlds. They differ not merely
infinitely in degree, but absolutely in kind; and a
risk of serious error must arise if the same term is
loosely and hastily applied to things which, in their
essential nature, lie so far apart.

Now, that there may be, or, rather, plainly are,
many modes in which belief is assisted by Divine
co-operation I have already admitted. That the
word 'inspiration' may, with advantage, be confined to one or more of these I do not desire to
deny. It is a question of theological phraseology,
on which I am not competent to pronounce; and if
I have seized upon the word for the purposes of my
argument, it is with no desire to confound any distinction which ought to be preserved, but because
there is no other term which so pointedly expresses

that Divine element in the formation of beliefs on which it was my business to lay stress. This, if my theory be true, does, after all, exist, howsoever it may be described, to the full extent which I have indicated; and though the beliefs which it assists in producing differ infinitely from one another in their nearness to absolute truth, the fact is not disguised, nor the honour due to the most spiritually perfect utterances in aught imperilled, by recognising in all some marks of Divine intervention.

But, in the second place, it may be objected that inspiration thus broadly conceived is incapable of providing mankind with any satisfactory criterion of religious truth. Since its co-operation can be traced in so much that is imperfect, the mere fact of its co-operation cannot in any particular case be a protection even against gross error. If, therefore, we seek in it not merely a Divinely ordered cause of belief, but also a Divinely ordered ground for believing, there must be some means of marking off those examples of its operation which rightfully command our full intellectual allegiance, from those which are no more than evidences of an influence towards the truth working out its purpose slowly through the ages.

This is beyond dispute. Nothing that I have said about inspiration in general as a source of belief affects in any way the character of certain instances of inspiration as an authority for belief. Nor was it intended to do so; for the problem, or group of problems, which would thus have been raised is altogether beside the main course of my argument. They belong, not to an Introduction to Theology, but to Theology itself. Whether there is an authority in religious matters of a kind altogether without parallel in scientific or ethical matters ; what, if it exists, is its character, and whence come its claims to our obedience, are questions on which theologians have differed, and still differ, and which it is quite beyond my province to decide.   For the subject of · this Essay is the 'foundations of belief,' and, as I have already indicated,[1] the kind of authority contemplated by theologians is never 'fundamental,' in the sense in which that word is here used.   The deliverances of no organisation, of no individual, of no record, can lie at the roots of belief as reason, whatever they may do as cause.   It is always possible to ask whence these claimants to authority derive their credentials, what titles the organisation or the individual possesses to our obedience, whether the records are authentic, and what is their precise import.   And the mere fact that such questions may be put, and that they can neither be thrust aside as irrelevant nor be answered without elaborate critical and historical discussion, shows clearly enough that we have no business with them here.

[1] See *ante*, chapter on Authority and Reason.

III

But although it is evidently beyond the scope
)f this work to enter upon even an elementary
liscussion of theological method, it seems right
hat I should endeavour, in strict continuation of
he argument of this chapter, to say something on
he source from which, according to Christianity,
.ny religious authority whatever must ultimately
lerive its jurisdiction. What I have so far tried to
:stablish is this—that the great body of our beliefs,
cientific, ethical, theological, form a more coherent
.nd satisfactory whole if we consider them in a
Theistic setting, than if we consider them in a Nat-
iralistic one. The further question, therefore,
nevitably suggests itself, Whether we can carry the
)rocess a step further, and say that they are more
:oherent and satisfactory if considered in a Chris-
ian setting than in a merely Theistic one?

The answer often given is in the negative. It is
ilways assumed by those who do not accept the
loctrine of the Incarnation, and it is not uncommonly
:onceded by those who do, that it constitutes an ad-
litional burden upon faith, a new stumbling-block
o reason. And many who are prepared to accom-
nodate their beliefs to the requirements of (so-called)
Natural Religion,' shrink from the difficulties and
)erplexities in which this central mystery of Revealed
Religion threatens to involve them. But what are

these difficulties? . Clearly they are not scientific. We are here altogether outside the region where scientific ideas possess any worth, or scientific categories claim any authority. It may be a realm of shadows, of empty dreams, and vain speculations. But whether it be this, or whether it be the abiding-place of the highest Reality, it evidently must be explored by methods other than those provided for us by the accepted canons of experimental research. Even when we are endeavouring to comprehend the relation of our own finite personalities to the material environment with which they are so intimately connected, we find, as we have seen, that all familiar modes of explanation break down and become meaningless. Yet we certainly exist, and presumably we have bodies. If, then, we cannot devise formulæ which shall elucidate the familiar mystery of our daily existence, we need neither be surprised nor embarrassed if the unique mystery of the Christian faith refuses to lend itself to inductive treatment.

But though the very uniqueness of the doctrine places it beyond the ordinary range of scientific criticism, the same cannot be said for the historical evidence on which, in part at least, it rests. Here, it will perhaps be urged, we are on solid and familiar ground. We have only got to ignore the arbitrary distinction between 'sacred' and 'secular,' and apply the well-understood methods of historic criticism to a particular set of ancient records, in order to extract from them all that is necessary to satisfy our curiosity. If they break down under cross-examination, we need trouble ourselves no further about the metaphysical dogmas to which they point. No immunity or privilege claimed for the subject-matter of belief can extend to the merely human evidence adduced in its support; and as in the last resort the historical element in Christianity does evidently rest on human testimony, nothing can be simpler than to subject this to the usual scientific tests, and accept with what equanimity we may any results which they elicit.

But, in truth, the question is not so simple as those who make use of arguments like these would have us suppose. 'Historic method' has its limitations. It is self-sufficient only within an area which is, indeed, tolerably extensive, but which does not embrace the universe. For, without taking any very deep plunge into the philosophy of historical criticism, we may easily perceive that our judgment as to the truth or falsity of any particular historic statement depends, partly on our estimate of the writer's trustworthiness, partly on our estimate of his means of information, partly on our estimate of the intrinsic probability of the facts to which he testifies. But these things are not 'independent variables,' to be measured separately before their results are balanced and summed up. On the contrary, it is manifest that, in many cases, our opinion on the trustworthiness and competence of the witnesses is modified by our opinion as to the inherent likelihood of what they tell us; and that our opinion as to the inherent likelihood of what they tell us may depend on considerations with respect to which no historical method is able to give us any conclusive information. In most cases, no doubt, these questions of antecedent probability have to be themselves decided solely, or mainly, on historic grounds, and, failing anything more scientific, by a kind of historic instinct. But other cases there are, though they be rare, to whose consideration we must bring larger principles, drawn from a wider theory of the world; and among these should be counted as first, both in speculative interest and in ethical importance, the early records of Christianity.

That this has been done, and, from their own point of view, quite rightly done, by various destructive schools of New Testament criticism, everyone is aware. Starting from a philosophy which forbade them to accept much of the substance of the Gospel narrative, they very properly set to work to devise a variety of hypotheses which would account for the fact that the narrative, with all its peculiarities, was nevertheless there. Of these hypotheses there are many, and some of them have occasioned an admirable display of erudite ingenuity, fruitful of instruction from every point of view, and for all time. But it is a great, though common, error to describe these learned efforts as examples of the unbiassed application of historic methods to historic documents. It would be more correct to say that they are endeavours, by the unstinted employment of an elaborate critical apparatus, to force the testimony of existing records into conformity with theories on the truth or falsity of which it is for philosophy, not history, to pronounce. What view I take of the particular philosophy to which these critics make appeal the reader already knows; and our immediate concern is not again to discuss the presuppositions with which other people have approached the consideration of New Testament history, but to arrive at some conclusion about our own.

How, then, ought the general theory of things at which we have arrived to affect our estimate of the antecedent probability of the Christian views of Christ? Or, if such a phrase as 'antecedent probability' be thought to suggest a much greater nicety of calculation than is at all possible in a case like this, in what temper of mind, in what mood of expectation, ought our provisional philosophy to induce us to consider the extant historic evidence for the Christian story? The reply must, I think, depend, as I shall show in a moment, upon the view we take of the ethical import of Christianity; while its ethical import, again, must depend on the degree to which it ministers to our ethical needs.

IV

Now·ethical needs, important though they are, occupy no great space, as a rule, in the works of ethical writers. I do not say this by way of criticism; for I grant that any examination into these needs would have only an indirect bearing on the essential subject-matter of ethical philosophy, since no inquiry into their nature, history, or value would help either to establish the fundamental principles of a moral code or to elaborate its details. But, after all, as I have said before, an assortment of 'categorical imperatives,' however authoritative and complete, supplies but a meagre outfit wherewith to meet the storms and stresses of actual experience. If we are to possess a practical system, which shall not merely tell men what they ought to do, but assist them to do it; still more, if we are to regard the spiritual quality of the soul as possessing an intrinsic value not to be wholly measured by the external actions to which it gives rise, much more than this will be required. It will not only be necessary to claim the assistance of those ethical aspirations and ideals which are not less effectual for their purpose though nothing corresponding to them should exist, but it will also be necessary, if it be possible, to meet those ethical needs which must work more harm than good unless we can sustain the belief that there is somewhere to be found a Reality wherein they can find their satisfaction.

These are facts of moral psychology which, thus broadly stated, nobody, I think, will be disposed to dispute, although the widest differences of opinion may and do prevail as to the character, number, and relative importance of the ethical needs thus called into existence by ethical commands. It is, further, certain, though more difficulty may be felt in admitting it, that these needs can be satisfied in many cases but imperfectly, in some cases not at all, without the aid of theology and of theological sanctions. One commonly recognised ethical need, for example, is for harmony between the interests of the individual and those of the community. In a rude and limited fashion, and for a very narrow circle of ethical commands, this is deliberately provided by the prison and the scaffold, the whole machinery of the criminal law. It is provided, with less deliberation, but with greater delicacy of adjustment, and over a wider area of duty, by the operation of public opinion. But it can be provided, with any approach to theoretical perfection, only by a future life, such as that which is assumed in more than one system of religious belief.

Now the question is at once suggested by cases of this kind whether, and, if so, under what limitations, we can argue from the existence of an ethical need to the reality of the conditions under which alone it would be satisfied. Can we, for example,

argue from the need for some complete correspondence between virtue and felicity, to the reality of
another world than this, where such a correspondence will be completely effected? A great ethical
philosopher has, in substance, asserted that we can.
He held that the reality of the Moral Law implied
the reality of a sphere where it could for ever be
obeyed, under conditions satisfactory to the 'Practical Reason'; and it was thus that he found a place
in his system for Freedom, for Immortality, and for
God. The metaphysical machinery, indeed, by which
Kant endeavoured to secure these results is of a kind
which we cannot employ. But we may well ask
whether somewhat similar inferences are not fitting
portions of the provisional philosophy I am endeavouring to recommend; and, in particular, whether
they do not harmonise with the train of thought we
have been pursuing in the course of this Chapter.
If the reality of scientific and of ethical knowledge
forces us to assume the existence of a rational and
moral Deity, by whose preferential assistance they
have gradually come into existence, must we not
suppose that the Power which has thus produced
in man the knowledge of right and wrong, and
has added to it the faculty of creating ethical ideals,
must have provided some satisfaction for the ethical
needs which the historical development of the spiritual life has gradually called into existence?

Manifestly the argument in this shape is one
which must be used with caution. To reason purely

a priori from our general notions concerning the working of Divine Providence to the reality of particular historic events in time, or to the preva- lence of particular conditions of existence through eternity, would imply a knowledge of Divine mat- ters which we certainly do not possess, and which, our faculties remaining what they are, a revelation trom Heaven could not, I suppose, communicate to us. My contention, at all events, is of a much humbler kind. I confine myself to asking whether, in a universe which, by hypothesis, is under moral governance, there is not a presumption in favour of facts or events which minister, if true, to our highest moral demands? and whether such a presumption, if it exists, is not sufficient, and more than sufficient, to neutralise the counter-presumption which has uncritically governed so much of the criticism di- rected in recent times against the historic claims of Christianity? For my own part, I cannot doubt that both these questions should be answered in the affirmative ; and if the reader will consider the variety of ways by which Christianity is, in fact, fitted effectually to minister to our ethical needs, I find it hard to believe that he will arrive at any dif- ferent conclusion.

V

I need not say that no complete treatment of this question is contemplated here. Any adequate survey of the relation in which Christianity stands to the moral needs of man would lead us into the very heart of theology, and would require us to consider topics altogether unsuited to these controversial pages. Yet it may, perhaps, be found possible to illustrate my meaning without penetrating far into territories more properly occupied by theologians; while, at the same time, the examples of which I shall make use may serve to show that, among the needs ministered to by Christianity, are some which increase rather than diminish with the growth of knowledge and the progress of science; and that this Religion is therefore no mere reform, appropriate only to a vanished epoch in the history of culture and civilisation, but a development of theism now more necessary to us than ever.

I am aware, of course, that this may seem in strange discord with opinions very commonly held. There are many persons who suppose that; in addition to any metaphysical or scientific objections to Christian doctrines, there has arisen a legitimate feeling of intellectual repulsion to them, directly due to our more extended perception of the magnitude and complexity of the material world. The discovery of Copernicus, it has been said, is the death-blow to Christianity: in other words, the recognition by the human race of the insignificant part which they and their planet play in the cosmic drama renders the Incarnation, as it were, intrinsically incredible. This is not a question of logic, or science, or history. No criticism of documents, no haggling over 'natural' or 'supernatural,' either creates the difficulty or is able to solve it. For it arises out of what I may almost call an æsthetic sense of disproportion. 'What is man, that Thou art mindful of him; and the son of man, that Thou visitest him?' is a question charged by science with a weight of meaning far beyond what it could have borne for the poet whose lips first uttered it. And those whose studies bring perpetually to their remembrance the immensity of this material world, who know how brief and how utterly imperceptible is the impress made by organic life in general, and by human life in particular, upon the mighty forces which surround them, find it hard to believe that on so small an occasion this petty satellite of no very important sun has been chosen as the theatre of an event so solitary and so stupendous.

Reflection, indeed, shows that those who thus argue have manifestly permitted their thoughts about God to be controlled by a singular theory of His relations to man and to the world, based on an unbalanced consideration of the vastness of Nature. They have conceived Him as moved by the mass of His own works; as lost in spaces of His own creation. Consciously or unconsciously, they have fallen into the absurdity of supposing that He considers His creatures, as it were, with the eyes of a contractor or a politician; that He measures their value according to their physical or intellectual importance; and that He sets store by the number of square miles they inhabit or the foot-pounds of energy they are capable of developing. In truth, the inference they should have drawn is of precisely the opposite kind. The very sense of the place occupied in the material universe by man the intelligent animal, creates in man the moral being a new need for Christianity, which, before science measured out the heavens for us, can hardly be said to have existed. Metaphysically speaking, our opinions on the magnitude and complexity of the natural world should, indeed, have no bearing on our conception of God's relation, either to us or to it. Though we supposed the sun to have been created some six thousand years ago, and to be 'about the size of the Peloponnesus,' yet the fundamental problems concerning time and space, matter and spirit, God and man, would not on that account have to be formally restated. But then, we are not creatures of pure reason; and those who desire the assurance of an intimate and effectual relation with the Divine life, and who look to this for strength and consolation, find that the progress of scientific knowledge makes it more and more difficult to obtain it by the aid of any merely speculative theism. The feeling of trusting dependence which was easy for the primitive tribes, who regarded themselves as their God's peculiar charge, and supposed Him in some special sense to dwell among them, is not easy for us; nor does it tend to become easier. We can no longer share their naïve anthropomorphism. We search out God with eyes grown old in studying Nature, with minds fatigued by centuries of metaphysic, and imaginations glutted with material infinities. It is in vain that we describe Him as immanent in creation, and refuse to reduce Him to an abstraction, be it deistic or be it pantheistic. The overwhelming force and regularity of the great natural movements dull the sharp impression of an ever-present Personality deeply concerned in our spiritual well-being. He is hidden, not revealed, in the multitude of phenomena, and as our knowledge of phenomena increases, He retreats out of all realised connection with us farther and yet farther into the illimitable unknown.

Then it is that, through the aid of Christian doctrine, we are saved from the distorting influences of our own discoveries. The Incarnation throws the whole scheme of things, as we are too easily apt to represent it to ourselves, into a different and far truer proportion. It abruptly changes the whole scale on which we might be disposed to measure the magnitudes of the universe. What we should otherwise think great, we now perceive to be relatively small. What we should otherwise think trifling, we now know to be immeasurably important. And the change is not only morally needed, but is philosophically justified. Speculation by itself should be sufficient to convince us that, in the sight of a righteous God, material grandeur and moral excellencies are incommensurable quantities; and that an infinite accumulation of the one cannot compensate for the smallest diminution of the other. Yet I know not whether, as a theistic speculation, this truth could effectually maintain itself against the brute pressure of external Nature. In the world looked at by the light of simple theism, the evidences of God's material power lie about us on every side, daily added to by science, universal, overwhelming. The evidences of His moral interest have to be anxiously extracted, grain by grain, through the speculative analysis of our moral nature. Mankind, however, are not given to speculative analysis; and if it be desirable that they should be enabled to obtain an imaginative grasp of this great truth; if they need to have brought home to them that, in the sight of God, the stability of the heavens is of less importance than the moral growth of a human spirit, I know not how this end could be more completely attained than by the Christian doctrine of the Incarnation.

A somewhat similar train of thought is suggested

by the progress of one particular branch of scien‑
tific investigation. Mankind can never have been
ignorant of the dependence of mind on body. The
feebleness of infancy, the decay of age, the effects
of sickness, fatigue, and pain, are facts too obvious
and too insistent ever to have passed unnoticed.
But the movement of discovery has prodigiously
emphasised our sense of dependence on matter. We
now know that it is no loose or variable connection
which ties mind to body. There may, indeed, be
neural changes which do not issue in consciousness;
but there is no consciousness, so far as accepted
observations and experiments can tell us, which is
not associated with neural changes. Looked at,
therefore, from the outside, from the point of view
necessarily adopted by the biologist, the psychic
life seems, as it were, but an intermittent phospho‑
rescence accompanying the cerebral changes in
certain highly organised mammals. And science,
through countless channels, with irresistible force
drives home to each one of us the lesson that we are
severally bound over in perpetual servitude to a
body for whose existence and qualities we have no
responsibility whatever.

As the reader is well aware, views like these
will not stand critical examination. Of all creeds,
materialism is the one which, looked at from the
inside—from the point of view of knowledge and
the knowing Self—is least capable of being philo‑
sophically defended, or even coherently stated.

Nevertheless, the burden of the body is not, in practice, to be disposed of by any mere process of critical analysis. From birth to death, without pause or respite, it encumbers us on our path. We can never disentangle ourselves from its meshes, nor divide with it the responsibility for our joint performances. Conscience may tell us that we *ought* to control it, and that we *can*. But science, hinting that, after all, we are but its product and its plaything, receives ominous support from our experiences of mankind. Philosophy may assure us that the account of body and mind given by materialism is neither consistent nor intelligible. Yet body remains the most fundamental and all-pervading fact with which mind has got to deal, the one from which it can least easily shake itself free, the one that most complacently lends itself to every theory destructive of high endeavour.

Now, what is wanted here is not abstract speculation or negative dialectic. These, indeed, may lend us their aid, but they are not very powerful allies in this particular species of warfare. They can assure us, with a well-grounded confidence, that materialism is wrong, but they have (as I think) nothing satisfactory to put in its place, and cannot pretend to any theoretic explanation which shall cover all the facts. What we need, then, is something that shall appeal to men of flesh and blood, struggling with the temptations and discouragements which flesh and blood is heir to : confused and baffled by theories of heredity: sure that the physiological view represents at least one aspect of the truth; not sure how any larger and more consoling truth can be welded on to it; yet swayed towards the materialist side less, it may be, by materialist reasoning than by the inner confirmation which a humiliating experience gives them of their own subjection to the body.

What support does the belief in a Deity ineffably remote from all human conditions bring to men thus hesitating whether they are to count themselves as beasts that perish, or among the Sons of God? What bridge can be found to span the immeasurable gulf which separates Infinite Spirit from creatures who seem little more than physiological accidents? What faith is there, other than the Incarnation, which will enable us to realise that, however far apart, they are not hopelessly divided? The intellectual perplexities which haunt us in that dim region where mind and matter meet may not be thus allayed. But they who think with me that, though it is a hard thing for us to believe that we are made in the likeness of God, it is yet a very necessary thing, will not be anxious to deny that an effectual trust in this great truth, a full satisfaction of this ethical need, are among the natural fruits of a Christian theory of the world.

One more topic there is, of the same family as those with which we have just been dealing, to which, before concluding, I must briefly direct the reader's attention. I have already said something about what is known as the 'problem of evil,' and the immemorial difficulty which it throws in the way of a completely coherent theory of the world on a religious or moral basis. I do not suggest now that the doctrine of the Incarnation supplies any philosophic solution of this difficulty. I content myself with pointing out that the difficulty is much less oppressive under the Christian than under any simpler form of Theism; and that though it may retain undiminished whatever speculative force it possesses, its moral grip is loosened, and it no longer parches up the springs of spiritual hope or crushes moral aspiration.

For where precisely does the difficulty lie? It lies in the supposition that an all-powerful Deity has chosen out of an infinite, or at least an unknown, number of possibilities to create a world in which pain is a prominent, and apparently an ineradicable, element. His action on this view is, so to speak, gratuitous. He might have done otherwise; He has done thus. He might have created sentient beings capable of nothing but happiness; He has in fact created them prone to misery, and subject by their very constitution and circumstances to extreme possibilities of physical pain and mental affliction. How can One of Whom this can be said excite our love? How can He claim our obedience? How can He be a fitting object of praise, reverence, and worship? So runs the familiar argument, accepted by some as a permanent element in their melancholy philosophy; wrung from others as a cry of anguish under the sudden stroke of bitter experience.

This reasoning is in essence an explication of what is supposed to be involved in the attribute of Omnipotence; and the sting of its conclusion lies in the inferred indifference of God to the sufferings of His creatures. There are, therefore, two points at which it may be assailed. We may argue, in the first place, that in dealing with subjects so far above our reach, it is in general the height of philosophic temerity to squeeze out of every predicate the last significant drop it can apparently be forced to yield; or drive all the arguments it suggests to their extreme logical conclusions. And, in particular, it may be urged that it is erroneous, perhaps even unmeaning, to say that the universality of Omnipotence includes the power to do that which is irrational; and that, without knowing the Whole, we cannot say of any part whether it is rational or not.

These are metaphysical considerations which, so long as they are used critically, and not dogmatically, negatively, not positively, seem to me to have force. But there is a second line of attack, on which it is more my business to insist. I have already pointed out that ethics cannot permanently flourish side by side with a creed which represents God as indifferent to pain and sin; so that, if our provisional philosophy is to include morality within its circuit (and what harmony of knowledge would that be which did not ?), the conclusions which apparently follow from the co-existence of Omnipotence and of Evil are not to be accepted. Yet this speculative reply is, after all, but a fair-weather argument; too abstract easily to move mankind at large, too frail for the support, even of a philosopher, in moments of extremity. Of what use is it to those who, under the stress of sorrow, are permitting themselves to doubt the goodness of God, that such doubts must inevitably tend to wither virtue at the root? No such conclusion will frighten them. They have already almost reached it. Of what worth, they cry, is virtue in a world where sufferings like theirs fall alike on the just and on the unjust? For themselves, they know only that they are solitary and abandoned ; victims of a Power too strong for them to control, too callous for them to soften, too far for them to reach, deaf to supplication, blind to pain. Tell them, with certain theologians, that their misfortunes are explained and justified by an hereditary taint; tell them, with certain philosophers, that, could they understand the world in its completeness, their agony would show itself an element necessary to the harmony of the Whole, and they will think you are mocking them. Whatever be the worth of speculations like these, it is not in the moments when they are most required that they come effectually to our rescue. What is needed is such a living faith in God's relation to Man as shall leave no place for that helpless resentment against the appointed Order so apt to rise within us at the sight of undeserved pain. And this faith is possessed by those who vividly realise the Christian form of Theism. For they worship One who is no remote contriver of a universe to whose ills He is indifferent. If they suffer, did He not on their account suffer also? If suffering falls not always on the most guilty, was He not innocent? Shall they cry aloud that the world is ill-designed for their convenience, when He for their sakes subjected Himself to its conditions? It is true that beliefs like these do not in any narrow sense resolve our doubts nor provide us with explanations. But they give us something better than many explanations. For they minister, or rather the Reality behind them ministers, to one of our deepest ethical needs: to a need which, far from showing signs of diminution, seems to grow with the growth of civilisation, and to touch us ever more keenly as the hardness of an earlier time dissolves away.

Here, then, on the threshold of Christian Theology, I bring my task to a conclusion. I feel, on looking back over the completed work, even more strongly than I felt during its progress, how hard was the task I have undertaken, and how far beyond my powers successfully to accomplish. For I have aimed at nothing less than to show, within a reasonable compass and in a manner to be understood by all, how, in face of the complex tendencies which sway this strange age of ours, we may best draw together our beliefs into a comprehensive unity which shall possess at least a relative and provisional stability. In so bold an attempt I may well have failed. Yet, whatever be the particular weaknesses and defects which mar the success of my endeavours, three or four broad principles emerge from the discussion, the essential importance of which I find it impossible to doubt, whatever errors I may have made in their application.

1. It seems beyond question that any system which, with our present knowledge and, it may be, our existing faculties, we are able to construct must suffer from obscurities, from defects of proof, and from incoherences. Narrow it down to bare science—and no one has seriously proposed to reduce it further—you will still find all three, and in plenty.

2. No unification of belief of the slightest theoretical value can take place on a purely scientific basis — on a basis, I mean, of induction from particular experiences, whether 'external' or 'internal.'

3. No philosophy or theory of knowledge (epistemology) can be satisfactory which does not find room within it for the quite obvious, but not sufficiently considered fact that, so far as empirical science can tell us anything about the matter, most

of the proximate causes of belief, and all its ultimate *}* causes, are non-rational in their character.

4. No unification of beliefs can be practically adequate which does not include ethical beliefs as well as scientific ones; nor which refuses to count among ethical beliefs, not merely those which have immediate reference to moral commands, but those also which make possible moral sentiments, ideals and aspirations, and which satisfy our ethical needs. Any system which, when worked out to its legitimate issues, fails to effect this object can afford no permanent habitation for the spirit of man.

To enforce, illustrate, and apply these principles has been the main object of the preceding pages. How far I have succeeded in showing that the least incomplete unification open to us must include the fundamental elements of Theology, and of Christian Theology, I leave it for others to determine; repeating only the conviction, more than once expressed in the body of this Essay, that it is not explanations which survive, but the things which are explained; not theories, but the things about which we theorise; and that, therefore, no failure on my part can imperil the great truths, be they religious, ethical, or scientific, whose interdependence I have endeavoured to establish.

APPENDIX

BELIEFS, FORMULAS, AND REALITIES

I

IT may be useful to add to the preceding argument on the foundations of belief some observations
on the formal side of their historical development,
which will not only serve, I hope, to make clearer
the general scheme here advocated, but may help to
solve certain difficulties which have sometimes been
felt in the interpretation of theological and ecclesiastical history.

Assuming, as we do, that Knowledge exists, we
can hardly do otherwise than make the further assumption that it has grown and must yet further
grow. In what manner, then, has that growth been
accomplished? What are the external signs of its
successive stages, the marks of its gradual evolution?
One, at least, must strike all who have surveyed,
even with a careless eye, the course of human speculation—I mean the recurring process by which the
explanations or explanatory formulas in terms of

which mankind endeavour to comprehend the universe are formed, are shattered, and then in some new shape are formed again. It is not, as we sometimes represent it, by the steady addition of tier to tier that the fabric of knowledge uprises from its foundation. It is not by mere accumulation of material, nor even by a plant-like development, that our beliefs grow less inadequate to the truths which they strive to represent. Rather are we like one who is perpetually engaged in altering some ancient dwelling in order to satisfy new-born needs. The ground-plan of it is being perpetually modified. We build here; we pull down there. One part is kept in repair, another part is suffered to decay. And even those portions of the structure which may in themselves appear quite unchanged, stand in such new relations to the rest, and are put to such different uses, that they would scarce be recognised by their original designer.

Yet even this metaphor is inadequate, and perhaps misleading. We shall more accurately conceive the true history of knowledge if we represent it under the similitude of a plastic body whose shape and size are in constant process of alteration through the operation both of external and of internal forces. The internal forces are those of reason. The external forces correspond to those non-rational causes on whose importance I have already dwelt. Each of these agencies may be supposed to act both by way of destruction and of addition. By their joint operation new material is deposited at one point, old material is eroded at another; and the whole mass, whose balance has been thus disturbed, is constantly changing its configuration and settling towards a new position of equilibrium, which it may approach, but can never quite attain.

We must not, however, regard this body of beliefs as being equally mobile in all its parts. Certain elements in it have the power of conferring on the whole something in the nature of a definite structure. These are known as 'theories,' 'hypotheses,' 'generalisations,' and 'explanatory formulas' in general. They represent beliefs by which other beliefs are co-ordinated. They supply the framework in which the rest of knowledge is arranged. Their right construction is the noblest work of reason ; and without their aid reason, if it could be exercised at all, would itself be driven from particular to particular in helpless bewilderment.

Now the action and reaction between these formulas and their contents is the most salient, and in some respects the most interesting, fact in the history of thought. Called into being, for the most part, to justify, or at least to organise, pre-existing beliefs, they can seldom perform their office without modifying part, at least, of their material. While they give precision to what would otherwise be indeterminate, and a relative permanence to what would otherwise be in a state of flux, they do so at the cost of some occasional violence to the beliefs with which they deal. Some of these are distorted to make them fit into their predestined niches. Others, more refractory, are destroyed or ignored. Even in science, where the beliefs that have to be accounted for have often a native vigour born of the imperious needs of sense-perception, we are sometimes disposed to see, not so much what is visible, as what theory informs us ought to be seen. While in the region of æsthetic (to take another example), where belief is of feebler growth, the inclination to admire what squares with some current theory of the beautiful, rather than with what appeals to any real feeling for beauty, is so common that it has ceased even to amuse.

But this reaction of formulas on the beliefs which they co-ordinate or explain is but the first stage in the process we are describing. The next is the change, perhaps even the destruction, of the formula itself by the victorious forces that it has previously held in check. The plastic body of belief, or some portion of it, under the growing stress of external and internal influences, breaks through, it may be with destructive violence, the barriers by which it was at one time controlled. A new theory has to be formed, a new arrangement of knowledge has to be accepted, and under changed conditions the same cycle of not unfruitful changes begins again.

I do not know that any illustration of this familiar process is required, for in truth such examples

are abundant in every department of Knowledge.
As chalk consists of little else but the remains of
dead animalculæ, so the history of thought consists
of little else but an accumulation of abandoned explanations. In that vast cemetery every thrust of the
shovel turns up some bone that once formed part of
a living theory; and the biography of most of these
theories would, I think, confirm the general account
which · I have given of their birth, maturity, and
· decay.

II

Now we may well suppose that under existing
circumstances death is as necessary in the intellectual world as it is in the organic. It may not always
result in progress, but without it, doubtless, progress would be impossible; and if, therefore, the
constant substitution of one explanation for another
could be effected smoothly, and as it were in silence,
without disturbing anything beyond the explanations themselves, it need cause in general neither
anxiety nor regret. But, unfortunately, in the case
of Theology, this is not always the way things happen. There, as elsewhere, theories arise, have their
day, and fall; but there, far more than elsewhere, do
these theories in their fall endanger other interests
than their own. More than one reason may be given
for this difference. To begin with, in Science the
beliefs of sense-perception, which, as I have implied,

are commonly vigorous enough to resist the warp‑
ing effect of theory, even when the latter is in its
full strength, are not imperilled by its decay. They
provide a solid nucleus of unalterable conviction,
which survives uninjured through all the mutations
of intellectual fashion. We do not require the as‑
sistance of hypotheses to sustain our faith in what
we see and hear. Speaking broadly, that faith is
unalterable and self-sufficient.

Theology is less happily situated. There it often
happens that when a theory decays, the beliefs to
which it refers are infected by a contagious weak‑
ness. The explanation and the thing explained are
mutually dependent. They are animated as it were
with a common life, and there is always a danger
lest they should be overtaken by a common de‑
struction.

Consider this difference between Science and
Theology in the light of the following illustration.
The whole instructed world were quite recently
agreed that heat was a form of matter. With equal
unanimity they now hold that it is a mode of motion.
These opinions are not only absolutely inconsistent,
but the change from one to the other is revolution‑
ary, and involves the profoundest modification of
our general views of the material world. Yet no
one's confidence in the existence of some quality in
things by which his sensations of warmth are pro‑
duced is thereby disturbed; and we may hold either
of these theories, or both of them in turn, or no

theory at all, without endangering the stability of our scientific faith.

Compare with this example drawn from physics one of a very different kind drawn from theology. If there be a spiritual experience to which the history of religion bears witness, it is that of Reconciliation with God. If there be an 'objective' cause to which the feeling is confidently referred, it is to be found in the central facts of the Christian story. Now, incommensurable as the subject is with that touched on in the last paragraph, they resemble each other at least in this—that both have been the theme of much speculation, and that the accounts of them which have satisfied one generation, to another have seemed profitless and empty. But there the likeness ends. In the physical case, the feeling of heat and the inward assurance that it is really connected with some quality in the external body from which we suppose ourselves to derive it, survive every changing speculation as to the nature of that quality and the mode of its operation. In the spiritual case, the sense of Reconciliation connected by the Christian conscience with the life and death of Christ seems in many cases to be bound up with the explanations of the mystery which from time to time have been hazarded by theological theorists. And as these explanations have fallen out of favour, the truth to be explained has too often been abandoned also.

This is not the place to press the subject further:

and I have neither the right in these Notes to assume the truth of particular theological doctrines,
nor is it my business to attempt to prove them.   But
this much more I may perhaps be allowed to say by
way of parenthesis.   If the point of view which this
Essay is intended to recommend be accepted, the
precedent set, in the first of the above examples, by
science is the one which ought to be followed by
theology.   No doubt, when a belief is only accepted
as the conclusion of some definite inferential process,
with that process it must stand or fall.   If, for instance, we believe that there is hydrogen in the sun,
solely because that conclusion is forced upon us by
certain arguments based upon spectroscopic observations, then, if these arguments should ever be discredited, the belief in solar hydrogen would, as a
necessary consequence, be shaken or destroyed.
But in cases where the belief is rather the occasion
of an hypothesis than a conclusion from it, the destruction of the hypothesis may be a reason for de-
vising a new one, but is certainly no reason for abandoning the belief.   Nor in science do we ever take
any other view.   We do not, for example, step over
a precipice because we are dissatisfied with all the
attempts to account for gravitation.   In theology,
however, experience does sometimes lean too tim_
idly on theory, and when in the course of time
theory decays, it drags down experience in its
fall.   How many persons are there who, because
they dislike the theories of Atonement propounded,

say, by Anselm, or by Grotius, or the versions of these which have imbedded themselves in the devotional literature of Western Europe, feel bound ' in reason ' to give up the doctrine itself? Because they cannot compress within the rigid limits of some semi-legal formula a mystery which, unless it were too vast for our full intellectual comprehension, would surely be too narrow for our spiritual needs, the mystery itself is to be rejected! Because they cannot contrive to their satisfaction a system of theological jurisprudence which shall include Redemption as a leading case, Redemption is no longer to be counted among the consolations of mankind!

III

There is, however, another reason beyond the natural strength of the judgments due to sense-perception which tends to make the change or abandonment of explanatory formulas a smoother operation in science than it is in theology; and this reason is to be found in the fact that Religion works, and, to produce its full results, must needs work, through the agency of organised societies. It has, therefore, a social side, and from this its speculative side cannot, I believe, be kept wholly distinct. For although feeling is the effectual bond of all societies, these feelings themselves, it would seem, cannot be properly developed without the aid of something which is, or which does duty as, a reason. They require some alien material on which, so to speak, they may be precipitated; round which they may crystallise and coalesce. In the case of political societies this reason is founded on identity of race, of language, of country, or even of mere material interest. But when the religious society and the political are not, as in primitive times, based on a common ground, the desired reason can scarcely be looked for elsewhere, and, in fact, never is looked for elsewhere, than in the acceptance of common religious formulas. Whence it comes about that these formulas have to fulfil two functions which are not merely distinct but incomparable. They are both a statement of theological conclusions and the symbols of a corporate unity. They represent at once the endeavour to systematise religious truth and to organise religious associations; and they are therefore subject to two kinds of influence, and involve two kinds of obligation, which, though seldom distinguished, are never identical, and may sometimes even be opposed.

The distinction is a simple one; but the refusal to recognise it has been prolific in embarrassments, both for those who have assumed the duty of contriving symbols, and for those on whom has fallen the burden of interpreting them. The rage for defining [1] which seized so large a portion of Christendom, both Roman and non-Roman, during the Reformation troubles, and the fixed determination to

[1] Cf. Note on page 369.

turn the definitions, when made, into impassable barriers between hostile ecclesiastical divisions, are among the most obvious, but not, I think, among the most satisfactory, facts in modern religious history. To the definitions taken simply as well-intentioned efforts to make clear that which was obscure, and systematic that which was confused, I raise no objections. Of the practical necessity for some formal basis of Christian co-operation I am, as I have said, most firmly convinced. But not every formula which represents even the best theological opinion of its age is therefore fitted to unite men for all time in the furtherance of common religious objects, or in the support of common religious institutions; and the error committed in this connection by the divines of the Reformation, and the counter-Reformation, largely consisted in the mistaken supposition that symbols and decrees, in whose very elaboration could be read the sure prophecy of decay, were capable of providing a convenient framework for a perpetual organisation.

It is, however, beyond the scope of these Notes to discuss the dangers which the inevitable use of theological formulas as the groundwork of ecclesiastical co-operation may have upon Christian unity, important and interesting as the subject is. I am properly concerned solely with the other side of the same shield, namely, the dangers with which this inevitable combination of theory and practice may threaten the smooth development of religious beliefs—dangers which do not follow in the parallel case of science, where no such combination is to be found.   The doctrines of science have not got to be discussed amid the confusion and clamour of the market-place; they stir neither hate nor love; the fortunes of no living polity are bound up with them; nor is there any danger lest they become petrified into party watchwords.   Theology is differently situated.   There the explanatory formula may be so historically intertwined with the sentiments and traditions of the ecclesiastical organisation; the heat and pressure of ancient conflicts may have so welded them together, that to modify one and leave the other untouched seems well-nigh impossible. Yet even in such cases it is interesting to note how unexpectedly the most difficult adjustments are sometimes effected; how, partly by the conscious, and still more by the unconscious, wisdom of mankind; by a little kindly forgetfulness; by a few happy inconsistencies; by methods which might not always bear the scrutiny of the logician, though they may well be condoned by the philosopher, the changes required by the general movement of belief are made with less friction and at a smaller cost— even to the enlightened—than might, perhaps, antecedently have been imagined.

IV

The road which theological thought is thus compelled to travel would, however, be rougher even than it is were it not for the fact that large changes and adaptations of belief are possible within the limits of the same unchanging formulas.   This is a fact to which it has not been necessary hitherto to call the reader's attention.   It has been more convenient, and so far not, I think, misleading, to follow familiar usage, and to assume that identity of statement involves identity of belief; that when persons make the same assertions intelligently and in good faith they mean the same thing.   But this on closer examination is seen not to be the case.   In all branches of knowledge abundant examples are to be discovered of statements which do not fall into the cycle of change described in the last section, which no lapse of time nor growth of learning would apparently require us to revise.   But in every case it will, I think, be found that, with the doubtful exception of purely abstract propositions, these statements, themselves unmoved, represent a moving body of belief, varying from one period of life to another, from individual to individual, and from generation to generation.

Take an instance at random.   I suppose that the world, so long as it thinks it worth while to

have an opinion at all upon the subject, will continue to accept without amendment the assertion that
Julius Cæsar was murdered at Rome in the first
century B.C.   But are we, therefore, to suppose
that this proposition must mean the same thing
in the mouths of all who use it?   Surely not.
Even if we refuse to take account of the associated
sentiments which give a different colour in each
man's eyes to the same intellectual judgment, we
cannot ignore the varying positions which the
judgment itself may hold in different systems of
belief.   It is manifestly absurd to say that a statement about the mode and time of Cæsar's death
has the same significance for the schoolboy who
learns it as a line in a *memoria technica*, and the historian (if such there be) to whom it represents a
turning-point in the history of the world.   Nor is it
possible to deny that any alteration in our views on
the nature of Death, or on the nature of Man, must
necessarily alter the import of a proposition which
asserts of a particular man that he suffered a particular kind of death.

This may perhaps seem to be an unprofitable
subtlety; and so, to be sure, in this particular case,
it is.   But a similar reflection is of obvious importance when we come to consider, for example, such
propositions as 'there is a God,' or 'there is a world
of material things.'   Both these statements might
be, and are, accepted by the rudest savage and by

the most advanced philosopher. They may, so far as we can tell, continue to be accepted by men in all stages of culture till the last inhabitant of a perishing world is frozen into unconsciousness. Yet plainly the savage and the philosopher use these words in very different meanings. From the tribal deity of early times to the Christian God, or, if you prefer it, the Hegelian Absolute; from Matter as conceived by primitive man to Matter as it is conceived by the modern physicist, how vast the interval! The formulas are the same, the beliefs are plainly not the same. Nay, so wide are they apart, that while to those who hold the earlier view the later would be quite meaningless, it may require the highest effort of sympathetic imagination for those whose minds are steeped in the later view to reconstruct, even imperfectly, the substance of the earlier. The civilised man cannot fully understand the savage, nor the grown man the child.

V

Now a question of some interest is suggested by this reflection. Can we, in the face of the wide divergence of meaning frequently conveyed by the same formula at different times, assert that what endures in such cases is anything more than a mere husk or shell? Is it more than the mould into which any metal, base or precious, may be poured at will? Does identity of expression imply anything which deserves to be described as community of belief? Are we here dealing with things, or only with words?

In order to answer this question we must have some idea, in the first place, of the relation of Language to Belief, and, in the second place, of the relation of Belief to Reality. That the relation between the first of these pairs is of no very precise or definite kind I have already indicated. And the fact is so obvious that it would hardly be worth while to insist on it were it not that Formal Logic and conventional usage both proceed on exactly the opposite supposition. They assume a constant relation between the symbol and the thing symbolised ; and they consider that so long as a word is used (as the phrase is) ' in the same sense,' it corresponds, or ought to correspond, to the same thought. But this is an artificial simplification of the facts; an hypothesis, most useful for certain purposes, but one which seldom or never corresponds with concrete reality. If in the sweat of our brow we can secure that inevitable differences of meaning do not vitiate the particular argument in hand, we have done all that logic requires, and all that lies in us to accomplish. Not only would more be impossible, but more would most certainly be undesirable. Incessant variation in the uses to which we put the same expression is absolutely necessary if the complexity of the Universe is, even in the most imperfect fashion, to find a response in thought. If terms were counters, each purporting always to represent the whole of one unalterable aspect of reality, language would become, not the servant of thought, nor even its ally, but its tyrant. The wealth of our ideas would be limited by the poverty of our vocabulary. Science could not flourish, nor Literature exist. All play of mind, all variety, all development would perish; and mankind would spend its energies, not in using words, but in endeavouring to define them.

It was this logical nightmare which oppressed the intellect of the Middle Ages. The schoolmen have been attacked for not occupying themselves with experimental observation, which, after all, was no particular business of theirs; for indulging in excessive subtleties—surely no great crime in a metaphysician; and for endeavouring to combine the philosophy and the theology of their day into a coherent whole—an attempt which seems to me to be entirely praiseworthy. A better reason for their not having accomplished the full promise of their genius is to be found in the assumption which lies at the root of their interminable deductions, namely, that language is, or can be made, what logic by a convenient convention supposes it to be, and that if it were so made, it would be an instrument better fitted on that account to deal with the infinite variety of the actual world.

VI

If language, from the very nature of the case, hangs thus loosely to the belief which it endeavours to express, how closely does the belief fit to the reality with which it is intended to correspond? To hear some persons talk one would really suppose that the enlightened portion of mankind, *i.e.* those who happen to agree with them, were blessed with a precise knowledge respecting large tracts of the Universe. They are ready on small provocation to embody their beliefs, whether scientific or theological, in a series of dogmatic statements which, as they will tell you, accurately express their own accurate opinions, and between which and any differing statements on the same subject is fixed that great gulf which divides for ever the realms of Truth from those of Error. Now I would venture to warn the reader against paying any undue meed of reverence to the axiom on which this view essentially depends, the axiom, I mean, that 'every belief must be either true or not true.' It is, of course, indisputable. But it is also unimportant; and it is unimportant for this reason, that if we insist on assigning every belief to one or other of these two mutually exclusive classes, it will be found that most, if not all, the positive beliefs which deal with concrete reality—the very beliefs, in short, about which a reasonable man may be expected principally to interest himself—

would in strictness have to be classed among the 'not true.' I do not say, be it observed, that all propositions about the concrete world must needs be erroneous; for, as we have seen, every proposition provides the fitting verbal expression for many different beliefs, and of these it may be that one expresses the full truth. My contention merely is, that inasmuch as any fragmentary presentation of a concrete whole must, because it is fragmentary, be therefore erroneous, the full complexity of any true belief about reality will necessarily transcend the comprehension of any finite intelligence. We know only in part, and we therefore know wrongly.

But it may perhaps be said that observations like these involve a confusion between the 'not true' and the 'incomplete.' A belief, as the phrase is, may be 'true so far as it goes,' even though it does not go far enough. It may contain the truth and nothing but the truth, but not the whole truth. Why should it under such circumstances receive so severe a condemnation? Why is it to be branded, not only as inadequate, but as erroneous? To this I reply that the division of beliefs into the True, the Incomplete, and the Wholly False may be, and for many purposes is, a very convenient one. But in the first place it is not philosophically accurate, since that which is incomplete is touched throughout with some element of falsity. And in the second place it does not happen to be the division on which we are engaged. We are dealing with the logical contra-

dictories ' True ' and ' Not True.'   And what makes
it worth while dealing with them is, that the particular classification of beliefs which they suggest lies
at the root of much needless controversy in all
branches of knowledge, and not least in theology ;
and that everywhere it has produced some confusion
of thought and, it may be, some defect of charity.
It is not in human nature that those who start from
the assumption that all opinions are either true or
not true, should do otherwise than take for granted
that their own particular opinions belong to the
former category ; and that therefore all inconsistent
opinions held by other people must belong to the
latter.   Now this, in the current affairs of life, and
in the ordinary commerce between man and man, is
not merely a pardonable but a necessary way of looking at things.   But it is foolish and even dangerous
when we are engaged on the deeper problems of
science, metaphysics, or theology ; when we are
endeavouring in solitude to take stock of our position in the presence of the Infinite.   However profound may be our ignorance of our ignorance, at
least we should realise that to describe (when using
language strictly) any scheme of belief as wholly
false which has even imperfectly met the needs of
mankind, is the height of arrogance ; and that to
claim for any beliefs which we happen to approve
that they are wholly true, is the height of absurdity.
   Somewhat more, be it observed, is thus required
of us than a bare confession of ignorance.   The

least modest of men would admit without difficulty
that there are a great many things which he does
not understand; but the most modest may perhaps
be willing to suppose that there are some things
which he does.   Yet outside the relations of abstract
propositions (about which I say nothing) this cannot
be admitted.   Nowhere else—neither in our knowledge of ourselves, nor in our knowledge of each
other, nor in our knowledge of the material world,
nor in our knowledge of God, is there any belief
which is more than an approximation, any method
which is free from flaw, any result not tainted with
error.   The simplest intuitions and the remotest
speculations fall under the same condemnation.
And though the fact is apt to be hidden from us
by the unyielding definitions with which alike in
science and theology it is our practice to register
attained results, it would, as we have seen, be a
serious mistake to suppose that any complete correspondence between Belief and Reality was secured
by the linguistic precision and the logical impecca-
·bility of the propositions by which beliefs themselves
are communicated and recorded.

To some persons this train of reflection suggests
nothing but sceptical misgiving and intellectual
despair.   To me it seems, on the other hand, to save
us from both.   What kind of a Universe would that
be which we could understand?   If it were intelligible (by us), would it be credible?   If our reason
could comprehend it, would it not be too narrow

for our needs? 'I believe because it is impossible'
may be a pious paradox. 'I disbelieve because it is
simple' commends itself to me as an axiom. An
axiom doubtless to be used with discretion: an
axiom which may easily be perverted in the interests of idleness and superstition; an axiom, nevertheless, which contains a valuable truth not always
remembered by those who make especial profession
of worldly wisdom.

VII

However this may be, the opinions here advocated may help us to solve certain difficulties occasionally suggested by current methods of dealing
with the relation between Formulas and Beliefs. It
has not always, for instance, been found easy to
reconcile the immutability claimed for theological
doctrines with the movement observed in theological ideas. Neither of them can readily be abandoned. The conviction that there are Christian
verities which, once secured for the human race,
cannot by any lapse of time be rendered obsolete
is one which no Church would willingly abandon.
Yet the fact that theological thought follows the
laws which govern the evolution of all other thought,
that it changes from age to age, largely as regards
the relative emphasis given to its various elements,
not inconsiderably as regards the substance of those
elements themselves, is a fact written legibly across

the pages of ecclesiastical history. How is this apparent contradiction to be accommodated?

Consider another difficulty—one quite of a different kind. The common sense of mankind has been shocked at the value occasionally attributed to uniformity of theological profession, when it is perhaps obvious from many of the circumstances of the case that this carries with it no security for uniformity of inward conviction. There is an unreality, or at least an externality about such professions which, to those who think (rightly enough) that religion, if it is to be of any value, must come from the heart, is apt not unnaturally to be repulsive. Yet, on the other hand, it is but a shallow form of historical criticism which shall attribute this desire for conformity either to mere impatience of expressed differences of opinion (no doubt a powerful and widely distributed motive), or to the perversities of Priestcraft. What, then, is the view which we ought to take of it? Is it good or bad? and, if good, what purpose does it serve?

Now these questions may be answered, I think, at least in part, if we keep in mind two distinctions on which in this and the preceding chapter I have ventured to insist—the distinctions, I mean, *in the first place*, between the function of formulas as the systematic expression of religious doctrine, and their function as the basis of religious co-operation; and the distinction, *in the second place*, between the accuracy of any formula and the real truth of the various beliefs which it is capable of expressing.

Uniformity of profession, for example, to take the last difficulty first, can be regarded as unimportant only by those who forget that, while there is no necessary connection whatever between the causes which conduce to successful co-operation and those which conduce to the attainment of speculative truth, of these two objects the first may, under certain circumstances, be much more important than the second. A Church is something more than a body of more or less qualified persons engaged more or less successfully in the study of theology. It requires a very different equipment from that which is sufficient for a learned society. Something more is asked of it than independent research. It is an organisation charged with a great practical work. For the successful promotion of this work unity, discipline, and self-devotion are the principal requisites; and, as in the case of every other such organisation, the most powerful source of these qualities is to be found in the feelings aroused by common memories, common hopes, common loyalties; by professions in which all agree; by a ceremonial which all share; by customs and commands which all obey. He, therefore, who would wish to expel such influences either from Church or State, on the ground that they may alter (as alter they most certainly will) the opinions which, in their absence, the members of the community, left to follow at will their own spec-

ulative devices, would otherwise form, may know
something of science or philosophy, but assuredly
knows little of human nature.

But it will perhaps be said that co-operation, if
it is only to be had on these terms, may easily be
bought too dear. So, indeed, it may. The history
of the Church is unhappily there to prove the fact.
But as this is true of religious organisations, so also
is it true of every other organisation—national, political, military, what you will—by which the work
of the world is rendered possible. There are circumstances which may make schism justifiable, as
there are circumstances which make treason justifiable, or mutiny justifiable. But without going into
the ethics of revolt, without endeavouring to determine the exact degree of error, oppression, or
crime on the part of those who stay within the
organisation which may render innocent or necessary the secession of those who leave it, we may rest
assured that something very different is, or ought to
be, involved in the acceptance or rejection of common formulas than an announcement to the world
of a purely speculative agreement respecting the
niceties of doctrinal statement.

This view may perhaps be more readily accepted
when it is realised that, as I have pointed out, no
agreement about theological or any other doctrine
insures, or, indeed, is capable of producing, same-
ness of belief. We are no more able to believe what
other people believe than to feel what other people

feel. Two friends read together the same description of a landscape. Does anyone suppose that it
stirs within them precisely the same quality of sentiment, or evokes precisely the same subtle associations? And yet, if this be impossible, as it surely
is, even in the case of friends attuned, so far as may
be, to the same emotional key, how hopeless must
it be in the case of an artist and a rustic, an Ancient
and a Modern, an Andaman islander and a European!
But if no representation of the splendours of Nature
can produce in us any perfect identity of admiration,
why expect the definitions of theology or science to
produce in us any perfect identity of belief? It may
not be. This uniformity of conviction which so
many have striven to attain for themselves, and to
impose upon their fellows, is an unsubstantial phan-
tasm, born of a confusion between language and the
thought which language so imperfectly expresses.
In this world, at least, we are doomed to differ even
in the cases where we most agree.

   There is, however, consolation to be drawn from
the converse statement, which is, I hope, not less true.
If there are differences where we most agree, surely
also there are agreements where we most differ. I
like to think of the human race, from whatever
stock its members may have sprung, in whatever
age they may be born, whatever creed they may
profess, together in the presence of the One Reality,
engaged, not wholly in vain, in spelling out some
fragments of its message. All share its being; to

none are its oracles wholly dumb. And if both in
the natural world and in the spiritual the advancement we have made on our forefathers be so great
that our interpretation seems indefinitely removed
from that which primitive man could alone comprehend, and wherewith he had to be content, it may
be, indeed I think it is, the case that our approximate guesses are still closer to his than they are to
their common Object, and that far as we seem to
have travelled, yet, measured on the celestial scale,
our intellectual progress is scarcely to be discerned,
so minute is the parallax of Infinite Truth.

These observations, however, seem only to render more distant any satisfactory solution of the
first of the difficulties propounded above. If knowledge must, at the best, be so imperfect; if agreement, real inner agreement, about the object of
knowledge can thus never be complete; and if, in
addition to this, the history of religious thought is,
like all other history, one of change and development, where and what are those immutable doctrines which, in the opinion of most theologians,
ought to be handed on, a sacred trust, from generation to generation? The answer to this question is,
I think, suggested by the parallel cases of science
and ethics. For all these things may be said of
them as well as of theology, and they also are the
trustees of statements which ought to be preserved
unchanged through all revolutions in scientific and
ethical theory. Of these statements I do not pre-

tend to give either a list or a definition. But without saying what they are, it is at least permissible,
after the discussion in the last chapter, to say what,
as a rule, they are not. They are not Explanatory.
Rare indeed is it to find explanations of the concrete
which, if they endure at all, do not require perpetual
patching to keep them in repair. Not among these,
but among the statements of things explained, of
things that want explanation, yes, and of things that
are inexplicable, we must search for the propositions about the real world capable of ministering
unchanged for indefinite periods to the uses of Mankind. Such propositions may record a particular
'fact,' as that 'Cæsar is dead.' They may embody
an ethical imperative, as that 'Stealing is wrong.'
They may convey some great principle, as that the
order of Nature is uniform, or that 'God exists.'
All these statements, even if accurate (as I assume,
for the sake of argument, that they are), will, no
doubt, as I have said, have a different import for
different persons and for different ages. But this is
not only consistent with their value as vehicles for
the transmission of truth—it is essential to it. If
their meaning could be exhausted by one generation, they would be false for the next. It is because
they can be charged with a richer and richer content as our knowledge slowly grows to a fuller harmony with the Infinite Reality, that they may be
counted among the most precious of our inalienable
possessions.

NOTE

The permanent value which the results of the great ecclesiastical controversies of the first four centuries have had for Christendom, as compared with that possessed by the more transitory speculations of later ages, illustrates, I think, the suggestion contained in the text.   For whatever opinion the reader may entertain of the decisions at which the Church arrived on the doctrine of the Trinity, it is at least clear that they were not in the nature of explanations.   They were, in fact, precisely the reverse. They were the negation of explanations.   The various heresies which it combated were, broadly speaking, all endeavours to bring the mystery as far as possible into harmony with contemporary speculations, Gnostic, Neoplatonic, or Rationalising, to relieve it from this or that difficulty : in short, to do something towards ' explaining ' it.   The Church held that all such explanations or partial explanations inflicted irremediable impoverishment on the idea of the Godhead which was essentially involved in the Christian revelation.   They insisted on preserving that idea in all its inexplicable fulness ; and so it has come about that while such simplifications as those of the Arians, for example, are so alien and impossible to modern modes of thought that if they had been incorporated with Christianity they must have destroyed it, the doctrine of Christ's Divinity still gives reality and life to the worship of millions of pious souls, who are wholly ignorant both of the controversy to which they owe its preservation, and of the technicalities which its discussion has involved.[1]

[1] [On this unoffending note Principal Fairbairn, writing as an expert theologian, has passed some severe comments (see ' Catholicism, Roman and Anglican,' p. 356 *et seq.*).   He seems to think the terms used in the definitions of Nicea and Chalcedon must, because they are technical, be therefore ' of the nature of explanations.'   I cannot agree.   I think they were used, not to explain the mystery they were designed to express, but to show with unmistakable precision wherein the rival formula, which was so much more in harmony with the ordinary philosophic thought of the day, fell short of what was required by the Christian consciousness.]

SUMMARY

1. ALL men who reflect at all, interpret their experiences in the light of certain broad theories and preconceptions as to the world in which they live. These theories and preconceptions need not be explicitly formulated, nor are they usually, if ever, thoroughly self-consistent. They do not remain unchanged from age to age; they are never precisely identical in two individuals. Speaking, however, of the present age and of the general body of educated opinion, they may be said to fall roughly into two categories—which we may call respectively the Spiritualistic and the Naturalistic. In the Naturalistic class are included by common usage Positivism, Agnosticism, Materialism, &c., though not always with the good will of those who make profession of these doctrines (pp. 1–8).

2. In estimating the value of any of these theories we have to take into account something more than their 'evidence' in the narrow meaning often given to that term. Their bearing upon the most important forms of human activity and emotion deserves also to be considered. For, as I proceed to show, there

may, in addition to the merely logical incongruities in which the essence of inconsistency is commonly thought to reside, be also incongruities between theory and practice, or theory and feeling, producing inconsistencies of a different, but, it may be, not less formidable description.

3. In the first chapter (pp. 11–32) I have endeavoured to analyse some of these incongruities as they manifest themselves in the collision between Naturalism and Ethical emotions. That there are emotions proper to Ethics is admitted on all hands (p. 11). It is not denied, for instance, that a feeling of reverence for what is right—for what is prescribed by the moral law—is a necessary element in any sane and healthy view of things : while it becomes evident on reflection that this feeling cannot be independent of the origin from which that moral law is supposed to flow, and the place which it is thought to occupy in the Universe of things (p. 13).

4. Now on the Naturalistic theory, the place it occupies is insignificant (p. 14), and its origin is quite indistinguishable from that of any other contrivance by which Nature provides for the survival of the race. Courage and self-devotion are factors in evolution which came later into the field than e.g. greediness or lust: and they require therefore the special protection and encouragement supplied by fine sentiments. These fine sentiments, however, are merely a device comparable to other devices,

often disgusting or trivial, produced in the interests
of race-preservation by Natural Selection; and when
we are under their sway we are being cheated by
Nature for our good—or rather for the good of the
species to which we belong (pp. 14-19).

5. The feeling of freedom is, on the Naturalist
theory, another beneficent illusion of the same kind.
If Naturalism be true, it is certain that we are not
free.   If we are not free, it is certain that we are not
responsible.   If we are not responsible, it is certain
that we are exhibiting a quite irrational emotion
when we either repent our own misdoings or reverence the virtues of other people (pp. 20-26).

6. There is yet a third kind of disharmony between the emotions permitted by Naturalism and
those proper to Ethics—the emotions, namely, which
relate to the *consequences* of action.   We instinctively
ask for some adjustment between the distribution of
happiness and the distribution of virtue, and for an
ethical end adequate to our highest aspirations.   The
first of these can only be given if we assume a future
life, an assumption evidently unwarranted by Naturalism (pp. 26-28); the second is rendered impossible
by the relative insignificance of man and all his
doings, as measured on the scale supplied by modern
science.   The brief fortunes of our race occupy but
a fragment of the range in time and space which is
open to our investigations; and if it is only in relation to them that morality has a meaning, our prac-

tical ideal must inevitably be petty, compared with the sweep of our intellectual vision (pp. 28–32).

7. With Chapter II. (p. 33) we turn from Ethics to Æsthetics; and discuss the relation which Naturalism bears to the emotions aroused in us by Beauty. A comparatively large space (pp. 35–61) is devoted to an investigation into the ' natural history' of taste. This is not only (in the author's opinion) intrinsically interesting, but it is a desirable preliminary to the contention (pp. 61–65) that (on the Naturalist view of things) Beauty represents no permanent quality or relation in the world as revealed to us by Science. This becomes evident when we reflect (a) that could we perceive things as the Physicist tells us they are, we might regard them as curious and interesting, but hardly as beautiful; (b) that differences of taste are notorious and, indeed, inevitable, considering that no causes exist likely to call into play the powerful selective machinery by which is secured an approximate uniformity in morals; (c) that even the apparent agreement among official critics represents no identity of taste; while (d) the genuine identity of taste, so often found in the same public at the same time, is merely a case of that ' tendency to agreement' which, though it plays a most important part in the general conduct of social life, has in it no element of permanence, and, indeed, under the name of *fashion*, is regarded as the very type of mutability.

8. From these considerations it becomes apparent (pp. 65, 66) that æsthetic emotion at its best and highest is altogether discordant with Naturalistic theory.

9. The advocates of Naturalism may perhaps reply that, even supposing the foregoing arguments were sound, and there is really this alleged collision between Naturalistic theory and the highest emotions proper to Ethics and Æsthetics, yet, however much we may regret the fact, it should not affect our estimate of a creed which, professing to draw its inspiration from reason alone, ought in no wise to be modified by sentiment. How far this contention can be sustained will be. examined later. In the meanwhile it suggests an inquiry into the position which that Reason to which Naturalism appeals occupies according to Naturalism itself in the general scheme of things (Chapter III. pp. 67-76).

10. According to the spiritual view of things, the material Universe is the product of Reason. According to Naturalism it is its source. Reason and the inlets of sense through which reason obtains the data on which it works are the products of non-rational causes; and if these causes are grouped under the guidance of Natural Selection so as to produce a rational or partially rational result, the character of this result is determined by our utilitarian needs rather than our speculative aspirations (pp. 67-72).

11. Reason therefore, on the Naturalistic hypoth-

esis, occupies no very exalted or important place in the Cosmos. It supplies it neither with a First cause nor a Final cause. It is a merely local accident ranking after appetite and instinct among the expedients by which the existence of a small class of mammals on a very insignificant planet is rendered a little less brief, though perhaps not more pleasurable, than it would otherwise be (pp. 72–76).

12. Chapter IV. (pp. 77–86) is a summary of the three preceding ones and terminates with a contrasted pair of catechisms based respectively on the Spiritualistic and the Naturalistic method of interpreting the world (pp. 83–86).

13. This incongruity between Naturalism and the higher emotions inevitably provokes an examination into the evidence on which Naturalism itself rests, and this accordingly is the task to which we set ourselves at the beginning of Part II. (See Part II., Chapter I., pp. 89–136.) Now on its positive side the teaching of Naturalism is by definition identical with the teaching of Science. But while Science is not bound to give any account of its first principles, and in fact never does so, Naturalism, which is nothing if not a philosophy, is in a different position. The essential character of its pretensions carries with it the obligation to supply a reasoned justification of its existence to any who may require it.

14. It is no doubt true that Naturalistic philosophers have never been very forward to supply this

reasoned justification (pp. 94–96), yet we cannot go wrong in saying that Naturalistic theory, in all its forms, bases knowledge entirely upon experiences; and that of these experiences the most important are those which are given in the 'immediate judgments of the senses' (pp. 106, 107), and principally of vision (p. 108).

15. A brief consideration, however, of this simple and common-sense statement shows that two kinds of difficulty are inherent in it. In the *first* place, the very account which Science gives of the causal steps by which the object experienced (e.g. the thing seen) makes an impression upon our senses, shows that the experiencing self, the knowing 'I,' is in no immediate or direct relation with that object (pp. 107–111); and it shows further that the message thus conveyed by the long chain of causes and effects connecting the object experienced and the experiencing self, is essentially mendacious (pp. 111–118). The attempt to get round this difficulty either by regarding the material world as being not the object immediately experienced, but only an inference from it, or by abolishing the material world altogether in the manner of Berkeley, Hume, and J. S. Mill, is shown (pp. 118–126) to be impracticable, and to be quite inconsistent with the teaching of Science, as men of science understand it.

16. In the *second* place, it is clear that we require in order to construct the humblest scientific edifice,

not merely isolated experiences, but general principles (such as the law of universal causation) by which
isolated experiences may be co-ordinated. How on
any purely empirical theory are these to be obtained?
No method that will resist criticism has ever been
suggested; and the difficulty, insuperable in any
case, seems enormously increased when we reflect
that it is not the accumulated experience of the race,
but the narrow experience of the individual on which
we have to rely. It must be *my* experience for *me*,
and *your* experience for *you*. Otherwise we should
find ourselves basing our belief in these general
principles upon our general knowledge of mankind
past and present, though we cannot move a step
towards the attainment of such general knowledge
without first assuming these principles to be true
(pp. 127–132).

17. It would not be possible to go further in the
task of exposing the philosophic insufficiency of the
Naturalistic creed without the undue employment
of philosophic technicalities. But, in my view, to
go further is unnecessary. If fully considered, the
criticisms contained in this chapter are sufficient,
without any supplement, to show the hollowness of
the Naturalistic claim, and as it is with Naturalism
that this work is mainly concerned, there seems no
conclusive necessity for touching on rival systems
of Philosophy.

As a precautionary measure, however, and to

prevent a flank attack, I have (in Part II. Chapter II.) briefly examined certain aspects of Transcendental Idealism in the shape in which it has principally gained currency in this country; while at the beginning of the succeeding chapter (pp. 163–170) I have indicated my reason for respectfully ignoring any other of the great historic systems of Philosophy.

18. The conclusion of this part of the discussion, therefore, is that neither in Naturalism, with which we are principally concerned, nor in Rationalism, which is Naturalism in the making (pp. 174–180), nor in any other system of thought which commands an important measure of contemporary assent, can we find a coherent scheme which shall satisfy our critical faculties. Now this result may seem purely negative; but evidently it carries with it an important practical corollary. For whereas the ordinary canons of consistency might require us to sacrifice all belief and sentiments which did not fully harmonise with a system rationally based on rational foundations, it is a mere abuse of these canons to apply them in support of a system whose inner weaknesses and contradictions show it to be at best but a halting and imperfect approximation to one aspect of absolute truth (pp. 180, 181).

19. Chapter IV. in Part II. (pp. 182–189) may be regarded as a parenthesis, though a needful parenthesis, in the course of the general argument. It is

designed to expose the absurdity of the endeavour to make rationalising theories (as defined on pp. 174–180) issue not in Naturalism but in Theology. Paley's 'Evidences of Christianity' is the best known example of this procedure; and I have endeavoured to show that, however valuable it may be as a supplement to a spiritualistic creed already accepted, it is quite unequal to the task of refuting Naturalism by extracting Spiritualism out of the Biblical narrative by ordinary historical and inductive methods.

20. With Part II. Chapter IV. ends the critical or destructive portion of the Essay. With Part III. (p. 194) begins the attempt at construction. The preliminary stage of this consists in some brief observations on the Natural History of beliefs. By the natural history of beliefs I mean an account of beliefs regarded simply as phenomena among other phenomena; not as premises or conclusions in a logical series, but as antecedents or consequents in a causal series. From this point of view we have to ask ourselves not whether a belief is true, but whence it arose; not whether it ought to be believed, but how it comes to be believed. We have to put ourselves, so to speak, in the position of a superior being making anthropological investigations from some other planet (p. 197), or into the position we ourselves occupy when examining opinions which have for us only an historic interest.

21. Such an investigation directed towards what may roughly be described as the 'immediate beliefs of experience'—those arising from perception and memory—shows that they are psychical accompaniments of neural processes—processes which in their simpler form appear neither to possess nor to require this mental collaboration. Physiological co-ordination, unassociated with any psychical phenomena worthy to be described as perception or belief, is sufficient for the lower animals or for most of them ; it is in many cases sufficient for man. Conscious experience and the judgments in which it is embodied seem, from this point of view, only an added and almost superfluous perfection, a finishing touch given to activities which often do excellently well with no such rational assistance (pp. 197–201).

22. Empirical philosophy in its cruder form would have us believe that by some inductive leger-demain there may be extracted from these psycho-logical accidents the vast mass of supplementary beliefs actually required by the higher social and scientific life of the race (pp. 200, 201). We have already shown as regards one great scientific axiom (the uniformity of Nature) that this is not logically possible. We may now say more generally that from the point of view of Natural History it is not what in fact happens. Not reasoning, inductive or deductive, is the true parent of this numerous off-spring: we should be nearer the mark if we looked

to Authority—using this as a convenient collective
name for the vast multitude of psychological causes
of belief, *not being also reasons for it*, which have their
origin in the social environment, and are due to the
action of mind on mind.

23. An examination into this subject carried out
at considerable length (Part III., Chapter II., pp.
202–240) serves to show not merely that this is so,
but that, if society is to exist, it could not be otherwise. Reasoning no doubt has its place both in the
formation of beliefs and in their destruction. But
its part is insignificant compared with that played
by Authority. For it is to Authority that we owe
the most fundamental premises on which our reason-
ings repose; and it is Authority which commonly
determines the conclusions to which they must in
the main adapt themselves.

24. These views, taken in connection with the
criticism on Naturalism contained in Part II., show
that the beliefs of which Naturalism is composed
must on its own principles have a non-rational source,
and on any principles must derive largely from Authority: that Naturalism neither owes its origin to
reason, nor has as yet been brought into speculative
harmony with it. Why, then, should t be regarded
as of greater validity than (say) Theology? Is there
any relevant difference between them? and, if not,
is it reasonable to act as if there were? (pp. 243-
246).

25. One difference there undoubtedly is (p. 246). About the judgments which form the starting-point of Science there is unquestionably an *inevitableness* lacking to those which lie at the root of Theology or Ethics. There may be, and are, all sorts of speculative difficulties connected with the reality or even the meaning of an external world; nevertheless our beliefs respecting what we see and handle, however confused they may seem on analysis, remain absolutely coercive in their assurance compared with the beliefs with which Ethics and Theology are principally concerned (pp. 246, 247).

26. There is here no doubt a real difference—though one which the Natural History of beliefs may easily explain (p. 249). But is it a relevant difference? Assuredly not. The coercion exercised by these beliefs is not a rational coercion. It is due neither to any deliberate act of reason, nor to any blind effect of heredity or tradition which reason *ex post facto* can justify. The necessity to which we bow, rules us by violence, not by right.

27. The differentiation which Naturalism makes in favour of its own narrow creed is thus an irrational differentiation, and so the great masters of speculative thought, as well as the great religious prophets, have always held (pp. 252–255).

28. And if no better ground for accepting as fact a material world more or less in correspondence with our ordinary judgments of sense perceptions can be

alleged than the practical need for doing so, there is nothing irrational in postulating a like harmony between the Universe and other Elements in our nature 'of a later, a more uncertain, but no ignobler growth' (pp. 256–260).

29. Nor can it be said that, in respect of distinctness or lucidity, fundamental scientific conceptions have any advantage over Theological or Ethical ones (pp. 261–265). Mr. Spencer has indeed pointed out with great force that 'ultimate scientific ideas,' like 'ultimate religious ideas,' are 'unthinkable.' But he has not drawn the proper moral from his discovery. If in the case of Science we accept unhesitatingly postulates about the material world as more certain than any reason which can be alleged in their defence; if the needs of everyday life forbid us to take account of the difficulties which seem on analysis to becloud our simplest experiences, practical wisdom would seem to dictate a like course when we are dealing with the needs of our spiritual nature.

30. We have now reached a point in the argument at which it becomes clear that the 'conflict between Science and Religion,' if it exists, is not one which in the present state of our knowledge can or ought to require us to reject either of these supposed incompatibles. For in truth the difficulties and contradictions are to be found rather within their separate spheres than between them. The conflicts from which they suffer are in the main

civil conflicts; and if we could frame a satisfying philosophy of Science and a satisfying philosophy of Religion, we should, I imagine, have little difficulty in framing a philosophy which should embrace them both (p. 273).

31. We may, indeed, go much further, and say that, unless it borrow something from Theology, a philosophy of Science is impossible. The perplexities in which we become involved if we accept the Naturalistic dogma that all beliefs ultimately trace their descent to non-rational causes, have emerged again and again in the course of the preceding argument. Such a doctrine cuts down any theory of knowledge to the root. It can end in nothing but the most impotent scepticism. Science, therefore, is at least as much as Theology compelled to postulate a Rational Ground or Cause of the world, who made *it* intelligible and *us* in some faint degree able to understand it (pp. 277–283).

32. The difficulties which beset us whenever we attempt to conceive how this Rational (and therefore Spiritual) cause acts upon or is related to the Material Universe, are no doubt numerous and probably insoluble. But they are common to Science and to Religion, and, indeed, are of a kind which cannot be avoided even by the least theological of philosophies, since they are at once suggested in their most embarrassing form whenever we try to realise the relation between the Self and the world of matter,

a relation which it is impossible practically to deny or speculatively to understand (pp. 283-286).

33. It is true that at first sight most forms of religion, and certainly Christianity as ordinarily held, seem to have burdened themselves with a difficulty from which Science is free—the familiar difficulty of Miracles. But there is probably here some misconception. Whether or not there is sufficient reason for believing any particular Wonder recorded in histories, sacred or profane, can only be decided by each person according to his general view of the system of the world. But however he may decide, his real difficulty will not be with any supposed violation of the principle of Uniformity (a principle not always accurately understood by those who appeal to it (pp. 289-292)), but with a metaphysical paradox common to all forms of religion, whether they lay stress on the 'miraculous' or not.

34. What is this metaphysical paradox? It is the paradox involved in supposing that the spiritual source of all that exists exercises 'preferential action' on behalf of one portion of his creation rather than another; that He draws a distinction between good and bad, and having created all, yet favours only a part. This paradox is implied in such expressions as 'Providence,' 'A Power that makes for Righteousness,' 'A Benevolent Deity,' and all the other phrases by which Theology adds something to the notion of the 'Infinite Substance,' or 'Universal

Idea or Subject,' which is the proper theme of a non-theological Metaphysic (pp. 297–302).

35. In this preferential action, however, Science and Ethics seem as much interested as Theology. For, in the first place, it is worth noting that if we accept the doctrine of a First Cause immanent in the world of phenomena, the modern doctrine of Evolution almost requires us to hold that there is in the Universe a purpose being slowly worked out—a 'striving towards something which is not, but which gradually becomes, and, in the fulness of time, will be' (pp. 301–302).

36. But, in truth, much stronger reasons have already been advanced for holding that both Science and Ethics must postulate not merely a universal substance or subject, but a Deity working by what I have ventured to call 'preferential methods.' So far as Science is concerned, we have already seen that at the root of every rational process lies a non-rational one, and that the least unintelligible account which can be given of the fact that these non-rational processes, physical, physiological, and social, issue in knowledge is, that to this end they were preferentially guided by Supreme Reason (pp. 303–306).

37. A like argument may be urged with even greater force in the case of Ethics. If we hold—as teachers of all schools profess to hold—that morality is a thing of intrinsic worth, we seem driven also to

assume that the complex train of non-moral causes which have led to its recognition, and have at the same time engendered the sentiments which make the practice of it possible, have produced these re-sults under moral—i.e. preferential—guidance (pp. 306, 307).

38. But if Science and Ethics, to say nothing of Æsthetics (pp. 307, 308), thus require the double presupposition of a Deity and of a Deity working by 'preferential' methods, we need feel no surprise if these same preferential methods have shown them-selves in the growth and development of Theology (p. 310).

39. The reality of this preferential intervention has been persistently asserted by the adherents of every religion. They have always claimed that their beliefs about God were due to God. The one ex-ception is to be found in the professors of what is rather absurdly called Natural Religion, who are wont to represent it as the product of 'unassisted reason.' In face, however, of the arguments already advanced to prove that there is no such thing as unassisted reason, this pretension may be summarily dismissed (pp. 309-311).

40. Though we describe, as we well may, this preferential action in matters theological by the word Inspiration, it does not follow, of course, that what is inspired is on that account necessarily true, but only that it has an element of truth due to the

Divine co-operation with our limited intelligences.
And for my own part I am unwilling to admit that
some such element is not to be found in all the great
religious systems which have in any degree satisfied
the spiritual needs of mankind (pp. 311–314).

41. So far the argument has gone to show that
the great body of our beliefs, scientific, ethical,
æsthetic, and theological, form a more coherent and
satisfactory whole in a Theistic than in a Naturalistic setting. Can the argument be pressed further?
Can we say that those departments of knowledge,
or any of them, are more coherent and satisfactory
in a distinctively Christian setting than in a merely Theistic one? (p. 317). If so, the *a priori* presuppositions which have induced certain learned
schools of criticism to deal with the Gospel narra-
tives as if these were concerned with events intrinsically incredible will need modification, and there
may even on consideration appear to be an *a priori*
presupposition in favour of their general veracity
(pp. 317–325).

42. Now it can, I think, be shown that the central
doctrine of Christianity, the doctrine which essentially differentiates it from every other religion, has
an ethical import of great and even of an increasing
value. The Incarnation as dogma is not a theme
within the scope of this work; but it may not be
amiss, by way of Epilogue, to enumerate three aspects of it in which it especially ministers, as noth-

ing else could conceivably minister, to some of the most deep-seated of our moral necessities.

43 (*a*). The whole tendency of modern discovery is necessarily to magnify material magnitudes to the detriment of spiritual ones. The insignificant part played by moral forces in the cosmic drama, the vastness of the physical forces by which we are closed in and overwhelmed, the infinities of space, time, and energy thrown open by Science to our curious investigations, increase (on the Theistic hypothesis) our sense of the power of God, but relatively impoverish our sense of his moral interest in his creatures. It is surely impossible to imagine a more effective cure for this distorted yet most natural estimate than a belief in the Incarnation (pp. 326–330).

44 (*b*). Again, the absolute dependence of mind on body, taught, and rightly taught, by empirical science, confirmed by each man's own humiliating experience, is of all beliefs the one which, if fully realised, is most destructive of high endeavour. Speculation may provide an answer to physiological materialism, but for the mass of mankind it can provide no antidote ; nor yet can an antidote be found in the bare theistic conception of a God ineffably remote from all human conditions, divided from man by a gulf so vast that nothing short of the Incarnation can adequately bridge it (pp. 330–333).

45 (*c*). A like thought is suggested by the 'prob-

lem of evil,' that immemorial difficulty in the way
of a completely consistent theory of the world on a
religious basis. Of this difficulty, indeed, the Incarnation affords no speculative solution, but it does
assuredly afford a practical palliation. For whereas
a merely metaphysical Theism leaves us face to face
with a Deity who shows power but not mercy, who
has contrived a world in which, so far as direct observation goes, the whole creation travails together
in misery, Christianity brings home to us, as nothing
else could do, that God is no indifferent spectator
of our sorrows, and in so doing affords the surest
practical alleviation to a pessimism which seems
fostered alike by the virtues and the vices of our
modern civilisation (pp. 333–337).

Lightning Source UK Ltd.
Milton Keynes UK
UKHW022035220119

336028UK00002B/8/P